75 GREAT HIKES
SEATTLE

MELISSA OZBEK

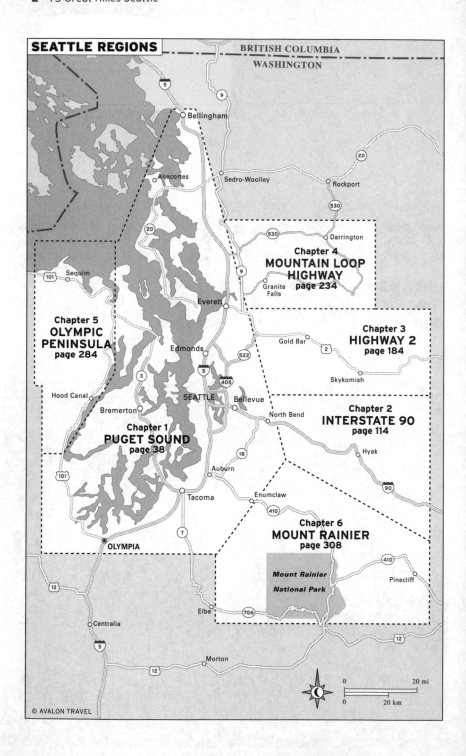

SEATTLE REGIONS

BRITISH COLUMBIA
WASHINGTON

Bellingham

Anacortes

Sedro-Woolley

Rockport

Darrington

Chapter 4
MOUNTAIN LOOP
HIGHWAY
page 234

Granite
Falls

Sequim

Everett

Chapter 5
OLYMPIC
PENINSULA
page 284

Gold Bar

Chapter 3
HIGHWAY 2
page 184

Edmonds

Skykomish

Hood Canal

SEATTLE

Bellevue

Bremerton

North Bend

Chapter 2
INTERSTATE 90
page 114

Chapter 1
PUGET SOUND
page 38

Hyak

Auburn

Tacoma

Enumclaw

Chapter 6
MOUNT RAINIER
page 308

OLYMPIA

Mount Rainier

National Park

Pinecliff

Centralia

Elbe

Morton

0   20 mi

0   20 km

© AVALON TRAVEL

Contents

How to Use This Book

ABOUT THE MAPS

This book is divided into chapters based on regions that are within close reach of the city; an overview map of these regions precedes the table of contents. Each chapter begins with a region map that shows the locations and numbers of the trails listed in that chapter.

Each trail profile is also accompanied by a detailed trail map that shows the hike route.

Map Symbols

– – – – – –	Featured Trail	(80)	Interstate Freeway	O	City/Town
– – – – – –	Other Trail	(101)	U.S. Highway	✕✈	Airfield/Airport
▒▒▒▒▒	Expressway	(21)	State Highway	⌇	Golf Course
▒▒▒▒▒	Primary Road	66	County Highway	🗻	Waterfall
▒▒▒▒▒	Secondary Road	★	Point of Interest	▒	Swamp
▫▫▫▫▫	Unpaved Road	P	Parking Area	▲	Mountain
··········	Ferry	T	Trailhead	♠	Park
— · — ·	National Border	A	Campground	)⌒	Pass
— · · —	State Border	▪	Other Location	✦	Unique Natural Feature

ABOUT THE TRAIL PROFILES

Each profile includes a narrative description of the trail's setting and terrain. This description also typically includes mile-by-mile hiking directions, as well as information about the trail's highlights and unique attributes.

The **mileage** and **elevation** for each hike was measured with a Garmin GPSMAP 64st. The elevation gain for each hike is cumulative; all the bumps and hills that you'll ascend throughout the hike are counted in the overall elevation gain.

In addition to the featured trail, each listing includes options on how to **shorten** or **lengthen** the hike, where to **hike nearby,** or how to extend the hike into a **day trip** or **get away for the weekend.**

Detailed driving **directions** are provided from the city center or from the intersection of major highways to the trailhead. Two GPS coordinates are included for each trailhead: The first can be entered online, while the second can be entered into your GPS. When public transportation is available, instructions are noted after the directions.

ABOUT THE ICONS

The icons in this book are designed to provide at-a-glance information on special features for each trail.

🦌 The trail offers an opportunity for wildlife watching.

🌼 The trail features wildflower displays in spring.

💧 The trail travels to a waterfall.

🏛 The trail visits a historic site.

🐕 Dogs are allowed.

👨‍👧 The trail is appropriate for children.

♿ The trail is wheelchair accessible.

🚌 The trailhead can be accessed via public transportation.

ABOUT THE DIFFICULTY RATING

Each profile includes a difficulty rating. Definitions for ratings follow. Remember that the difficulty level for any trail can change due to weather or trail conditions, so always phone ahead to check the current state of any trail.

Easy: Easy hikes are 5 miles or less and with an elevation gain of 500 feet. They are generally suitable for beginner hikers, those recovering from an injury, and families with young children.

Easy/Moderate: Easy/Moderate hikes are 2–8 miles long and with an elevation gain of up to 1,200 feet. They are generally suitable for reasonably fit hikers and families with active children age 6 or older.

Moderate: Moderate hikes are 3–9 miles long and with an elevation gain of up to 2,500 feet. They are suitable for fit hikers.

Moderate/Strenuous: Moderate/Strenuous hikes are 3–11 miles long and with an elevation gain of up to 3,500 feet. They are suitable for fit and experienced hikers seeking a workout.

Strenuous: Strenuous hikes are 6–12 miles long with an elevation gain of up to 5,300 feet. They are suitable for very fit, advanced hikers.

INTRODUCTION

Author's Note

The best-kept secret about living in the Seattle area is its natural surroundings. Cocooned among the Pacific Ocean, Puget Sound, the Olympics, and the Cascades, Seattle's dynamic topography ranges from beaches and river valleys to rainforests and snowcapped mountains. This is a playground for hikers of all shapes and sizes: kids, naturalists, fitness fanatics, weekend warriors, and everyday people looking to experience the natural wonders of Washington state. Easy trails to surging waterfalls and spooky ghost towns, moderate hikes to undulating waves of wildflowers and mountain-rimmed alpine lakes, and hard-core climbs to spired peaks with 360-degree views barely scratch the surface of hiking options.

Few cities can boast a hiking community as experienced, engaged, and interwoven as Seattle can. A wide range of hiking groups, friendly outdoor organizations, conservation societies, and passionate, experienced locals enhance our community by sharing their knowledge of the local landscape. Seattle residents gain further inspiration from a vibrant community of outdoor writers, filmmakers, photographers, and bloggers. Sometimes it's so much information that it's hard to know where to start. That's where this book comes in.

At your fingertips is a library of classic hikes and hidden gems for a range of abilities, including those traveling with a wheelchair, families with children, and experienced hiking enthusiasts. Organized by geographic area, these hikes help pinpoint where to go and highlight trail features such as wildflowers, waterfalls, or berry picking. Included within are notable hikes nearby and options to turn your hike into a day trip or a weekend getaway. Everything you need to know about your next hike has been thoroughly researched, taking the guesswork out of your planning so that you can relax and enjoy your time on the trail.

After logging hundreds of miles throughout the state, hiking has become more than just a walk in the woods for me. It is a quiet space to gather my thoughts, an outlet for the frustrations of everyday life, and a shared sense of wonder with friends. Sometimes a valuable experience—where we learn about ourselves, grow our self-confidence, and feel personal fulfillment—can happen right in our own backyard. Your adventure is waiting for you. Go out and get it.

—Melissa Ozbek

Best Hikes

Can't decide where to hike this weekend? Try these unique hikes, grouped into some of my favorite categories.

Best Beach Hikes

Rosario Head to Lighthouse Point, Deception Pass State Park, Puget Sound, page 48

West Beach to Goose Rock, Deception Pass State Park, Puget Sound, page 53

Joseph Whidbey State Park, Whidbey Island, Puget Sound, page 57

Ebey's Landing, Ebey's Landing National Historical Reserve, Puget Sound, page 61

Dungeness Spit, Dungeness National Wildlife Refuge, Olympic Peninsula, page 286

Best for Berry Picking

Granite Mountain, Mount Baker-Snoqualmie National Forest, I-90, page 157

Lake Dorothy, Mount Baker-Snoqualmie National Forest, Highway 2, page 221

Johnson Ridge-Scorpion Mountain, Mount Baker-Snoqualmie National Forest, Highway 2, page 213

Cutthroat Lakes, Mount Baker-Snoqualmie National Forest, Mountain Loop Highway, page 254

Mount Dickerman, Mount Baker-Snoqualmie National Forest, Mountain Loop Highway, page 266

Best Day Trips

Oyster Dome via Samish Overlook, day trip to Bow-Edison, Puget Sound, page 40

Padilla Bay Shore Trail, day trip to La Conner, Puget Sound, page 44

Ebey's Landing, day trip to Coupeville, Puget Sound, page 61

South Whidbey State Park, day trip to Greenbank Farm, Puget Sound, page 65

Norse Peak, day trip to Crystal Mountain Resort, Mount Rainier, page 334

Best Easy Hikes

Cama Beach State Park, Camano Island, Puget Sound, page 69

Wildside-Red Town Loop, Cougar Mountain Regional Wildland Park, Puget Sound, page 87

Gold Creek Pond, Mount Baker-Snoqualmie National Forest, I-90, page 175

Big Four Ice Caves, Mount Baker-Snoqualmie National Forest, Mountain Loop Highway, page 258

Staircase Rapids Loop, Olympic National Park, Olympic Peninsula, page 299

Best Historical Hikes

Ebey's Landing, Ebey's Landing National Historical Reserve, Puget Sound, page 61

Discovery Park Loop, Discovery Park, Puget Sound, page 76

Anti-Aircraft Peak, Cougar Mountain Regional Wildland Park, Puget Sound, page 91

Wellington Ghost Town-Windy Point, Mount Baker-Snoqualmie National Forest, Highway 2, page 225

Lime Kiln Trail, Robe Canyon Historic Park, Mountain Loop Highway, page 236

Best Kid-Friendly Hikes

Padilla Bay Shore Trail, Padilla Bay National Estuarine Research Reserve, Puget Sound, page 44

Foster and Marsh Islands, Washington Park Arboretum, Puget Sound, page 80

Nisqually Estuary Boardwalk Trail, Billy Frank Jr. Nisqually National Wildlife Refuge, Puget Sound, page 108

Denny Creek Trail to Melakwa Lake, Mount Baker-Snoqualmie National Forest, I-90, page 164

Franklin Falls, Mount Baker-Snoqualmie National Forest, I-90, page 168

Best Hikes to Lakes

Ira Spring Trail-Mason Lake, Mount Baker-Snoqualmie National Forest, I-90, page 147

Snow Lake, Mount Baker-Snoqualmie National Forest, I-90, page 172

Lake Serene, Mount Baker-Snoqualmie National Forest, Highway 2, page 198

Lake Valhalla, Okanogan-Wenatchee National Forest, Highway 2, page 230

Lake Twentytwo, Mount Baker-Snoqualmie National Forest, Mountain Loop Highway, page 250

Best for Mountain Views

Heybrook Lookout, Mount Baker-Snoqualmie National Forest, Highway 2, page 202

Mount Dickerman, Mount Baker-Snoqualmie National Forest, Mountain Loop Highway, page 266

Tolmie Peak Lookout, Mount Rainier National Park, Mount Rainier, page 310

Second Burroughs, Mount Rainier National Park, Mount Rainier, page 338

Dege Peak, Mount Rainier National Park, Mount Rainier, page 343

Best Hikes Off the Beaten Path

Teneriffe Falls, hike to Mount Teneriffe, I-90, page 128

Rachel Lake, hike to Alta Mountain, I-90, page 179

Lake Valhalla, hike to Mount McCausland, Highway 2, page 230

Upper Big Quilcene-Marmot Pass, hike to Buckhorn Mountain, Olympic Peninsula, page 295

Second Burroughs, hike to Third Burroughs, Mount Rainier, page 338

Best Strenuous Hikes

Mailbox Peak, Middle Fork Snoqualmie Natural Resources Conservation Area, I-90, page 139

Bandera Mountain, Mount Baker-Snoqualmie National Forest, I-90, page 151

Blanca Lake, Mount Baker-Snoqualmie National Forest, Highway 2, page 194

Gothic Basin, Mount Baker-Snoqualmie National Forest, Mountain Loop Highway, page 270

Mount Pugh via Stujack Pass, Mount Baker-Snoqualmie National Forest, Mountain Loop Highway, page 278

Best for Waterfalls

Twin Falls, Olallie State Park, I-90, page 132

Franklin Falls, Mount Baker-Snoqualmie National Forest, I-90, page 168

Woody Trail to Wallace Falls, Wallace Falls State Park, Highway 2, page 190

view of Big Four Mountain from the Mount Dickerman Trail

Lake Serene, Mount Baker-Snoqualmie National Forest, Highway 2, page 198

Boulder River, Mount Baker-Snoqualmie National Forest, Mountain Loop Highway, page 240

Best for Wildflowers

Mount Townsend, Olympic National Forest, Olympic Peninsula, page 290

Upper Big Quilcene-Marmot Pass, Olympic National Forest, Olympic Peninsula, page 295

Spray Park, Mount Rainier National Park, Mount Rainier, page 314

Grand Park via Lake Eleanor, Mount Rainier National Park, Mount Rainier, page 327

Tipsoo Lake-Naches Peak Loop, Mount Rainier National Park, Mount Rainier, page 347

Hiking Tips

THE 10 ESSENTIALS

The 10 Essentials are a set of systems designed by The Mountaineers (www. mountaineers.org) to help hikers respond safely to an emergency and to prepare for spending the night outdoors.

1. Nutrition: Bring enough food for a day plus extra in case of an emergency.

2. Hydration: Carry an ample supply of water (at least one gallon per person per day) and a water treatment system.

3. First Aid: Keep a first-aid kit sealed in a waterproof plastic bag.

4. Emergency Shelter: Carry a reflective emergency blanket, bivy sack, or waterproof tarp.

5. Insulation: Pack extra clothing layers for varying weather conditions.

6. Illumination: Have a headlamp or flashlight and bring extra batteries.

7. Fire: Keep waterproof matches and a fire starter handy.

8. Sun Protection: Wear a hat, sunglasses, and sunscreen.

9. Navigation: Bring a topographic map and compass.

10. Repair Kit and Tools: A multipurpose tool, knife, scissors, and duct tape can come in handy on the trail.

Beyond the 10 Essentials

PERSONAL LOCATOR BEACONS AND SATELLITE MESSENGERS

Personal locator beacons (PLBs) and satellite messengers are electronic devices for communicating with others (friends, family, emergency services) when no cell reception is available, enabling you to signal for help in the event of an emergency. Devices differ in many ways, from the satellite networks they use to text messaging features to varying subscription options.

PLBs and satellite messengers are supported by different satellite networks (non-profit COSPAS/SARSAT for PLBs, for-profit Iridium or Globalstar for satellite messengers) that vary in coverage. Some devices have two-way text messaging, while others have one-way text messaging or no text messaging options.

PLBs do not require an annual subscription, while satellite messengers have a variety of subscription options. Before you invest in a device, evaluate their functions, satellite networks, and total costs carefully, focusing on what features are most important to you. Check out **Outdoor Gear Lab** (www.outdoorgearlab.com) for a helpful side-by-side comparison of PLBs and satellite messengers.

EXERCISE GOOD JUDGMENT

Use good judgment on the trail to make smart, informed decisions that will keep you and your fellow hikers safe. Turn around early in poor weather conditions,

HIKING APPS

There are lots of great apps that can enhance your hike, from predicting the weather to tracking your mileage to identifying what the heck you're looking at. Here are my favorites and why I love them.

- **Bugle** (www.gobugle.com) makes it easy to share your hiking plans with an emergency contact and to notify them when you've made it home safe. The app will email your hiking itinerary to your designated emergency contacts. Once you've finished your hike, use it to notify your emergency contacts that you're safe. If you don't check in, your emergency contacts are sent text and email alerts, and advised of the next steps to take.

- **PeakFinder** (www.peakfinder.org) is a great tool for identifying mountains while hiking. Before you head out, download a custom map for the area you want to be able to identify peaks in (such as Washington State). While you're out hiking, use the app's viewfinder to match the mountain shapes you see to the mountain shapes in the app, and voilà, you've identified a mountain.

- **Gaia GPS** (www.gaiagps.com) lets you track, save, and share your hiking information. View your mileage, speed, and elevation gain and track your trail in real time for instant feedback. I love being able to see how far I've hiked, how far I have left to go, and to check my average speed. Sync your hikes online to view them later, or download a gpx track.

- **WSDOT** (www.wsdot.wa.gov) The Washington State Department of Transportation app is a great one-stop shop for real-time travel and traffic information in the state.

- **First Aid by American Red Cross** (www.redcross.org) can help you recognize and treat medical conditions such as heat stroke, an asthma attack, hypothermia, and sprains that can happen while out on the trail.

- **Dark Sky** (www.darkskyapp.com) allows you to easily check hourly precipitation forecasts for your hiking area, get notified when showers begin, and check hourly temperatures.

and stop to use a map and compass if a route feels "off" or you're unsure which junction to take. Think ahead and be prepared to pivot in adverse conditions.

WHISTLE

A whistle can be useful to communicate with others about your location—whether it's your hiking group or a search and rescue team. Its loud, high-pitched sound carries farther than a shout. Many backpacks even come with a small, built-in whistle on the chest strap buckle.

INSECT REPELLENT

While long pants and sleeves are the best deterrent to warding off pesky bugs, insect repellent for your skin, clothing, and gear can give you an extra boost of

Hiking poles help with balance and leverage at water crossings.

protection. Products containing DEET or Picaridin are considered the most effective; however, they vary in texture, odor, protection time, which insects they repel, and the harshness of ingredients. Check product guidelines and labels carefully.

Purchase clothing made with insect-repellent fabric, such as Insect Shield, or use a repellent specifically designed for clothing and gear such as Permethrin (follow instructions on the product's label). Stash a bug net in your backpack to wear over your hat when you come across swarms.

TREKKING POLES
Trekking poles are not just handy for swatting at thick branches and pesky spider webs, but they also help propel you forward, provide balance and traction in snow or during stream crossings, and offer relief to knees and the lower body by redistributing pack load. These convenient tools allow you to poke a puddle, mud, or loose rock to see what's what. When selecting trekking poles, check for comfort, collapsibility, durability, and ease of adjustment (lever-locking poles are generally easier to adjust than twist-lock). Most hikers appreciate a comfortable grip, being able to strap poles easily to their pack, and changing the length of the poles to suit the terrain. A sturdy pair of trekking poles will last several seasons.

ELECTRONICS
With better camera technology and the proliferation of outdoor apps and tools, it's hard to turn your back on the usefulness of bringing your phone on a hike. Take

thoughtful steps to keep your device protected. Your phone is fragile—susceptible to failing in a variety of scenarios, from extreme temperatures to loss of battery life. Lengthen battery life by putting your phone in airplane mode, dimming the screen, and closing nonessential apps. Keep your device warm in cold weather by stowing it in an inside pocket close to your body. Use a protective case and pack a portable phone charger (with any necessary connector cables) in case you run out of juice.

ON THE TRAIL
Wildlife

Observing wildlife can be a thrilling experience—there's nothing quite like seeing a nanny goat feed alongside the trail with her kid or a bear shoot across a meadow. However, wildlife are as advertised: wild. While many hikers have positive experiences observing wildlife, animals can act unpredictably. A little knowledge about what to do when encountering black bears, cougars, and mountain goats can prevent a negative experience, protect you in the event of an unlikely attack, and keep wildlife safe from negative human impacts.

BEARS

According to the **Department of Fish and Wildlife** (WDFW, www.wdfw.wa.gov), Washington State has a healthy black bear population of roughly 25,000-30,000 bears. While a very small number of grizzly bears can be found in North Cascades National Park, you're more likely to encounter a black bear than a grizzly bear when hiking in Washington.

Despite the name, black bears come in a range of colors—from cinnamon brown to dusty black. These omnivores feast on plants, nuts, and berries as well as rodents and fish. They are great swimmers and tree climbers, often taking a dip in a lake to cool off or sending their cubs up a tree if danger is present. Black bears are also creatures of opportunity, and items such as trash, bird feeders, and smells from campgrounds can be a powerful motivator to approach humans for the chance at food—especially if they've lost their fear of humans. The WDFW estimates that 95 percent of the calls they receive about conflicts with black bears are due to human behavior, such as not storing food properly at a campsite or not taking steps to prevent animal access to trash.

No one wants to imagine being attacked by a bear. Fortunately, attacks are unlikely and black bears prefer to avoid you. To avoid a bear encounter: make your presence known while you're on the trail, maintain a safe distance from any bears or cubs, and keep children and pets close. When camping in bear country, pitch your tent at least 100 yards away from any cooking and food storage site. Clear tents of any items with an aroma, including food, garbage, toothpaste, and hygiene products; deposit these items in a bear-resistant container or hang them in a bear-resistant sack at least 12 feet off the ground and 4 feet from the tree trunk.

While hiking, periodically hum, whistle, sing, or talk to a hiking buddy to avoid spooking a bear. If you do spot a bear in the distance, keep at least 100 yards (about the length of a football field) between you and the bear. If you unexpectedly cross a bear, stay calm. Avoid eye contact and do not run—bears can reach speeds of 35 miles per hour. Back away slowly or move in a wide arc around the bear. Wave your arms and talk loudly to identify yourself as human. In the unlikely event that a bear attacks, bear spray can also be used to deter a charging bear. If that fails, play dead by curling into a ball or lie face down with your hands laced behind your head (to protect it). Be still, calm, and quiet. Your goal is to get the bear to stop its attack by letting it know that you are not a threat.

Cougars

Cougars (also known as pumas or mountain lions) are large members of the cat family and are native to Washington State. These shy, solitary animals can measure up to eight feet long (from nose to tail) and range in numbers roughly 1,800-2,100.

Cougar attacks on humans are uncommon. If you do encounter a cougar, stay calm. Pick up any children immediately and keep pets close. Face the cougar and back away slowly. Try to make yourself look bigger by opening up your jacket and spreading your arms—do not crouch or try to hide. If a cougar threatens, yell, shout, and throw objects to discourage an attack. If a cougar does attack, fight back vigorously by using your hands, rocks, sticks, and any gear at hand.

Cougars are classified as a game animal; a hunting license is required for hunting them in open season. Cougars can generally be found throughout the state, with the exception of the Columbia River Basin.

Mountain Goats

Roughly 2,400-3,200 mountain goats inhabit Washington State and are typically found near or above the tree line in high-elevation areas with steep, rocky cliffs and alpine meadows. Male and female mountain goats have shaggy, white coats, sharp, black horns, and short tails and generally have a shy, unassuming disposition. While it can be a memorable experience to observe a mountain goat, be aware of the mountain goat guidelines issued by the forest service and WDFW to help maintain a balanced relationship between hikers and goats.

Mountain goats crave salt (commonly found in human sweat, urine, and food); hikers who feed mountain goats or urinate next to the trail may unknowingly encourage their interactions with humans as normal. This can lead to goats boldly approaching other hikers and may lead to aggressive behavior. Keep a distance of at least 50 yards from any goats and avoid approaching, chasing, or feeding them.

If a goat persistently follows you, then stand your ground. Wave your arms, yell, and throw small rocks to establish your personal space and discourage the

If you encounter a mountain goat on the trail, give it plenty of space.

goat from following you. To learn more about mountain goats and to watch an informative video, visit WDFW (www.wdfw.wa.gov) online.

Poison Ivy and Poison Oak

Hikers are more likely to run into poison oak in the Puget Sound area, northern Olympic Peninsula, and Columbia Gorge than to encounter poison ivy, found east of the Cascades. Both plants can be shrubs or vines, with greenish-white flowers that develop into small, off-white berries. Poison oak and poison ivy leaves are made up of three leaflets that turn red in autumn. Poison oak leaflets look like mittens or oak leaves, while poison ivy leaflets are oval-shaped with a pointed tip. Both plants can cause a red, itchy rash, swelling, and blisters when skin comes into contact with an oil in the sap (urushiol) found on the plants' leaves, roots, and stems. Urushiol can transfer to a person from hiking clothing and even pet fur.

Protect your skin by wearing long-sleeved shirts, long pants, and socks. Stick to clear, established paths and practice identifying poison ivy and oak so that you can recognize the plants on the trail. If you do come into contact with poison ivy or poison oak, wash the skin immediately with soap and water and wash any clothing or gear on hand at the time of contact. To help relieve itchiness, use an anti-itch cream, a cold compress, or take a cool shower. Rashes normally go away after 2-3 weeks, but contact your doctor if you have concerns.

Ticks

Ticks are found throughout Washington State, usually in wooded, grassy, and brushy areas, but tick-borne diseases are rare. Ticks are members of the arachnid

OUTDOOR PHOTOGRAPHY TIPS

It can be a challenge to capture images in nature, whether it's a group photo or mountain vista. These tips from photographer Ken Stanback (www.kenstanback.com) can help you take better pictures while on the trail.

- **Use a polarized filter.** The best lighting is usually near sunrise or sunset; however, hikers often take photos midday. A polarized filter can tone down the high-contrast sunlight, darkening the sky and giving the image a more dramatic look. If you don't have a polarized filter, try aiming the camera lens through your sunglasses or shooting with the sun at your back.

- **Create an entry for the viewer's eyes to focus on.** Use a leading line to draw a viewer's eyes into your photograph. First determine the focal point of the scene: Is it a mountain peak, the trees? Then look for something leading toward the focal point—like a tree branch hanging over the scene or a river—that will direct the viewer's eyes.

- **Use the rule of thirds.** If you want your fellow hikers to be a part of a vista, place them in one-third of the image. This allows people to be part of the scene without overpowering it. Placing your subject to the left or the right of the image's center also gives the viewer an entry into your photo.

- **In a group shot, fill the frame.** The focal point of a group image should be on the people, so get in close for a really tight shot—zoom in or walk right up. One option is to leave a little scenery around the image's edges to show the location.

And most important, slow down and enjoy the scene!

family; they have large bodies, tiny heads, and eight legs. Ticks can latch on to human and animal skin, embedding part of their mouth into skin to feed on blood. When this occurs, diseases (such as Lyme disease) can transfer from the tick to humans and animals. Yep, dogs can get Lyme disease and other infectious diseases from ticks, too.

Take a few simple steps before, during, and after your hike to help protect against ticks. Wear long sleeves and long pants and tuck your pant legs into your socks. Choose light colors that can make spotting a tick easier. Pretreating clothes with Permethrin can help repel ticks, as can using an insect repellent that contains DEET (follow instructions on the product's label). While hiking, stick to cleared trails and avoid grassy areas and low-hanging branches. Hit the shower soon after you get home, thoroughly checking your body, clothes, hiking gear, and furry friend for ticks.

If you do spot a tick, use fine-tipped tweezers to grip the tick as close to the skin as possible. Pull upward with firm pressure; you want to pull the tick out in one piece. Once removed, disinfect your hands and the bite area with soap and warm water or rubbing alcohol.

If any part of the tick remains in your skin, use tweezers for further removal. Save the tick in an airtight container and bring it to your doctor so that it can be tested for Lyme disease. The **Centers for Disease Control** (www.cdc.gov) recommends contacting your doctor if a rash, fever, aches, or pains develop within a few weeks of the bite.

HEALTH AND SAFETY
Hiking Fitness

Fitness plays a major part in helping you safely begin and complete a hike. Whether seeking solitude, exercise, or quality time with family and friends, we all hike at different paces for different reasons. Give yourself permission to progress at your own pace and acknowledge your own personal hiking journey. What's important is to get outside and be active in a way you can enjoy, setting yourself up for a safe and fun hike.

If you're new to hiking, start with easy 2-3-mile hikes to gain confidence and experience in the outdoors. Build up your hiking experience through a steady progression of easy, moderate, and strenuous hikes in order to warm up to longer distances. If you're looking to up your hiking game, pick a goal hike. Find a regular hiking buddy or a group to join, and set up a series of increasingly challenging hikes until you accomplish your goal.

Hiking through the Seasons

The Pacific Northwest hiking experience runs in a unique seasonal cycle. It helps to have a general sense of what to expect in each season so that you are prepared to handle varying conditions. It's also fun to get a feel for which hikes work well in which season so that you can enjoy a hike at its "peak" time.

Spring

Though your favorite summer summits are still covered in lingering snow and it feels like the rain will never end, spring is actually a great time to hit up those waterfall and riverside hikes (typically raging from snowmelt and the rainy season). Hiking in late spring is also great for wildflowers.

Expect trails to be muddy from the rain and overgrown from plants enjoying their spring growth spurt. Pack layers, gloves, and warm clothing; though temperatures may have warmed, it can still be quite cold on spring hikes. If it's been a long, stormy winter, roads and trails may be icy or have experienced blowdowns, high water levels, and bridge washouts. Check trip reports online at **Washington Trails Association** (WTA, www.wta.org) for updates.

Above all, be patient. It's tempting to get a running start on your favorite summer hike, even if there is snow. But if you're not prepared with the proper gear, traction, and knowledge for snow travel, it's best to wait.

SUMMER

Snow and cooler conditions may still be present into the summer on popular hikes such as Mount Pilchuck, Snow Lake, and Granite Mountain. Check road and trail conditions, and don't assume hikes are snow-free just because it's June or July. When conditions are good, hit the summits on the Mountain Loop Highway and Olympic Peninsula, take in wildflowers and mountain views at Mount Rainier, and go berry picking in mid-August.

Take advantage of your winter and spring fitness regimen to explore new places and push yourself to challenging distances and elevations. Enjoy the few short months when summits like Mount Pugh are snow-free.

Keep an eye on temperatures and sun exposure and pack bug spray, a sun hat, sunscreen, and plenty of water to stay hydrated in hot temperatures. Higher elevations can still be chilly, though—always prepare with an extra layer for the summit.

FALL

Early to mid-fall is a wonderful season for hikes to mountain views and alpine lakes set amid brightly colored fall foliage—think Rachel Lake, Granite Mountain, and Lake Valhalla—as well as savoring the changing season with a crisp coolness in the air, rolling fog, salmon spawning, and—finally!—less pesky bugs to swat. By mid-October, the rainy season is typically in full swing, with dropping temperatures, rising water levels, and snow dusting the mountains. This time of year is another opportunity to visit those lower-elevation waterfall and riverside hikes, as well as evaluate your rain gear. It's also a good idea to wear bright colors as hunting season gears up. Sign up early in the season for an avalanche awareness class, mountaineering class, snowshoe class, or even a mushroom-foraging class to mix up your summer routine and prepare for winter hiking.

WINTER

Even when the high country is covered in thick blankets of snow, there are still hikes you can do; it just means adjusting your gear, the location and elevation of your hikes, and your expectations. Try low-elevation hikes (wildlife refuges, state parks, the Issaquah Alps), coastal hikes (Padilla Bay, Rosario Head to Lighthouse Point), and areas that benefit from the rain shadow effect, such as Whidbey Island.

Take an **avalanche awareness class** (www.rei.com, www.avalanche.org, www.avtraining.org) and visit the Northwest Avalanche Center's website (www.nwac.us) to educate yourself about avalanche conditions. Explore guided snowshoe walks in the Mount Baker-Snoqualmie National Forest (www.fs.usda.gov) or Mount Rainier National Park or Olympic National Park (www.nps.gov) as a way to get outside in the wintertime and breathe in the distant snowcapped peaks.

When traveling, make sure your car is prepped for winter conditions. Pack warm layers and carry traction devices, such as microspikes, in case you encounter snow and ice.

THE RAINY SEASON

The rainy season in the greater Seattle area typically starts in mid-October and feels like we just can't shake it until early July—it's a joke that around here we call June "Junuary." But there are lots of great reasons to keep hiking in the rainy season: Trails are typically less crowded, previously hidden views of lakes and mountains open up due to the lack of leaves on the trees, the opportunity to establish or maintain a solid hiking fitness base to build on once the summer season rolls around, and feeling pretty darn good about yourself for getting outside in not-so-ideal conditions. Here are some tips for hiking in the rainy season.

- **Become a weather forecasting ninja.** Check the National Oceanic and Atmospheric Administration's (NOAA, www.weather.gov) hourly weather forecast graph—a solid source of information about hourly temperatures, precipitation potential, cloud cover, wind, and thunder. I use it to figure out if there will be rain during my hike, what time I need to get to the summit in order to have the best shot at a view, and what layers and gear to pack according to the forecasted temperature.
- **Be rain-ready.** Keeping your hands, feet, head, and body warm and dry can be the difference between a safe, rainy-day hike and a miserable, hazardous one. Investing in rain gear is one way to stay safe in rainy weather and elongate your hiking season. If you're buying rain gear for the first time, start with the basics: waterproof boots/shoes, waterproof jacket with hood, waterproof pants, and waterproof gloves. Choose layers that will help retain heat, wick away sweat, and dry quickly: There is no worse feeling than hiking in cold, soggy, wet clothing that sticks to your skin. Not only that—it can lead to hypothermia by preventing you from getting warm. Cotton is comfy in pajamas and our favorite sweats, but it dries slowly and sucks up moisture like a sponge. Leave your favorite cotton T-shirt at home and pick fabrics such as merino wool or polyester instead. Line the inside of your pack with a garbage bag or use a waterproof backpack cover to help keep items inside your pack dry while you hike.
- **Have a Plan B.** A road closure, bridge washout across a raging creek, stormy weather, or unanticipated snow can turn your plans upside down. Have an idea of an alternate hike nearby before you set out, or use the Washington Trails Association's Trailblazer App to search for hikes nearby when your planned hike doesn't work out. Expect that trails will generally be muddier and more waterlogged during the rainy season, and be prepared with the appropriate footwear.
- **Just go!** It's so tempting to spend a rainy afternoon on the couch or write off your hiking plans if it looks overcast outside. While it's true that hiking in the

rain requires a little more thought and a certain mindset, it can feel great to brave the weather, and even be fun when you're prepared with the right gear. If you're not convinced, check the hourly precipitation forecast—you may be able to squeak out an hour or two on a nearby park or trail in between showers. Packing a thermos of hot chocolate and hand warmers can be a nice rainy-day-hike boost and provide some extra warmth.

Hiking Prep

It's all too easy to forget a map, a water bottle, or even a rain jacket on a rainy day (true story). Miscalculating the weather conditions, how much water you'll need, or how long a hike will take could also lead to a potentially hazardous situation. Thinking about your hike before you start will give you a great head start at having a fun, safe, and successful outing. Here are some tips before hitting the trail.

- **Share your plans.** Give a friend or emergency contact a timeline of your day, the name and location of the trail, and your expected return time. I love using the Bugle app for this; it's easy to send my hiking plans to my emergency contacts, and the check-in feature alerts them when I'm safely back home.

- **Check weather conditions.** Be prepared to hike in the forecasted weather on your hiking day! Knowing the forecast tells you how to dress, what layers and rain gear to pack, and how much food and water to bring, and helps you mentally prepare for your hike. My go-to is NOAA (www.weather.gov) to get an idea of the weather for the region I'll be hiking in, as well as WSDOT (www.wsdot.com) to understand what's happening at the mountain passes. In winter, check NWAC (www.nwac.us) for avalanche forecasts.

- **Check road conditions.** It's a bummer when you've driven all the way to an access road only to find it inaccessible for some reason—it's closed for the season, closed for construction, washed out, blocked by a tree, or snowed in. Save yourself the aggravation and check the conditions before you go. Sometimes it's as easy as checking a recent trip report on WTA's website or social media sites. When in doubt, call the land manager affiliated with the hike or check their corresponding website. The Washington State Department of Transportation (www.wsdot.gov) is a great resource for traffic, ferries, and highway conditions.

- **Check trail conditions.** Checking trail conditions helps you learn if wildflowers or fall foliage are popping, if bugs are swarming your favorite lake hike, how much foot traffic a trail is seeing, if there is snow on the trail or muddy conditions, or if there have been animal sightings such as bears or mountain goats. Check trip reports on www.wta.org, social media, and online forums, or call up the land manager affiliated with the hike. Checking Instagram and Facebook feeds can be a great way to gauge the trail conditions and popularity of a trail, helping you decide whether to tackle it now or wait another week—or even later in the season—to go for it.

- **Organize your parking pass and driving directions.** Double-check which pass (if any) is required before you hit the trail. If you need to purchase a day pass, you can purchase and print out day passes for the Discover Pass (www. discoverpass.wa.gov) and Northwest Forest Pass (www.discovernw.org) ahead of time. Have the driving directions to a trailhead handy so that you're ready to go. Forest roads can have unsigned junctions; knowing where you're going can keep you from driving in circles.
- **Pack thoughtfully.** Customize what goes into your pack to the environment and conditions you'll be hiking in. Think about the trail's location, length, elevation gain, exposure, temperature, and difficulty: bring extra water and food for more difficult hikes and hotter or colder days. A significant chance of rain? Pack that rain gear. A high-elevation hike in the shoulder season? Pack a winter hat, winter gloves, and traction devices. Adjust clothing, layers, and gear depending on the trail and weather conditions.
- **Familiarize yourself.** Pack a trail map and review your route for a sense of where you're heading and in which direction. Practice using your water filter, hiking apps, and compass. Test the waterproofing of your backpack, boots, and rain gear if you're heading out in the rain.
- **Respect your limits.** Truthfully acknowledge your hiking fitness and ability before attempting an ambitious hike. If you're with a group and it's unclear how quickly or slowly the group will hike, ask. Speak up if you need to slow down and share pertinent medical conditions with the trip leader or a trustworthy hiking buddy before you start. Don't be afraid to call it a day if it goes beyond your comfort zone—we've all been there, and it's not worth risking your health, safety, or the safety of others in your group.
- **Protect your valuables.** Lock your car. Don't leave your wallet, laptop, camera equipment, or anything of value sitting in plain sight inside your vehicle at a trailhead. Pack them in your backpack, or remove them from your car before you leave home.

WILDERNESS ETIQUETTE
Trail Etiquette

With more and more people hitting the trails, it's important to practice good trail etiquette so that hikers can have positive interactions with each other. Be a good trail steward and set a good example for other hikers by observing the following guidelines.

- **Acknowledge other hikers.** A nod, smile, or friendly "Hello" is a simple gesture that helps foster a sense of community on the trails. Your fellow hikers are often a great source of information for trail conditions and wildlife sightings, as well as for rescuers if something were to happen to you. Of course, if a person makes you uncomfortable, move along.
- **Be aware of your surroundings.** For many people, hiking is an escape from the pace and pressures of everyday life. Keep a low voice when having a conversation, enjoying the natural sights and sounds on the trail. Use earphones when listening to music. Keep your ears open for hikers that may be coming up behind you, and step aside to let them pass.
- **Stick to established trails.** Trails wind uphill in a zigzag pattern called switchbacks, and some people cut straight through them, known as "cutting switchbacks." This can cause erosion on the mountainside and be misleading for other hikers, who may see a rough trail and think it's an alternative to the established trail. Avoid cutting switchbacks to set a good example for other hikers and to protect the environment.
- **Yield like a champ.** If you're going downhill, step aside for uphill hikers so that they can continue their upward momentum without breaking their rhythm. An uphill hiker may be happy for a break and wave you on, but offer to step aside first in a show of respect and to encourage others to follow the precedent—increasingly important as trails get busier. Mountain bikers always yield to hikers.
- **Step aside for horses.** Hikers, trail runners, and mountain bikers—basically, everybody!—yields to horses. When you see a horse and rider approaching, step to the downhill side of the trail to let them pass. If you are coming up behind a horse and rider, call out to let them know you're there and ask the rider if it is okay to pass. Give them plenty of space.
- **Minimize your impact.** As the saying goes, "Take only pictures, leave only footprints." Pack out all your garbage and take care of your business at least 200 feet from water sources, trails, and campsites to help preserve the environment and hiking experience for everyone.

Hiking with Kids

Hitting the trail with children brings a different energy than hiking alone or with other adults. Add kids into the mix and an excursion becomes playful, whimsical,

SEARCH AND RESCUE Q&A

No one wants to be in a situation where search and rescue is called, but unfortunately accidents do happen—even to well-prepared and experienced hikers. Here are some insights from Larry Colagiovanni, chair of **Seattle Mountain Rescue** (www.seattlemountainrescue.org), on how to stay safe while hiking.

Which trails near Seattle does search and rescue get called out to? Rattlesnake Ledge, Mailbox Peak, Mount Si, and Mount Pilchuck.

What are the most common reasons hikers call? Getting caught in the dark without a headlamp, slipping and tweaking an ankle or knee, and accidentally taking a wrong turn/getting off-trail and becoming lost.

What should you do if you or someone is lost or injured? Ask yourself, "Are you and your friend safe?" If you're not, get to the safest place you can. Assess the situation calmly and determine whether you can safely and reasonably help yourself or your friend. If not, call for help by activating your SPOT device, personal locator beacon, or by calling 911.

Take shelter and stay put, but remain visible to rescuers. Wear bright clothing, yell, blow a whistle, or set your headlamp to blink mode. While waiting for help to arrive, stay warm: wear all your layers, eat a snack, and (safely) move your body to generate heat.

Is there a fee for search and rescue services? Search and rescue is free in King County. However, when you return to the trailhead, you may need to be transported by ambulance or critical air transport, which may incur charges.

and full of discovery! Of course, children are also unpredictable and require a lot of care. Here are some tips and tricks from Kate Spiller, author of *Wild Tales Of* (www.wildtalesof.com) to help you make the most of their time outdoors.

Build prior knowledge. Raise excitement and help your child understand what to expect by talking about the hike before venturing off. Read books about the environment, study a local field guide, or watch online videos or trip reports. The more your child knows, the more connected they will feel and thus more likely to have a positive experience.

Be prepared. Timing is of the essence with kids—there is so much to occupy *your* mind (and hands) that it's best to be as prepared as possible. Pack snacks, lunches, and backpacks the night before, print directions to the trailhead in advance, and research any passes and permits.

Wear appropriate gear and clothing. Have appropriate footwear for the weather and trail conditions and choose clothing that protects from the elements. Avoid cotton in favor of technical fabric or merino wool to help regulate body

Do you have any advice for hikers new to Washington? Consider taking a class. The Mountaineers (www.mountaineers.org), REI (www.rei.com), and Mount Baker-Snoqualmie National Forest (www.fs.usda.gov) offer great introductory classes and field trips.

- Don't go alone. Join a hiking group (page 356).
- Carry the 10 Essentials (page 15).
- Learn how to navigate using a map and compass. GPSs are a great idea too.
- When there's snow on the trail, especially the popular ones, it becomes extremely slick. Carry traction devices like microspikes or Yaktrax.
- Take a class on navigating avalanche terrain. Carry a beacon, probe, and shovel and know how to use them. Practice often.

Great suggestions, thanks! Any other tips you'd like to share?
Always check trail conditions and weather forecasts before heading out.

Don't assume you'll have cell phone service. Instead, consider getting a SPOT device or personal locator beacon in case of an emergency.

Summer hikes can become quite hazardous in the winter. Granite Mountain and Source Lake are notorious for avalanches. It's easy to get lost at places like Mason Lake, where multiple trails come together and become harder to follow in the snow with footprints going in all directions.

Prepare your vehicle for winter hiking. Always have a first-aid kit, warm clothes and a blanket, drinking water, and a flashlight in your car.

temperature. If you're hiking with babies and toddlers, be prepared to carry your children. Invest in a soft-structured or frame carrier that is comfortable and fits well.

Choose goal-oriented destinations. Kids often feel more motivated on the trail when an exciting destination awaits. Waterfalls, historical landmarks, viewpoints, beaches, and creeks all help entice young hikers along the trail.

Consider mileage and elevation. Hikes should accommodate your young companion's ability and maturity. Take into consideration the total mileage, elevation gain, and other technical aspects before heading off on an adventure. It's often best to start small, or choose a trail with multiple options so you can add on if interest and energy are high. Even short distances can be very sweet!

Pack plenty of trail fuel. Pack plenty of water and take frequent snack breaks to keep energy and spirits high. For longer hikes, consider packing a full lunch to enjoy at the halfway point. Young hikers might be encouraged by a special snack reserved just for hikes!

Play games and sing songs! Play trail games and sing songs as you hike. Scavenger hunts, counting critters (or natural elements), playing follow the leader and I-Spy all help to engage children in the world around them and add fun to the hiking experience.

Now go! All the preparation in the world won't add up to anything unless you take the bold step to actually get out the door. Be brave, and go enjoy the outdoors with your children!

Hiking with Dogs

Dogs can be wonderful hiking companions, but, like us, are susceptible to injuries and health conditions. Below are some tips to help you and your pup have a safe hike. A special thank-you goes to Michaela Eaves, public information officer at the **Washington State Animal Response Team** (WASART,

Franklin Falls is a wonderful hike for families.

www.washingtonsart.org), for her insights and recommendations.

Know before you go. While dogs are welcome on many trails in national forests and state parks, they are prohibited in other places, such as Dungeness Spit, to protect wildlife and environmentally sensitive areas. For each trail description in this book, check for the dog icon, indicating that dogs are allowed on that trail.

Prepare a pet first-aid kit. Pack a pet first-aid kit in case your pup gets injured, such as tearing his or her paw pad on snow and ice. Items like maxi pads, vet wrap, a plastic bag, and duct tape can come in handy for paw wrapping. Visit WASART's YouTube channel to learn how to wrap an injured paw, and consider taking a pet first-aid class (www.walksnwags.com).

Pack water and snacks. Bring plenty of water and a snack to help keep your pup hydrated and nourished. If cool creeks are in short supply, dogs can overheat or get dehydrated. Give them lots of drink breaks to help keep them happy and healthy.

Rock that leash. Leash your dog to prevent him or her from running into unsafe terrain, getting into an altercation with a fellow dog or with wildlife, and to help other hikers have a positive experience on the trail. Dogs are creatures of accepting "what is"—your dog is happy to be on an adventure with you whatever the terms.

Have a poop system. Make packing out poop less stinky. Use a doggie pack or a special dog waste bag to help stifle the smell of a filled poo bag, and keep it away from food and clothing. Alternatively, dig a cat hole and bury the poop at least 200 feet from a water source.

Be emergency ready. WASART recommends the following steps in an emergency:

- Take a deep breath and remain calm.
- Call 911 or WASART's (425/681-5498). Sometimes you can text when a call can't make it through.
- Stay with your dog. Tethering an injured dog to a tree or leaving it with a stranger can leave him or her vulnerable if a rescue takes longer than planned.
- If you send someone else for help, then stay with your pet. Leaving your original location can mean additional hours and confusion for a rescue team.
- If your dog runs over a steep embankment, you must evaluate your safety first. Use caution to check

Give your pup plenty of breaks to keep them happy and healthy on the trail.

the dog's location. If you are with a buddy, send them for help and stay put. If you are alone, mark the spot where the dog went over, whether or not you can see your dog. Consider leaving a note in case someone finds your dog. Stay put if you can, but go for help if it's the only way.

Protect the Outdoors

It's hard sometimes to picture the impact you have on the environment when you're hiking alone or in a small group. But when you consider the number of people that visit a trail each year, it becomes clear how the actions of many can snowball. Mount Rainier National Park receives up to two *million* visitors per year—nearly 1.9 million people in 2015 alone. If even a fraction of those people decided to leave their toilet paper behind a bush or step into a protected meadow to get a better photograph of Mount Rainier, can you picture the impact that would have?

We can help protect the outdoors by leaving as little trace of our outdoor excursions as possible. This concept is known as Leave No Trace (LNT) and is embodied in a set of seven principles, outlined by the **Leave No Trace Center for Outdoor Ethics** (www.lnt.org):

- **Plan ahead and prepare.** Research group size limits and follow them. Leave a little extra time for finding a durable campsite. Pick a less popular trail or area to explore to minimize your impact. Pack clothing and gear responsibly for weather and trail conditions.
- **Travel and camp on durable surfaces.** Hike on established trails to help

prevent erosion. Avoid cutting switchbacks and trampling vegetation. Camp on durable surfaces, such as hard, bare ground, 200 feet from water.

- **Dispose of waste properly.** Bury waste in a 6-8-inch cat hole 200 feet away from a trail, campsite, or water source. Bring some kind of bag for packing out toilet paper, hygiene products, and garbage—including orange peels, banana peels, and nut shells.
- **Leave what you find.** Leave wildflowers and historical artifacts for other hikers to enjoy—take photographs or sketch them instead. Keep trees as nature intended—never use nails or make carvings in a tree's bark.
- **Minimize campfire impacts.** Learn the campfire rules for a trail and follow them. Where campfires are allowed, use established campfire rings. Never leave a campfire unattended, and make sure ashes are cool to the touch before leaving.
- **Respect wildlife.** Observe wildlife from a distance and do not feed them— they can lose their fear of humans and subsequently approach humans more aggressively for food. Keep your dog leashed to avoid disturbing wildlife.
- **Be considerate of other visitors.** Keep your voice low, step away if you need to make a call, and use earphones when listening to music. Step aside for horses and uphill hikers.

Another way to take action and protect the outdoors is to support outdoor organizations such as **The Mountaineers** (www.mountaineers.org) and **Washington Trails Association** (www.wta.org). Sign up for a volunteer work party, write a trip report, take a class, or help by becoming a member.

Taking Care of Business

Nature can call at any time, even if there's a vault toilet at the trailhead or a pit toilet along the trail. Coming prepared with the knowledge and supplies to take care of yourself not only helps keep trails clean and protects outside spaces, but frees you up to focus on having a great hike—without using extra energy thinking about handling a pit stop. It also helps your fellow hikers have a positive experience too. No one wants to stumble across wads of used toilet paper, maxi pads, and yep—even feces—next to a trail, but it has become an increasingly common experience, especially on popular trails. Sure, it takes some practice, but stick with it and experiment to find a system that works for you; soon enough it will become part of your hiking routine.

Before you set out, stash a trowel and plastic bag in your backpack for burying poop and packing out used toilet paper. (I've found a gardening trowel with a narrow shaft, purchased at my local hardware store, works well). Try to pee on rocks or bare ground instead of vegetation to avoid attracting animals. For poop, either bury it or pack it out. For burying, try to find a spot 200 feet—100 big steps—from the trail, water, and campsites that isn't already being used. Dig a hole 6-8 inches deep, do your business, and cover it back up. For packing out waste, make your own double-bag or use bags designed specifically for packing out waste, such as RESTOP bags. Some land managers may have special systems and regulations for waste disposal, so it's good to check before you go to see what your options are.

Ladies, always pack out used pads, tampons, and hygiene products. There are lots of clever ideas out there for packing out these items—experiment to see which you prefer. Personally, I pack two small plastic bags—one with wet wipes and one for sticking garbage in—inside a gallon-sized bag and find this system works for me on day hikes. I'll also put extra supplies in the gallon-sized bag, which helps keep the garbage from coming in contact with items in my backpack.

PASSES, PERMITS, AND FEES

Though the pass system in Washington State can be confusing, it can help to think about it in terms of the type of land a hike is on. Generally, there are three major categories of lands that require passes: state lands, national forests, and national parks. For state lands like Washington State Parks, a Discover Pass is required. Hikes in national forests with developed trailheads, such as Annette Lake and the Ira Spring Trail, require a Northwest Forest Pass. A national park fee is required at entrances to national parks. Trails on county land or local parks don't normally require passes. Below is the key information you need to know about each pass, and their corresponding websites for more information. Each trail in the book notes which pass (if any) is needed for a particular hike.

Discover Pass

A **Discover Pass** (866/320-9933, www.discoverpass.wa.gov or www.dol.wa.gov, $10 for day pass, $30 for annual pass) is required on state lands managed by Washington State Parks, the Washington Department of Natural Resources, and the Washington Department of Fish and Wildlife. The Discover Pass provides access to more than 1,000 trails, 100 state parks, 80 natural areas, and 30 wildlife areas, including Twin Falls, Little Si, and Mount Si. The pass is relatively new, created in 2011 by the Washington State Legislature. The pass was meant to generate revenue for these state lands in order to make up for sharp decreases in funding. Washington State Parks alone saw their funding from Washington State's General Fund dwindle from $94.5 million in the 2007-2009 budget to $8.7 million in the 2013-2015 budget—a 90.7 percent reduction over a period of six years (source: www.parks.state.wa.us). This led to a dramatic shift for Washington State Parks, which not only had to trim its programs and personnel, but also take creative steps to make up for the reduction in resources.

When you purchase a Discover Pass, 84 percent of those funds go to Washington State Parks to help keep the parks open. The other 16 percent is split between the Department of Fish and Wildlife and Department of Natural Resources. Purchasing a Discover Pass, or making a modest donation when you renew your vehicle tabs with the Washington State Department of Licensing, is a small yet vital action we can take to help support our state parks and lands.

You can purchase a pass online, in person, over the phone, or when you renew your vehicle tags through the Washington State Department of Licensing. When purchasing your pass through a participating retailer or licensed vendor, such as REI or Fred Meyer, a transaction fee and dealer fee applies, making the actual cost $11.50 for a day pass and $35 for an annual pass. Passes that are purchased from the Washington State Department of Licensing, automated pay stations, and staff at state parks are not subject to the fees.

A pass can be shared between two vehicles, and you do not need a pass if you enter a park on bicycle, horseback, or on foot. Certain passes and permits for hunting, fishing, disabled veterans, and people with disabilities do not require a Discover Pass on certain state lands.

The fine for not displaying a Discover Pass where required is $99, which can be reduced to $59 if you show proof to the court that you've paid for an annual Discover Pass within 15 days after the violation.

Northwest Forest Pass

A **Northwest Forest Pass** (www.discovernw.org or www.fs.usda.gov, $5 for day pass, $30 for annual pass) is needed at developed recreation sites in Washington and Oregon that are managed by the Forest Service and require a day-use fee. Each recreation site generally has certain amenities, such as signs, a toilet, ample parking, a picnic table, and a garbage receptacle. In the Mount Baker-Snoqualmie National Forest alone, there are 81 such sites, including Mount Pilchuck, Snow Lake, and Blanca Lake. Some sites don't require a fee because they don't meet a set of criteria needed for the Northwest Forest Pass—this is the case, for example, with Mount Townsend. Your dollars from the Northwest Forest Pass go into maintaining trailhead amenities, repairing trails, and providing visitor services.

A Northwest Forest Pass can be shared among cars in the same household. You can purchase passes online from **Discover Your Northwest** (www.discovernw.org) or in person at a Forest Service office or vendor such as REI. You must print your ePass within two days of buying it; otherwise, the link to print expires. Clearly display your pass on the driver's side dashboard. The fine for not displaying a Northwest Forest Pass where it is required is $85.

National Park Passes, Fees, and Permits

Our national parks are a treasure—preserving and protecting stunning American landscapes. Washington State has three national parks: Mount Rainier National Park, Olympic National Park, and North Cascades National Park. Hikes in Mount Rainier National Park and Olympic National Park are featured in this book.

Entrance fees are required for **Mount Rainier National Park** and **Olympic**

HIKING GEAR CHECKLIST

- Backpack
- Blister treatment
- Lip balm
- Clothing layers
- Emergency communication device (personal locator beacon or satellite messenger)
- Emergency shelter
- Extra batteries or a charger for electronics
- Extra pair of socks
- First-aid kit
- Flashlight or headlamp
- Food
- Hat
- Insect repellent
- Lightweight jacket
- Rain gear
- Sunglasses
- Sunscreen
- Tissues
- Trail map and compass
- Water
- Waterproof matches
- Whistle and signaling mirror

National Park (vehicles $25, hikers and cyclists $10, good for seven consecutive days).

Annual passes ($50) provide unlimited entry for one year. First-come, first-served wilderness permits are required for backcountry camping at Mount Rainier National Park (free) and Olympic National Park (fee). Permits can be picked up at any ranger station or wilderness information station within the parks.

AMERICA THE BEAUTIFUL PASS

America the Beautiful Passes (www. nps.gov) cover entrance fees and amenity fees at sites managed by six federal agencies—the National Park Service, U.S. Fish & Wildlife Service, Bureau of Land Management, Bureau of Reclamation, U.S. Forest Service, and the U.S. Army Corps of Engineers—where an entrance fee or amenity fee is required. The pass can be used for hikes in this book where a Northwest Forest Pass, a national park pass, or a U.S. Fish & Wildlife Service (not to be confused with the Washington State Department of Fish and Wildlife!) fee is required. The pass admits the pass holder plus an extra three adults traveling in a personal vehicle to an area requiring a vehicle fee. The pass is a great alternative to purchasing a Northwest Forest Pass if you expect to hike fairly often in national forests and national parks—this pass covers them both for unlimited visits for the duration of the pass.

The **Interagency Annual Pass** (www.usgs.gov, $80) is the standard annual pass and is valid for one year. Seniors over the age of 62 who are U.S. citizens or permanent residents can purchase a lifetime **Senior Pass** (www.usgs.gov, $10)—an incredible deal. (The cost gets bumped up to $20 if you purchase your pass online or through the mail. To avoid the extra $10 processing fee, purchase your pass in person at a federal recreation site.)

Active members of the U.S. military (or their dependents) are eligible for the

Annual Military Pass (free), valid for one year. Children entering 4th grade (including home-schooled children) are eligible for an **Annual 4th Grade Pass** (free). The pass is valid for the length of the 4th grade school year, through the following summer (Sept.-Aug.).

U.S. citizens and permanent residents with a permanent disability may be eligible for a free, lifetime **Access Pass.**

VOLUNTEER PASS

Volunteer to earn a free Discover Pass, Northwest Forest Pass, or America the Beautiful Pass. Volunteers accrue a certain number of hours or volunteer days on eligible projects in order to qualify, and then will need to submit their hours—sometimes in the form of a voucher—to the appropriate organization to redeem them for a pass.

At the **Washington Trails Association** (WTA, www.wta.org), you can earn a Discover Pass or Northwest Forest Pass by volunteering on trail work parties. Work parties (8:30am-3:30pm) repair and maintain trails by cutting back overgrown plants, clearing debris, constructing new trails and bridges, and much more. No experience is required. To sign up for a WTA trail work party, go to the "Find a Work Party" page on the WTA's website. It will say "Earn Discover Pass" or "Earn Northwest Forest Pass" if the work party is eligible for either.

Volunteer directly with Washington State Parks, the Washington Department of Natural Resources, or the Washington Department of Fish and Wildlife to earn a free **Discover Pass** (www.discoverpass.wa.gov.). Qualify by performing 24 hours of volunteer work on eligible projects.

You can also earn a free **America the Beautiful Volunteer Pass** (www.nps.gov) by performing 250 hours of service with agencies that participate in the pass program.

Free Access Days

Each year, **Washington State Parks** (www.discoverpass.wa.gov), the **U.S. Forest Service** (www.fs.usda.gov), and the **National Park Service** (www.nps.gov) publish a list of days throughout the year where entrance fees are waived at state parks, Forest Service-managed day-use sites, and national parks. Typically these include Martin Luther King Jr. Day, National Public Lands Day, and Veterans Day, as well as others.

PUGET SOUND

The waterways of the Salish Sea make for wonderful hikes beside beaches, bluffs, inlets, creeks, and sloughs. Along high mountain perches, sparkling fresh- and saltwater flows ripple in unending miles beneath you. Lowland hikes showcase solitude and nature via winding pathways through canopied forests, a historic prairie, and estuaries frequented by great blue herons. Day-hikers can take the ferry over to Whidbey Island for a different perspective. The peaks of the Cascades and the Olympics are visible from the sound, solidly and magnificently anchoring the water-filled views.

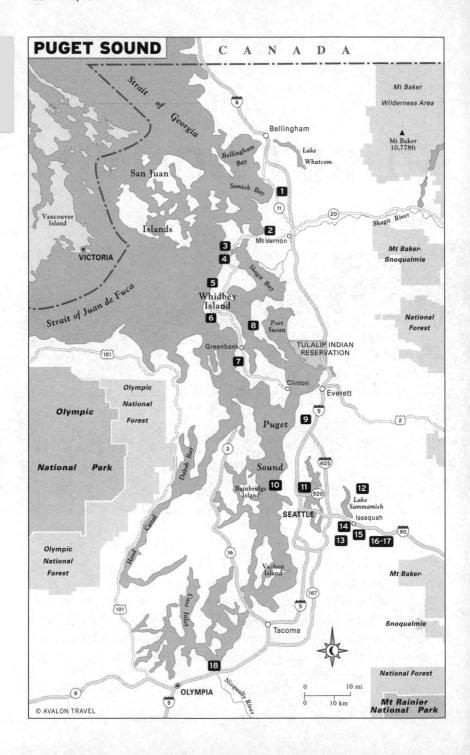

	TRAIL NAME	LEVEL	DISTANCE	TIME	ELEVATION	PAGE
1	Oyster Dome via Samish Overlook	Moderate	3.8 mi	2 hr 15 min	1,250 ft	40
2	Padilla Bay Shore Trail	Easy	4.2 mi	2 hr	80 ft	44
3	Rosario Head to Lighthouse Point	Easy/moderate	3.7 mi	1 hr 45min	675 ft	48
4	West Beach to Goose Rock	Easy/moderate	3.2 mi	1 hr 45 min	675 ft	53
5	Joseph Whidbey State Park	Easy	2 mi	1 hr	125 ft	57
6	Ebey's Landing	Easy/moderate	5.2 mi	2 hr 45 min	300 ft	61
7	South Whidbey State Park	Easy	2.4 mi	1.5 hr	325 ft	65
8	Cama Beach State Park	Easy	2.2 mi	1 hr 15 min	250 ft	69
9	Meadowdale Beach Park	Easy	2.3 mi	1 hr 15 min	425 ft	73
10	Discovery Park Loop	Easy	2.9 mi	1 hr 15 min	300 ft	76
11	Foster and Marsh Islands	Easy	2.2 mi	1 hr	100 ft	80
12	Evans Creek Preserve	Easy	1.8 mi	1 hr	200 ft	84
13	Wildside-Red Town Loop	Easy	2.6 mi	1hr 15 min	275 ft	87
14	Anti-Aircraft Peak	Easy/moderate	3.5 mi	2 hr	675 ft	91
15	Squak Mountain Loop	Moderate	6.2 mi	4 hr	1,900 ft	95
16	Poo Poo Point	Moderate	3.8 mi	2.5 hr	1,650 ft	100
17	West Tiger 3	Moderate	5.3 mi	3 hr	2,000 ft	104
18	Nisqually Estuary Boardwalk Trail	Easy	3.9 mi	2 hr	85 ft	108

1 OYSTER DOME VIA SAMISH OVERLOOK
Blanchard State Forest, Bow

Best: Day Trips

Distance: 3.8 miles round-trip

Duration: 2 hours 15 minutes

Elevation Change: 1,250 feet

Effort: Moderate

Trail: Dirt trail, stream crossings, rocky and rooty stretches

Users: Hikers, mountain bikers, horses, leashed dogs

Season: Year-round

Passes/Fees: Discover Pass

Maps: USGS topographic maps for Bellingham South and Bow

Contact: Washington State Department of Natural Resources, Northwest Region, www.dnr.wa.gov, sunrise-sunset daily

---

This forest hike has exceptional views of Skagit Valley, Samish Bay, and San Juan Islands from the summit.

Samish Overlook is that rare treat—a trailhead with a view. The Skagit Valley, the San Juan Islands, and Samish Bay unfurl beneath, and the views only get better from the rocky promontory at Oyster Dome. The trail from Samish Overlook to Oyster Dome is a bit of a shortcut (it joins the route to Oyster Dome from the Chuckanut Drive 1.5 miles in), offering a shorter option that's good for out-of-town guests.

Start the Hike
From Samish Overlook, take the **Chuckanut Trail** 0.4 mile north toward Oyster Dome. Notice the PNT sign at the start of the trail; the Chuckanut Trail is part of the Pacific Northwest Trail (PNT), a trail system that stretches 1,200 miles from Glacier National Park in Montana to Olympic National Park on the Olympic Peninsula. The PNT was designated a National Scenic Trail in 2009, joining the ranks of the Appalachian Trail and Pacific Crest Trail as one of 11 National Scenic Trails in the United States.

Merge onto the **Samish Bay Trail** toward Oyster Dome and continue 1.2 miles. Moss, ferns, Douglas fir, and cedars surround the straightforward trail as you ascend. Hopscotching over several streams, you'll soon start switchbacking

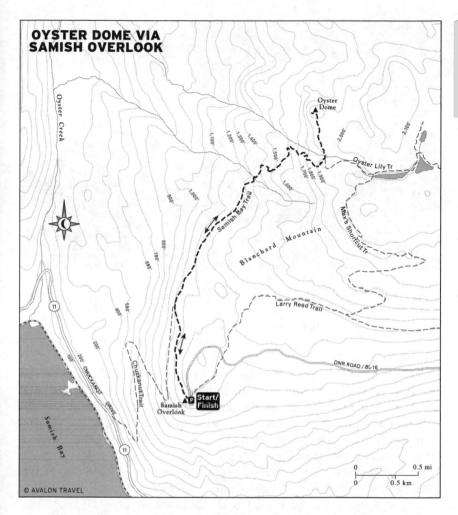

OYSTER DOME VIA SAMISH OVERLOOK

earnestly past large sandstone boulders. Bear right at a Y-junction to climb a path that switchbacks gently up the mountain. Offer a silent tip of your hat to the Washington Conservation Corp for their work on this path, a nice, rolling alternative to the steep, eroded trail on your left.

Arrive at a three-way intersection with the Samish Bay Trail, Oyster Dome Trail, and Oyster Lily Trail. Continue straight on the **Oyster Dome Trail** for 0.3 mile to the summit. The trail is a little ambiguous through this clearing, but picks up on the other side of a creek. For your final ascent, climb a particularly rocky and rooty section of trail to the promontory at the summit. On a clear day, spot the Olympics, Anacortes, the San Juan Islands, and the Salish Sea as they stretch out indefinitely before you. Hang out on one of the rocky ledges before heading back

A paraglider takes off from Samish Overlook.

to Samish Overlook. Be extra cautious here; it is a steep drop-off from the ledge and the rocks can be slippery in rain and icy weather.

Extend the Hike

Make this a loop hike to **Samish Overlook** for a 5.2-mile round-trip. From the three-way intersection of the Samish Bay Trail, Oyster Dome Trail, and Oyster Lily Trail, take the Oyster Lily Trail east toward Lily Lake. Bear right at the intersection with Lily Lake Campground and continue the trail to Max's Shortcut Trail ahead on the right. Descend Max's Shortcut Trail and bear right to continue on Larry Reed Trail toward Samish Overlook.

Alternatively, start your hike to Oyster Dome from the **Chuckanut Drive Trailhead** for a 6-mile hike (3.5 hours) with a 1,900-foot elevation gain. To get there from Seattle, take I-5 north to exit 236. Turn left onto Bow Hill Road and continue 3.7 miles. Turn right onto State Route 11/Chuckanut Drive and drive north for 3.1 miles. The trailhead will be on the right past milepost 10. Park on the shoulder of southbound State Route 11/Chuckanut Drive and carefully cross the road (no pedestrian crosswalk) to the trailhead. No facilities are available. **GPS Coordinates:** 48.608686, -122.433366 / N48° 36.531' W122° 25.997'

Make It a Day Trip

Drive to the small agricultural community of Bow-Edison to sample products from local farmers. Pick up a to-go cup of melt-in-your-mouth blueberry ice cream at family-run **Bow Hill Blueberries** (15628 Bow Hill Rd., Bow, 360/399-1006, www.bowhillblueberries.com, 10am-5pm daily, but call to confirm) or to pick blueberries in summer. Nearby **Samish Bay Cheese** (15115 Bow Hill Rd., Bow, 360/766-6707, www.samishbay.com, 10am-4pm Mon.-Fri., noon-4pm Sat.-Sun.) offers complimentary tastings of their organic cheeses—I love their Ladysmith with chives and queso fresco. For a caffeine fix, the **Farm to Market Bakery** (5507 Chuckanut Dr., Bow, 360/766-6240, www.rhodycafe.com, 9am-4pm Wed.-Sun., cash or check only) offers coffee, tea, and espresso drinks as well as baked goods. Farther west on Bow Hill Road is the pint-sized village of Edison, where you can pick up fresh bread, homemade crackers, and other treats at **Breadfarm** (5766 Cains Ct., Bow, 360/766-4065, www.breadfarm.com, 9am-7pm daily, cash or check only).

Directions
From Seattle, take I-5 north to exit 240 for Alger. Turn left at the stop sign onto Lake Samish Road and drive 0.5 mile. Turn left onto Barrell Springs Road and drive 0.6 mile. Turn right onto a dirt and gravel DNR road at a brown sign for Blanchard Hill Trail. Take your time and drive slowly on the rough, moderately potholed road for 1.6 miles. Turn left at a brown sign for Samish Overlook and continue 2.1 miles to the parking lot. Two vault toilets are next to the parking lot. **GPS Coordinates:** 48.609653, -122.426424 / N48° 36.585' W122° 25.578'

2 PADILLA BAY SHORE TRAIL

Padilla Bay National Estuarine Research Reserve, Mount Vernon

Best: Kid-Friendly, Day Trips

Distance: 4.2 miles round-trip

Duration: 2 hours

Elevation Change: 80 feet

Effort: Easy

Trail: Crushed gravel path

Users: Hikers, mountain bikers, hunters (Oct.-Jan.), leashed dogs

Season: Year-round

Passes/Fees: None

Maps: USGS topographic map for La Conner

Contact: Padilla Bay National Estuarine Research Reserve, www.ecy.wa.gov, dawn-dusk daily

---

Hike along an embankment with windswept views of Padilla Bay, San Juan Islands, and Cascades.

The Padilla Bay Shore Trail may seem like a simple walk along the water, but it has much more to offer. The wide, mostly flat trail includes lovely views of Padilla Bay, but what makes this hike a treat are the wildlife-watching opportunities and habitat variety—from farmland to sloughs and mudflats. The trail crosses the top of a dike, and the slightly perched view means that you can spy great blue herons, the peaks of the Cascades, and the San Juan Islands in the distance, and enjoy the ever-changing shoreline as it ebbs and flows with the tide.

The exposed trail can get quite windy; plan to bring sun and wind protection, especially on clear days. While the trail is a great year-round destination, it's particularly scenic on a clear winter day when you can walk along the water with views of distant snowcapped mountains.

Start the Hike

From the north parking lot, head downhill along the shoulder of Second Street. At the end of the road, turn left onto the shoulder of Bay View-Edison Road, followed by a right on a pedestrian crosswalk to join the **Padilla Bay Shore Trail.** Breathe in the salty sea air as you step onto the crushed gravel trail. Looking across the water, notice the height of the tide; the bay floods during high tide and retreats during low tide, revealing large stretches of mudflats that are hotbeds of activity for burrowing shrimp and clams. In 0.25 mile, benches appear near the water's edge, offering an opportunity to take in water-filled views of the birds and wildlife.

The bay hosts more than 200 species of birds—from bald eagles to owls to woodpeckers—serving as a pit stop along the Pacific Flyway, the bird migration route that stretches from Alaska to South America. Rippling beneath the surface of the water are meadows of eelgrass, an underwater grass developed from a unique mix of freshwater, saltwater, tide conditions, and mudflats. Eelgrass shelters marine life like salmon and provides a direct source of food for the black brant, a goose with a white-colored ring around its neck. Because of this special ecosystem, Padilla Bay was designated a National Estuarine Research Reserve by the federal government in 1980, one of only 28 such sites in the United States and the only one in Washington State.

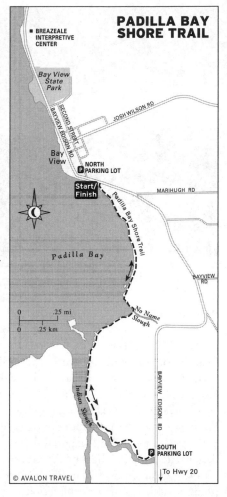

As you make your way along the bay's edge, enjoy the hip-high swaying grasses that line the trail, the small salt marsh pedestals just off shore, and the mountain views that open up near **No Name Slough,** about 1 mile into your hike. On a clear day, you may spot Mount Erie on Fidalgo Island across the bay to the west, the snow-white top of Mount Baker peeking out to the northeast, the sharp outline of Three Fingers to the southeast, and a scant peek of the Olympics to the southwest.

In about 1.7 miles, the trail passes an old, gray boathouse perched at the edge of **Indian Slough** with rusted equipment nearby. The boathouse used to warehouse grain, and the rusted equipment (a former pile driver) was used to hammer logs vertically into the mud to protect the dike from crashing waves. Enjoy the view

Enjoy a peaceful hike along Indian Slough on the Padilla Bay Shore Trail.

from the path as it parallels the slough, soon arriving at your turnaround point:
the south trailhead.

Extend the Hike

Visit the **Breazeale Interpretive Center** (10441 Bayview-Edison Rd., Mount
Vernon, 360/428-1558, www.ecy.wa.gov, 10am-5pm Tues.-Sat., but call to confirm),
just one mile up the road from the north parking lot. The center has thoughtful,
child-friendly exhibits about the estuary and its history; pamphlets, trail maps, and
information about the surrounding area; and a small network of trails behind the
building. A short, 0.5-mile, paved ADA-accessible trail leads from the center to a
deck overlooking Padilla Bay, the San Juan Islands, and the tips of the Olympics;
it's also a great option for families with strollers. A set of stairs leads to the beach
from the deck for further exploration.

Make It a Day Trip

Drive into the friendly village of La Conner for a waterfront stroll, a bite to eat at
The Oyster & Thistle (205 E. Washington St., La Conner, 360/766-6179, www.
theoysterandthistle.com, 3pm-9pm Tues.-Thurs., 11:30am-9pm Fri.-Mon.), or
window-shopping along First Street.

If visiting in spring, check out the fields of daffodils during the **La Conner
Daffodil Festival** (www.visitskagitvalley.com, Mar.) or do a tulip crawl at the
annual **Skagit Valley Tulip Festival** (www.tulipfestival.org, Apr.).

While in Mount Vernon, stop by **Snow Goose Produce** (15170 Fir Island Rd.,
Mount Vernon, 360/445-6908, www.snowgooseproducemarket.com, hours vary

seasonally, cash only) for generous dollops of Lopez Island Creamery ice cream heaped on handmade waffle cones.

Get Away for the Weekend

Just 0.5 mile up the road from the Padilla Bay Shore Trail, **Bay View State Park** (10901 Bay View-Edison Rd., Mount Vernon, 888/226-7688, www.parks.state. wa.us) has 46 tent sites, 29 utility spaces, and six homey cabins within walking distance of the park's beach.

Directions

From Seattle, take I-5 north to exit 230 for State Route 20 toward Burlington. At the end of the exit ramp, turn left onto State Route 20, heading west toward Whidbey Island. After 6.3 miles, turn right onto Bayview-Edison Road and follow the brown signs for Padilla Bay National Reserve and Bay View State Park. In 0.7 mile, pass the south trailhead on the left and continue 2.3 miles to Second Street. Turn right onto Second Street, then turn left into a large parking lot. There is one portable toilet in both the north and south parking lots.

Those with wheelchairs can pick up a gate key at the **Breazeale Interpretive Center** (10441 Bayview-Edison Rd., Mount Vernon, 360/428-1558, www.ecy. wa.gov), which opens the gates in front of the trailhead.

GPS Coordinates: 48.480569, -122.473164 / N48° 28.800' W122° 28.384'

3 ROSARIO HEAD TO LIGHTHOUSE POINT
Deception Pass State Park, Fidalgo Island

Best: Beaches

Distance: 3.7 miles round-trip

Duration: 1 hour 45 minutes

Elevation Change: 675 feet

Effort: Easy/moderate

Trail: Dirt paths with rocky sections, cliff edges with sharp drop-offs

Users: Hikers, leashed dogs

Season: Year-round

Passes/Fees: Discover Pass

Maps: Green Trails Map 41S for Deception Pass, USGS topographic map for Deception Pass

Contact: Deception Pass State Park, www.parks.state.wa.us, 6:30am-dusk daily in summer, 8am-dusk daily in winter

---

A rolling trail along beaches and bluffs offers outstanding views of Bowman Bay, Deception Pass, and Puget Sound.

Fidalgo Island is a small island just north of Whidbey Island and west of mainland Skagit County. This rolling seaside hike offers exceptional views of Deception Pass Bridge, Deception Pass, the Strait of Juan de Fuca, Bowman Bay, the San Juan Islands, and the Olympics. Brush up on your history with a visit to the Civilian Conservation Corps Interpretive Center and bring a picnic to enjoy at the many tables scattered at Bowman Bay. Take care hiking with young, nimble children; the trail winds close to the edge of the bluffs, and there are no fences or barriers between the bluff and sea below. The Naval Air Station Whidbey Island sits just south, so you may see and hear jets fly by as you hike.

Start the Hike
From the parking lot, bear right to explore **Rosario Head.** The beach on the left (with the small pier) is Sharpe Cove; to the right is Rosario Beach, where you may spot a starfish in the tide pools. Stop to admire the tall cedar carving of a woman holding a fish over her head; this story pole is about a Samish maiden who saved her tribe from starvation. Past the story pole, climb 60 feet to Rosario Head on a

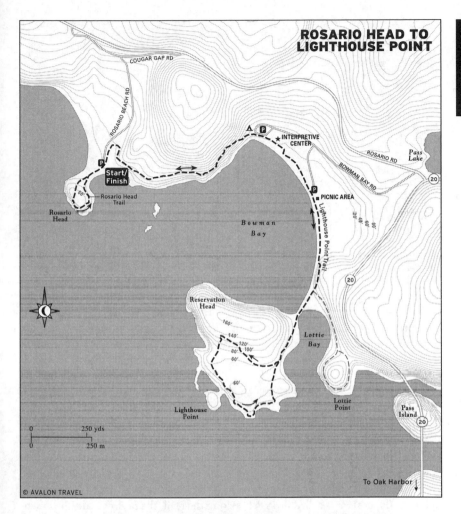

narrow, 0.3-mile loop that weaves along a small open meadow. Enjoy the endless water-filled views of Whidbey Island and Deception Island, as well as the Olympics. To the east, Bowman Bay beckons—the next leg of your hike.

Make your way down from Rosario Head and follow the gravel trail as it winds toward the parking lot and past a brown sign for Bowman Bay. The next 0.5 mile is a treat as you hike into a partially shaded forest of Douglas fir and cedar perched high above Bowman Bay with peekaboo views of the bay. A small, well-placed bench just off the main trail is a hidden gem; take a break to watch the sunset over the endless water views and try to spot cormorants, bald eagles, and herons.

Descend to Bowman Bay and stop at the **Civilian Conservation Corps Interpretive Center** (Apr.-Sept., hours vary) to check out exhibits about the Corps'

Deception Pass Bridge as seen from Lighthouse Point

work in Washington State. The Corps was instrumental in the development of Deception Pass State Park; in the 1930s, they built roads and trails and helped construct approach routes to Deception Pass Bridge. Past the interpretive center, enjoy the wide, pebbly, crescent-shaped beach at **Bowman Bay.** The bay is named for Amos Bowman, an early settler on Fidalgo Island who established a post office there in 1877. (A fun bit of trivia: The city name of Anacortes is a play on Bowman's wife's maiden name, Anna Curtis.) The fishing pier and open field, a playground, and plentiful picnic tables make this a nice destination and is an alternate starting place for a shorter hike to Lighthouse Point.

Upon reaching the southern edge of Bowman Bay, begin climbing up, over, and down a short, forested section of the trail as you follow signs for **Lighthouse Point.** Look carefully at the rocks lining the trail; the blue-gray, fan-shaped lichen with spikes on the bottom is called Frog Pelt. Along the trail, the peeling reddish-brown bark of madrones reveal the smooth trunk beneath. Down at sea level, make your way along a narrow isthmus lined with tall grasses that separates Lottie Bay to the south and Bowman Bay to the north.

The dirt trail follows a lollipop-shape for 1 mile as it climbs up and around Lighthouse Point with views of Deception Pass and Deception Pass Bridge. Reaching a Y-junction, bear right to follow the loop in a counterclockwise direction, taking in the 1,487-foot Deception Pass Bridge and churning water of Deception Pass before you. Keep left as you make your way around the loop, staying on the main path toward the fantastic views.

Deception Pass was named by explorer George Vancouver to commemorate his "deception" when exploring Puget Sound on the HMS *Discovery* in 1792.

Vancouver thought that the land south of Deception Pass was a peninsula, when in fact it was an island. Today, that island is known as Whidbey Island after the HMS *Discovery*'s sailing master, Joseph Whidbey.

Completing your loop, head back to Bowman Bay and Rosario Head to your starting point. Enjoy the views of the water and coastline in the changing light of day.

Shorten the Hike

Park at Bowman Bay for a 1.8-mile round-trip hike to **Lighthouse Point.** To reach the parking lot, take State Route 20 west for Deception Pass State Park. Turn right onto Rosario Road, then make a quick left onto Bowman Bay Road. In 0.25 mile, turn left at a stop sign and enter the large parking lot. There are two restrooms at Bowman Bay. A Discover Pass is required.

Hike Nearby

Head to nearby **Sharpe Park** (14692 Rosario Rd., Anacortes, www.skagitcounty. net) for a 1.4-mile round-trip hike to Sares Head, boasting 180-degree views from Whidbey Island to the San Juans. From the parking lot, take the main trail west, following signposts marked with a red dot for the Sares Head Trail. Past a pond, bear left at a Y-junction to continue southwest on the Sares Head Trail. Upon reaching a junction with the Upper Trail or the Lower Trail, bear right to take the Lower Trail to Sares Head. (Either way will work; the Upper Trail is slightly rougher and syncs up with the Lower Trail in 0.2 mile). There is an information kiosk with a map at the trailhead and an ADA-accessible vault toilet next to the parking lot. No pass is required to park in the lot.

Get Away for the Weekend

Spend the weekend by camping by the beach next to Bowman Bay. **Deception Pass State Park** (888/226-7688, www.parks.state.wa.us, open seasonally) has 18 tent sites and two utility sites, as well as shower and restroom facilities. Camping is popular in summer, so make a reservation months in advance.

Directions

From Seattle, head north on I-5 to exit 230 for State Route 20. Turn left at the end of the exit ramp onto State Route 20 and drive west toward Whidbey Island. In 11.6 miles, turn left to continue on State Route 20 West toward Oak Harbor (past the brown sign for Deception Pass State Park). In 5 miles, turn right onto Rosario Road at the sign for Deception Pass State Park. Drive for 0.7 mile, then turn left onto Cougar Gap Road. In about 0.1 mile, turn left onto Rosario Beach Road and drive 0.2 mile to the parking lot.

The gated parking lot for Rosario Head is closed November-February; however, you can park outside the gate on the wide dirt shoulder of Rosario Beach Road. No pass or permit is required when parking outside the lot. Restrooms are available inside the park, but are closed November-February.

GPS Coordinates: 48.418052, -122.662526 / N48° 25.090' W122° 39.743'

4 WEST BEACH TO GOOSE ROCK
Deception Pass State Park, Whidbey Island

Best: Beaches

Distance: 3.2 miles round-trip

Duration: 1 hour 45 minutes

Elevation Change: 675 feet

Effort: Easy/moderate

Trail: Sandy, pebbly beach, dirt paths, rooty sections

Users: Hikers, leashed dogs

Season: Year-round

Passes/Fees: Discover Pass

Maps: Green Trails Map 41S for Deception Pass, USGS topographic map for Deception Pass

Contact: Deception Pass State Park, www.parks.state.wa.us, 6:30am-dusk daily in summer, 8am-dusk daily in winter

---

Hike along a wide beach, then climb past the Deception Pass Bridge to a scenic overlook from Goose Rock.

Located on the northern edge of Whidbey Island in Deception Pass State Park, the trail from West Beach to Goose Rock combines waterfront exploration with perched mountain views. This breezy hike on wide North Beach, beside Deception Pass, passes underneath Deception Pass Bridge to take in views of the Cascades, the Olympics, and Whidbey Island from the summit of Goose Rock. Several picnic tables and stacks of driftwood line West Beach, making this a nice spot for a post-hike picnic or a snack while gazing at the Strait of Juan de Fuca to the west and the Olympics to the southwest.

With more than two million visitors annually, this is one of the state's most popular parks. Plan to visit in winter or get an early start in summer to avoid the crowds.

Start the Hike
Start your hike at the north end of the **West Beach** parking lot, following a brown sign with arrows toward the amphitheater and North Beach. You have two options as you make your way east: stroll along sandy North Beach or hike through the

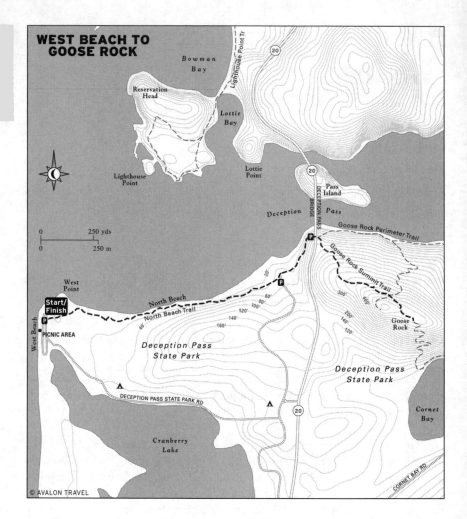

woods on a trail that parallels it to the south. **North Beach** is the obvious choice, a sandy walk next to the water on a long stretch of coastline with views of Deception Pass, Deception Island, and Deception Pass Bridge. As you walk along the eastern edge of North Beach, pick up a spur trail to connect to the main hiking trail toward Deception Pass Bridge.

After 1 mile, climb about 100 feet along a fenced path to **Deception Pass Bridge.** Pausing at a small clearing near the bridge, take in views of Deception Island and the San Juan Islands; tiny, ant-sized boats zip in and out of Deception Pass below. Following the trail under the bridge, notice stairways that lead to sidewalks on both sides of Deception Pass Bridge, a fun detour to stomach-dropping views of the churning current 180 feet below. Before the bridge was built in 1935,

looking east toward Deception Pass Bridge from North Beach

a small ferry owned and operated by the first female ferry captain in Washington State (Berte Olson) transferred residents between the islands.

Cross under the bridge and bear right to join the **NW Goose Rock Summit Trail,** a wide dirt path lined with Douglas fir, western redcedar, and red-flowering currant. The trail ascends steeply, gaining 325 feet over the last 0.4 mile. Reaching the summit in 1.6 miles, take in views of the Whidbey Island coastline, Cranberry Lake, and the Olympics in the southwest. To the east, you can see prominent peaks of the Cascades, including Whitehorse Mountain, Three Fingers, and Mount Pilchuck. Return the way you came, or continue on the trail past the summit for a loop hike on the Goose Rock Perimeter Trail.

Shorten the Hike

For a quick, 1-mile round-trip hike to **Goose Rock,** park in the lot at the southern end of the Deception Pass Bridge. Descend the staircase next to the bridge and follow the dirt trail, bearing right for signs to the NW Goose Rock Summit Trail. A Discover Pass is required, and restrooms are available in the parking lot.

Extend the Hike

Add an extra mile by making a loop around Goose Rock. Continue on the **Goose Rock Summit Trail** past the summit, following the trail as it descends several switchbacks along the south side of Goose Rock. Bear left to join the **Goose Rock Perimeter Trail,** a mild but pleasant trail that mingles forest-covered paths with views of Cornet Bay, Ben Ure Island, and Mount Baker. The loop rejoins the original trail next to Deception Pass Bridge.

Get Away for the Weekend

Located between North Beach and Cranberry Lake, **Cranberry Campground** (Deception Pass State Park, 888/226-7688, www.parks.state.wa.us, open seasonally) has 147 tent sites and 83 utility sites split between the lower loop and the forest loop. Camping is popular in summer; make reservations several months in advance. Another overnight option is spending the night at the **Ben Ure Cabin,** a one-room log cabin located on Ben Ure Island on the eastern side of Deception Pass. This adventurous accommodation is reachable only by a human-powered vessel, such as a rowboat. The cabin has a furnished kitchen, a queen-size futon, a small toilet and outdoor shower, and a deck. Guests must bring drinking water and bed linens.

Directions

From Seattle, take I-5 north to exit 230 for State Route 20 West. At the end of the exit ramp, turn left onto State Route 20 and drive west toward Whidbey Island. In 11.6 miles, turn left onto State Route 20 West for Deception Pass State Park. Continue on State Route 20 for 6 miles. Cross Deception Pass Bridge; 1 mile past the bridge, turn right into Deception Pass State Park. In 0.4 mile, bear left at a stop sign and follow signs for West Beach. Restrooms (open spring-fall) are located near the trailhead. Restrooms are located at the south end of the parking lot and are open in winter.

GPS Coordinates: 48.400266, -122.664002 / N48° 24.068' W122° 39.835'

5 JOSEPH WHIDBEY STATE PARK
Whidbey Island

Best: Beaches

Distance: 2 miles round-trip

Duration: 1 hour

Elevation Change: 125 feet

Effort: Easy

Trail: Dirt and grass paths

Users: Hikers, mountain bikers, leashed dogs

Season: Year-round

Passes/Fees: Discover Pass

Maps: USGS topographic map for Oak Harbor

Contact: Joseph Whidbey State Park, www.parks.state.wa.us, 8am-dusk daily

---

This quiet walk through an airy forest and grassy fields includes an option to explore a sandy beach.

Joseph Whidbey State Park is a hidden treasure about a 15-minute drive south of Deception Pass Bridge. Picturesque and mostly flat trails wind around open meadows and shaded, woody corridors while a sandy beach beckons on the park's western border. Plan your visit in summer to avoid the muddy, swamp-like conditions that plague the park in the rainy season (and as a quieter option to the crowds at Deception Pass State Park). The route is partially ADA-accessible; while the trail is generally wide and flat, it does have small rocks, roots, and potential wet patches that might require a little extra oomph.

Start the Hike
Start hiking on the **Moyers Trail,** located next to the restroom in the main parking lot. Head east on the wide, roomy path through an airy forest of tall Douglas fir, western redcedar, and red alder that is filled in by an understory of white-flowered Indian plum and cherry. The verdant path is a portal to the pastoral field that awaits in 0.4 mile.

Reaching a windswept meadow, bear right at a Y-junction and hike the 1.2-mile loop counterclockwise. Enjoy peekaboo views of the Strait of Juan de Fuca as you wind your way past blackberry and Nootka rose shrubs; their tender pink

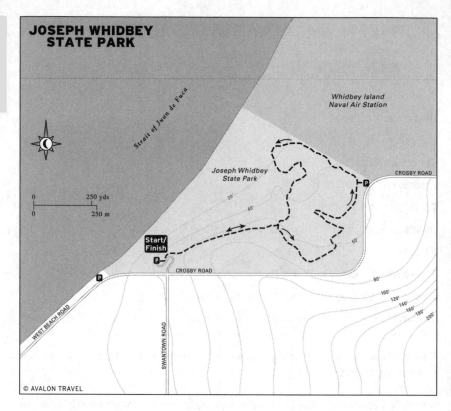

flowers bloom in late spring and early summer. In 0.4 mile, bear right to stay on the outer loop encircling the park. Small wooden benches line the path at regular intervals, inviting short breaks to soak in the views. Finish your loop then rejoin the Moyers Trail, heading west to the parking lot. For a wonderful beach walk, take the gravel trail from the parking lot down to the water's edge. In addition to the sandy shoreline, several picnic tables line the beach area—a nice option for a waterfront picnic with a view.

Extend the Hike

Time your hike to coincide with low tide for a wide and sandy 1.2-mile round-trip walk on the beach. Park in the small lot next to the beach or follow the obvious gravel trail from the main parking lot down to the beach. Expansive views of the Strait of Juan de Fuca are to the west, of the San Juan Islands to the north, and of the Olympics to the south. At 0.6 mile, a warning sign is posted near the state park boundary, your turnaround point. If a red flag is raised, live firing at the Naval Air Station may occur beyond this point; enter at your own risk.

prairielike fields at Joseph Whidbey State Park

Make It a Day Trip

Stop by **Lavender Wind** (2530 Darst Rd., Coupeville, 360/544-4132, www.lavenderwind.com, June-Aug., hours vary), a small lavender farm five miles south of Joseph Whidbey State Park. In summer, you can pick your own lavender and browse their on-site shop. In the off-season, visit their store in Coupeville (15 Coveland St., 360/544-4132, 10am-5pm daily) for lavender-infused products and specialty foods. While in Coupeville, stop in at **Kapaws Iskreme** (21 Front St., Coupeville, 360/929-2122, 11:30am-5pm daily Mar.-Dec.), a friendly parlor with delicious ice cream. If coffee is more your style, head to **Sunshine Drip Coffee Lounge** (306 N. Main St., Coupeville, 360/682-6201, www.sunshinedrip.com, hours vary seasonally) for Moka Joe organic coffee, a breakfast bagel, and kid-friendly menu items.

Directions

From Seattle, take I-5 north to exit 230 for State Route 20 West. At the end of the exit ramp, turn left onto State Route 20 and head west toward Whidbey Island. In 11.6 miles, turn left onto State Route 20 West and follow the signs for Oak Harbor and Deception Pass State Park. Continue straight on State Route 20 West for 6 miles to the Deception Pass Bridge, continuing past the bridge for another 7 miles. Turn right onto Ault Field Road at the City of Oak Harbor sign. Drive 2 miles, bearing right at the curve in the road to continue onto Clover Valley Road. Drive 1.8 miles (the road becomes Golf Course Rd.), then turn right onto Crosby Road. In 0.4 mile, pass an optional dirt parking lot on the right. In 0.7 mile, turn

the Whidbey Island coast at Joseph Whidbey State Park

right at the sign for Swanton Road and enter the main parking lot. The vault toilet in the parking lot is ADA-accessible.

The gate to the main parking lot is closed October 1-April 1; when closed, park at the beach lot 0.25 mile down the road or at the dirt lot that you passed on your way to the main lot. The main parking lot and the beach parking lot require a Discover Pass; the dirt lot does not.

GPS Coordinates: 48.308379, -122.713063 / N48° 18.510' W122° 42.800'

6 EBEY'S LANDING

Ebey's Landing National Historical Reserve, Whidbey Island

Best: Historical, Day Trips, Beaches

Distance: 5.2 miles round-trip

Duration: 2 hours 45 minutes

Elevation Change: 300 feet

Effort: Easy/moderate

Trail: Dirt, sand, and gravel paths, sandy beach with rocks

Users: Hikers, leashed dogs

Season: Year-round

Passes/Fees: Discover Pass required for the parking lot next to the beach

Maps: USGS topographic map for Coupeville

Contact: Trust Board of Ebey's Landing National Historical Reserve, www.nps.gov/ebla

---

Hike to sweeping views of a historic prairie, Admiralty Inlet, and the Olympics.

This spectacular hike is located on Ebey's Landing National Historical Reserve near Coupeville. A compelling history, the sweeping prairie, and views of the Cascades and the Olympics make Ebey's Landing one of the best hikes on Whidbey Island. The beach stretches for almost two miles, making this a nice option for a waterfront stroll and a great, kid-friendly destination. Plan your hike for low tide and prepare for windy weather—they don't call it "Windy Whidbey" for nothing. As you hike, please respect the private property on the reserve and stay on the publicly posted trails.

Start the Hike

Start your hike on the wide path next to a cottage, following the signs for the **Jacob Ebey House.** Jacob Ebey was the father of Isaac Neff Ebey, a prominent resident who was the first in his family to settle on Whidbey Island. Isaac Ebey arrived in 1850 after making the arduous journey west on the Oregon Trail. Soon after, he sent for his wife, two sons, his parents, Jacob and Sarah Ebey, and members of his extended family—all of whom joined him over the course of the next four years. The Jacob Ebey House was built in 1856 on land that Jacob Ebey claimed

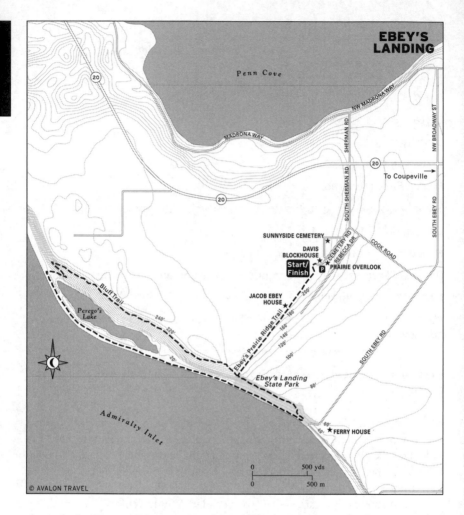

through the Oregon Donation Land Law of 1850. The house has been preserved over the years and is open seasonally for visitors.

Passing the Jacob Ebey House, head toward the fence ahead to continue on the **Ebey's Prairie Ridge Trail.** Follow the tractor-like dirt tracks for 0.5 mile, enjoying the mosaic patches of prairie land to the south. See if you can spot a gray building near the base of the prairie—this is known as the Ferry House. Built in the early 1860s, the house served as a traveler's inn from the mid-1800s to the early 1900s. Its construction, however, was a somber affair; it was built as a means to support Isaac Ebey's sons, Eason and Ellison Ebey, after he was brutally killed in 1857.

At the end of the Ebey's Prairie Ridge Trail, bear right to join the **Bluff Trail.** The narrow, sandy trail climbs 60 feet to the top of the bluff with spectacular

views of the beach and coastline from the Bluff Trail at Ebey's Landing

views of the Whidbey Island coastline to the south, as well as Admiralty Inlet, Port Townsend, and the Olympics to the southwest. Bald eagles may coast high above in the breeze as you wind your way past weathered, storm-twisted branches of Douglas fir. After 1 mile, descend long switchbacks on the Bluff Trail to the beach (step carefully past an eroded area that drops off steeply). The lagoon-like body of water below is Perego's Lake, a coastal wetland outlined by large piles of driftwood.

Reaching the sandy beach, bear left to continue south past **Perego's Lake.** The next 1.75 miles follows the beach, with smooth rocks atop the sand ranging in size from a small pebble to a bowling ball. Enjoy the wind-whipped views of the sea as it meets the bluffs and the new vantage point of the Olympics. Keep your eyes peeled for vessels traveling through Admiralty Inlet, as well as waterfowl and shorebirds trawling the sea and shore.

Arriving at the lower parking lot and information kiosk, make a U-turn to follow the trail 0.5 mile up a set of wooden stairs and along the edge of the bluff. A bench is a welcome spot for resting and sea-gazing. At the intersection with the Robert Y. Pratt Reserve sign, bear right to head back on the **Ebey's Prairie Ridge Trail** toward the Jacob Ebey house for 0.8 mile to the trailhead.

Shorten the Hike

For a simple walk on the beach, drive to the lower parking lot next to the beach. From State Route 20, drive north just past the town of Coupeville and turn left onto Ebey Road. Stay straight at a junction with Terry Road and, in 1.6 miles, the parking lot will be on the right at a bend in the road. This part of the reserve is on state land; a Discover Pass is required to park in this lot. A vault toilet is located in the parking lot.

Make It a Day Trip

Stop by **Fort Ebey State Park** (400 Hill Valley Dr., Coupeville, www.parks. state.wa.us, 360/678-4636, 8am-dusk daily) to check out a former World War II gun battery and take a scenic walk along a bluff with expansive views of the Strait of Juan de Fuca to the west. From Ebey's Landing, head north on State Route 20 and follow the signs for Fort Ebey and Gun Battery. The gun battery sits on a wide overlook with picnic tables, grills, and restrooms nearby. For a mostly flat, kid-friendly walk, pick up the Bluff Trail from the picnic area. (Take care with small children, as the trail winds close to the edge of the bluff.) A Discover Pass is required to park in Fort Ebey. Leashed dogs are allowed.

For a post-hike pick-me-up, the nearby town of **Coupeville** has several restaurants—from pub food to pizza—as well as a coffee shop, an ice-cream shop, and specialty stores that are fun to browse.

Directions

From Seattle, take I-5 north to exit 182 for State Route 525 North toward State Route 99 and Mukilteo. Merge onto State Route 525 and drive 8 miles north to the Mukilteo Ferry Terminal. Take the Mukilteo-Clinton ferry (888/808-7977, www.wsdot.wa.gov, fares vary) to Clinton and continue 28 miles north on State Route 525. Stay straight as the road turns into State Route 20. Past Coupeville, turn left onto Sherman Road (just past the sign for Ebey's Landing Overlook). In 0.3 mile, turn right onto Cemetery Road at the sign for Prairie Overlook. In 0.2 mile, park in the lot on the left. If the lot is full, there are additional parking spaces past the lot. A portable toilet is located on the trail near the Jacob Ebey House.
GPS Coordinates: 48.204673, -122.706553 / N48° 12.276' W122° 42.438'

7 SOUTH WHIDBEY STATE PARK

Whidbey Island

Best: Day Trips

Distance: 2.4 miles round-trip

Duration: 1.5 hours

Elevation Change: 325 feet

Effort: Easy

Trail: Dirt paths, some wooden paths and steps

Users: Hikers, leashed dogs

Season: Year-round

Passes/Fees: Discover Pass

Maps: USGS topographic map for Freeland

Contact: South Whidbey State Park, www.parks.state.wa.us, 8am-dusk daily

---

This quiet, shady hike winds through an old-growth forest to a 500-year-old cedar tree.

South Whidbey State Park features quiet, winding trails through a forest of towering Douglas fir to a 500-year-old cedar tree. (Note: A trail leading to the beach suffered severe damage in a 2016 landslide. As of this writing, the trail is closed as officials work to locate a stable reroute; check the state park website for updates.)

For maps and information about special programs in the park, visit **The Friends of South Whidbey State Park** (www.foswsp.org) and download their helpful brochure.

Start the Hike

From the parking lot, cross Smugglers Cove Road on the pedestrian crossing and walk toward the brown **Wilbert Trail** sign. Enter the forest and bear right for the **Ridge Loop Trail,** hiking under a canopy of Douglas fir, hemlock, and red alder. This forest was originally pegged for logging in 1977; however, a group of concerned Whidbey Island residents stymied the loggers' progress by physically standing in front of the trees and pursuing legal action to protect the forest. Their tactics worked, and in 1985 Governor Booth Gardner signed a bill adding the forest to the state park system. The forest officially became part of South Whidbey

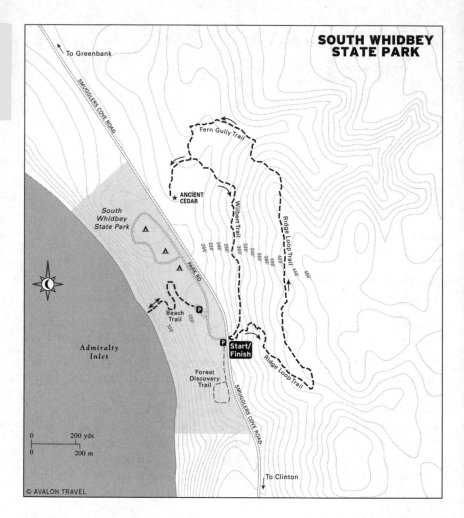

SOUTH WHIDBEY
STATE PARK

To Greenbank

SMUGGLERS COVE ROAD

Fern Gully Trail

ANCIENT
CEDAR

South
Whidbey
State Park

Wilbert Trail

Ridge Loop Trail

PARK RD

Beach
Trail

P

P

Start/
Finish

Ridge Loop Trail

Admiralty
Inlet

Forest
Discovery
Trail

SMUGGLERS COVE ROAD

0   200 yds
0   200 m

To Clinton

© AVALON TRAVEL

State Park in 1992. For more information, read *Whidbey Island: Reflections on People and the Land* by Elizabeth Guss, Janice O'Mahony, and Mary Richardson.

After hiking through a grove of young red alders and salmonberry shrubs, bear right onto the **Fern Gully Trail** in 1.1 miles. Descend 120 feet past moss-covered nurse logs and stumps to an unmarked junction with the **Wilbert Trail.** Bear right to join the trail and, in 0.1 mile, spot a sign on the left marked Ancient Cedar. Follow the short spur trail to an impressive 500-year-old cedar tree protected by a wooden fence.

After marveling at the size of the tree, turn around to head back on the **Wilbert Trail,** passing your earlier junction with the Fern Gully Trail. In 0.4 mile, arrive at a junction with the Ridge Loop Trail and bear right to stay on the Wilbert

an ancient, 500-year-old cedar tree

Trail for 0.4 mile back to the trailhead. The Wilbert Trail is named for local citizens Harry and Meryl Wilbert, members of the nonprofit group Save the Trees, who championed the forest's preservation.

Shorten the Hike

A direct hike to the **Ancient Cedar** shortens the hike to 1.6 miles round-trip. Start from the parking lot, crossing Smugglers Cove Road on the pedestrian crossing toward the brown Wilbert Trail sign. Veer left to head north on Wilbert Trail for 0.8 mile to the Ancient Cedar.

Make It a Day Trip

Visit **Greenbank Farm** (765 Wonn Rd., Greenbank, 360/222-3151, www.greenbankfarm.com) for lunch and a stroll on the farm's trails to sweeping views of Admiralty Inlet, the Saratoga Passage, and the Cascades. **Whidbey Pies & Cafe** (765 Wonn Rd., Greenbank, 360/678-1288, www.whidbeypies.com, hours vary seasonally) is located at the farm and serves fantastic sandwiches, salads, soups, fresh pie, tea, and espresso beverages. Stop at nearby **Double Bluff Beach** (6325 Double Bluff Rd., Freeland, www.islandcounty.net) during low tide for a 2-mile beach walk (and an off-leash dog area). Top off your day trip with a walk through **Langley** (Langley Chamber of Commerce, 208 Anthes Ave., Langley, 360/221-6765, www.visitlangley.com), a cozy seaside town with restaurants, cafés, and specialty shops.

Get Away for the Weekend

The campgrounds at South Whidbey State Park are closed indefinitely due to old, hazardous trees, but you can head north to camp at **Fort Ebey State Park** (400 Hill Valley Dr., Coupeville, 360/678-4636, www.parks.state.wa.us) or **Fort Casey State Park** (1280 Engle Rd., Coupeville, 360/678-4519, www.parks.state.wa.us). Fort Ebey has 39 standard campsites and 11 utility campsites with water and electricity. One ADA-accessible restroom and two showers (one ADA-accessible) are also available. Fort Casey has 21 standard campsites and 14 utility campsites with water and electricity. One restroom and one shower are available. Reservations are accepted at 888/226-7688.

Directions

From Seattle, take I-5 north to exit 182 for State Route 525 North toward State Route 99 and Mukilteo. Merge onto State Route 525 and drive 8 miles north to the Mukilteo Ferry Terminal. Take the Mukilteo-Clinton ferry (888/808-7977, www.wsdot.wa.gov, fares vary) to Clinton. Follow State Route 525 North for 10.3 miles, turning left onto East Bush Point Road. Drive 4.8 miles, staying straight as the road turns into Smugglers Cove Road. Turn left at the brown sign for South Whidbey State Park and head into the park, making a quick left into the first parking lot. A vault toilet is available next to the parking lot.

Public transit option: **Island Transit** (360/678-7771, www.islandtransit.org) Bus Route 1 services South Whidbey State Park on weekdays.

GPS Coordinates: 48.056168, -122.590953 / N48° 03.374' W122° 35.452'

8 CAMA BEACH STATE PARK
Camano Island

Best: Easy Hikes

Distance: 2.2 miles round-trip

Duration: 1 hour 15 minutes

Elevation Change: 250 feet

Effort: Easy

Trail: Dirt and gravel paths, stairway, pebbly beach

Users: Hikers, mountain bikers, leashed dogs

Season: Year-round

Passes/Fees: Discover Pass

Maps: USGS topographic map for Camano

Contact: Cama Beach State Park, www.parks.state.wa.us, 6:30am-dusk daily

---

Hike through an upland forest and down to the beach for a tour of historic Cama Beach State Park.

Cama Beach State Park is a former fishing resort on the southwestern shore of Camano Island; it opened as a Washington State Park in 2008. While the parking lot, welcome center, and trails all have a fresh, new feeling to them, the waterfront area is somewhat of a throwback: Cabins are only reachable on foot or via shuttle from the parking lots above, and the resort has the feel of a simpler time when beach vacations revolved around sports, games, and watching wildlife from the shore. Stop in at the **Welcome Center** (9am-5pm daily) for maps and park information before you head out.

Start the Hike
Start your hike at the signed **Bluff Trail** next to the drop-off shelter for a 1.7-mile lollipop loop. The pleasant, meandering dirt path winds through a forest of red-flowering currant, Indian plum, red alder, Douglas fir, and western redcedar, passing two wooden platforms along the way. The platforms offer a teasing view of Saratoga Passage and include colorful interpretive signs about common berries, ferns, trees, and shrubs in the Pacific Northwest. In 0.3 mile, bear left onto the **Marine View Loop Trail** to head toward a third wooden platform, this one with

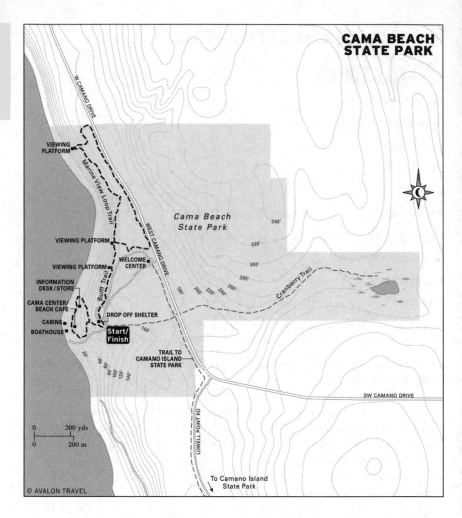

a view of the coastline and the cabins at Cama Beach. Continue on the loop or turn around to head back on the Bluff Trail toward the drop-off shelter and beach.

From your starting place near the drop-off shelter, finish the loop by following signs for the **Beach Trail** as it heads down to the beach. Bear right onto a gravel service road and, in 200 feet, turn left toward the **Cama Center and Beach Cafe** (360/387-3266, www.camabeachcafe.com, hours vary seasonally). Past the café, follow signs for the **Cama Center Trail** to the cabins and waterfront.

Emerge near the **Center for Wooden Boats** to views of the Saratoga Passage, Whidbey Island, and a peek at the Olympics. The long seawall stretching in front of the cabins was built in the 1950s to protect the cabins from driftwood, waves, and debris that might wash ashore. In mid-April, the park opens a seagate on the

a rocky beach walk along the western coast of Camano Island

southern end of the seawall allowing for easy beach access. There is also a small step on the northern end of the beach to help you climb over the wall.

Bear right and head north to explore the resort. At the **general store,** you can pick up a snack, get information about cabin rentals, and learn about the history of Cama Beach and Camano Island. Wander along the crushed-shell and pebble beach, enjoying the views of the bluff to the north. In spring, spy gray whales close to the shore; the whales divide their time between the bays in the north and south end of the island, feeding on ghost shrimp. In summer, spot Orca whales closer to the Whidbey Island side of the Saratoga Passage, where they like to stay in the deep water and feed on salmon. When done exploring, head back up the service road on the Beach Trail toward the drop-off shelter and parking lot area.

Hike Nearby
Camano Island State Park (2269 S. Lowell Point Rd., Camano Island, 360/387-3031, www.parks.state.wa.us, 6:30am-dusk in summer, 8am-dusk in winter, Discover Pass required) is reachable via a 1-mile connector trail from Cama Beach State Park or a short drive. A highlight of the park is the kid-friendly, 0.5-mile Al Emerson Nature Trail; pick up an informative trail brochure and identify the plants as you hike. From Cama Beach State Park, drive south on Camano Drive for 0.4 mile and turn right onto Lowell Point Road. Drive 0.8 mile then bear left at a signed Y-junction toward the campground and amphitheater. The Al Emerson Nature Trail is about 0.5 mile down the road on the left. Lowell Point is at the end of the road.

Make It a Day Trip

Rent a sailboat, motorboat, rowboat, kayak, or canoe from the **Center for Wooden Boats** (1880 SW Camano Dr., Camano Island, 360/387-9361, www.cwb.org, 10am-6pm daily June 15-Sept. 15, 10am-6pm Thurs.-Mon. Sept. 15-June 15) on Cama Beach.

Get Away for the Weekend

For an affordable, family-friendly getaway, spend the weekend in a rustic cabin at **Cama Beach** (360/387-1550, www.parks.state.wa.us, cama.beach@parks.wa.gov). Cabins have a living room, kitchen area, and bedroom; guests must bring their own bedding, pillows, towels, dishes, cookware, and utensils. Standard cabins have external restroom and coin-operated shower facilities, while deluxe cabins and bungalows have a shower, toilet, and sink. Pets are allowed in some cabins for an extra fee. Nearby **Camano Island State Park** (2269 S. Lowell Point Rd., Camano Island, 360/387-1550, www.parks.state.wa.us) offers 88 first-come, first-served campsites, as well as five cabins.

Directions

From Seattle, take I-5 north to exit 212 for State Route 532 West toward Stanwood and Camano Island. At the end of the exit ramp, turn left onto State Route 532. Drive 9.6 miles, passing through Stanwood and over the Stillaguamish River onto Camano Island. At a split in the road, bear left for East Camano Drive and follow signs for Cama Beach and Camano Island State Park. Drive 8 miles, staying straight as East Camano Drive turns into Elger Bay Road. Just past Elger Bay Grocery, turn right onto Mountain View Road and continue 2.1 miles (the road turns into Camano Drive). Turn left at the sign for Cama Beach State Park and continue past the drop-off shelter. Bear left at the Exit Parking sign, then left again to park in the Alder Lot (or one of the nearby lots if it is full). Day-users can park at the Cama Center and Beach Cafe.

Public transit option: **Island Transit** (360/678-7771, www.islandtransit.org) Bus Route 1 West stops at Cama Beach by request. To request a pick-up from Cama Beach, call Island Transit and select option 2.

GPS Coordinates: 48.145324, -122.508726 / N48° 08.565' W122° 30.784'

9 MEADOWDALE BEACH PARK

Snohomish County, Edmonds

Distance: 2.3 miles round-trip

Duration: 1 hour 15 minutes

Elevation Change: 425 feet

Effort: Easy

Trail: Dirt paths, wooden steps

Users: Hikers, leashed dogs

Season: Year-round

Passes/Fees: None required

Maps: USGS topographic map for Edmonds East

Contact: Snohomish County Parks & Recreation, www.snocoparks.org, 7am-dusk daily

---

Hike through a leafy, second-growth forest beside a bubbling creek with the option to continue to a scenic beach.

Second-growth forest, the sights and sounds of Lund's Gulch Creek, bird- and salmon-watching opportunities, and views of the Olympics and Whidbey Island are just some of the gratifying features along this short but scenic trail. Visit in late fall for salmon and trout spawning in the creek, or in winter when the weather is lousy in the mountains. Spring and summer are perfect for a local hike with friends and family. Whenever you visit, bring a used book to donate to the Little Library located next to the caretaker's home in the meadow.

Start the Hike

From the parking lot, descend the wide dirt trail into a forest dominated by towering old Douglas firs, leafy shrubs, and massive western redcedar stumps. In 0.25 mile, head down a section of wooden steps packed into the dirt trail, descending farther into steep-sided **Lund's Gulch.** Enjoy the sights and sounds of Lund's Gulch Creek, an important habitat for the chum salmon, Coho salmon, and cutthroat trout that swim up the creek from the Puget Sound to spawn.

The trail splits 1 mile into the hike, marked by an information kiosk and a **wooden bridge.** Head left over the bridge, keeping an eye out below for spawning salmon and trout in late November. Passing the caretaker's house and **Little**

MEADOWDALE BEACH PARK

PICNIC AREA

Lunds Gulch Creek

Meadowdale County Park

Start/Finish

152ND ST SW

156TH ST SW

60TH AVE W

60TH AVE W

75TH PLACE W

N MEADOWDALE RD

© AVALON TRAVEL

0   200 yds

0   200 m

Library on the left, make your way around the meadow on a paved loop trail before returning to the trailhead.

Extend the Hike

At the edge of the meadow, a miniature tunnel leads under the train tracks to the **beach.** The path under the tunnel has a narrow concrete walkway on one side for hikers; however, the tunnel can flood with several inches of water. Plan to bring a pair of tall, waterproof boots to protect your feet if you decide to explore the beach, or come back when the water has receded. Avoid crossing the train tracks to reach the beach; trains run this route on a regular basis and it is considered trespassing to cross the tracks. At the beach, soak in the views of Browns Bay to the southwest, the Olympics and Kitsap Peninsula directly west, and Whidbey Island to the northwest. Breathe in the sea air as you walk among the sand, pebbles, and driftwood before returning to the trail. The gate to the parking lot closes at dusk, so leave time to return to your vehicle if starting your hike later in the day.

Make It a Day Trip

Drive 3 miles north to **Picnic Point Park** (7231 Picnic Point Rd., Edmonds, 425/388-6600, www.snocoparks.org) to watch the sunset after your hike. A paved pedestrian bridge leads over the train tracks directly to the beach from the parking lot. No pass or permit is required to park in the lot; find portable toilets next to the parking lot.

Catch sight of a train heading south from Picnic Point.

For a bite to eat nearby, **Tubs Gourmet Subs** (4400 168th St. SW #201, Lynnwood, 425/741-9800, www.tubssubs.com, 10:30am-7pm Mon.-Sat., 11am-5pm Sun.) sells warm, thick, toasted subs at reasonable prices.

Directions

From Seattle, take I-5 north to exit 183 for 164th Street. Turn left onto 164th Street and continue 1.9 miles, staying on the main road as it curves into 44th Avenue West. Turn right at a stoplight onto 168th Street and drive for 0.5 mile, crossing State Route 99. Turn right onto 52nd Avenue and continue 0.7 mile, then turn left onto 156th Street. Drive 0.5 mile to the park entrance. A portable toilet is available in the parking lot; an ADA-accessible portable toilet is available in the picnic area at the bottom of the trail.

An ADA-accessible parking lot is located 0.5 mile north of the intersection of 75th Place West and North Meadowdale Road in Edmonds. The road is gated at the end of 75th Place West; call (425/388-6600, www.snocoparks.org) to apply for gate access.

Public transit option: **King County Metro Bus** (www.tripplanner.kingcounty. gov) Route 119 services 52nd Avenue West and 156th Street Southwest about 0.6 mile east of the park.

GPS Coordinates: 47.857390, -122.316837 / N47° 51.433' W122° 18.973'

10 DISCOVERY PARK LOOP
Discovery Park, Seattle

Best: Historical

Distance: 2.9 miles round-trip

Duration: 1 hour 15 minutes

Elevation Change: 300 feet

Effort: Easy

Trail: Dirt, gravel, and paved paths

Users: Hikers, bicyclists, leashed dogs (on path next to beach)

Season: Year-round

Passes/Fees: None

Maps: USGS topographic map for Shilshole Bay

Contact: Seattle Parks and Recreation, www.seattle.gov, 4am-11:30pm daily

---

Follow this loop with scenic viewpoints around Discovery Park and visit the beach and a lighthouse.

Perched on the edge of Magnolia Bluff in northwest Seattle, Discovery Park is a recreational tour de force. Forests, meadows, a scenic overlook, beaches, and former military buildings weave the park's present with its past as the Fort Lawton military base. The Discovery Park Loop Trail circumnavigates Discovery Park with the option for a detour to the beach and the West Point Lighthouse. While you can hike the loop trail in either direction, heading clockwise gives a nice progression of sights and viewpoints. The name Discovery Park is a reference to explorer George Vancouver's ship, the HMS *Discovery,* as well as to the park being a place of "discovery" for visitors.

Start the Hike
Pick up a map at the information kiosk in the east parking lot near the visitors center. Turn left to head up a paved pedestrian road for 0.1 mile. At the top of the road, turn left; veer past the staircase onto a dirt path and follow signs for the **Loop Trail.** A mix of young conifers, older red alders, and bigleaf maples lines the trail, a remnant of logging activity here in the early 1900s.

In 0.5 mile, pass the south parking lot and cross the driveway to pick up the **Loop Trail** on the other side. Ahead is the **View Point Trail,** a short, ADA-accessible trail

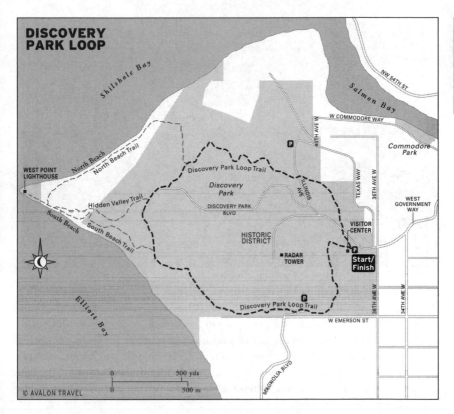

to views of Puget Sound and the Historic District. The large, soccer-ball-shaped tower you see from the View Point Trail is an FAA radar dome that was built in 1959 for Fort Lawton and used as backup by the Seattle-Tacoma International Airport. Look down the slope and you'll spy yellow, former military buildings, including a Post Exchange, a guardhouse, and an administrative building built between the late 1890s and the early 1900s. Other brick and yellow buildings nearby are private homes; please respect their signed boundaries as you explore the district.

Back on the **Loop Trail,** continue west toward the South Meadow. The views slowly open up, revealing grassy meadows, a bluff, and wide-angle vistas of Puget Sound. Old logs line the bluff along the gravel path; stay behind the logs as the bluff drops off sharply on the other side. Two benches overlook the sound, offering a stop for views of the seaplanes, barges, and sailboats that may pass by. Bainbridge Island sits directly across to the west; on a clear day, Mount Rainier can be seen to the south.

In about 0.25 mile, arrive at a junction with the **South Beach Trail.** Turn left on this trail for a detour to the beach or stay straight to continue on the **Loop Trail.** Cross Discovery Park Boulevard and pick up the **Loop Trail** on the other

the West Point Lighthouse and Olympics as seen from South Beach

side, heading toward the north parking lot. Over the next 0.4 mile, the loop crosses a series of roads before entering a rainforest-like section of the trail with trees draped in kryptonite-green moss and blue-gray lichen, croaking wildlife, and nurse logs. Wind 0.5 mile along this section, crossing Illinois Avenue on the pedestrian walkway toward the **visitors center** (8:30am-5pm Tues.-Sun.). After passing under a tunnel, continue straight to the visitors center and the information kiosk to complete your loop.

Extend the Hike

Take the **South Beach Trail** or head down the sidewalk on Discovery Park Boulevard for a 0.5-mile hike to South Beach. You can walk along South Beach right up to West Point Lighthouse, enjoying grand views of the Olympics on a clear day. If the tide is out, wander the tide pools to spot sea anemone, small crabs, and starfish. A trail connects to North Beach for more beach wandering with views of Shilshole Bay and Shilshole Marina. When you're done exploring, take the Hidden Valley Trail, North Beach Trail, or the sidewalks along Discovery Park Boulevard to pick up the Loop Trail.

This detour adds roughly 1.2 miles round-trip to the loop hike if continuing to the lighthouse. Visitors over age 62, those with children under age 8, or guests with limited mobility can request a three-hour parking permit to park in a small lot by the beach. Pick up the permit at the visitors center in the east parking lot.

Make It a Day Trip

While in Magnolia, stop by **Commodore Park** (3330 W. Commodore Way, Seattle,

206/684-4075, www.seattle.gov, 4am-11:30pm daily) for a waterfront walk beside the Lake Washington Ship Canal and a visit to the **Hiram Chittenden Locks** (www.nws.usace.army.mil, 7am-9pm daily). In addition to viewing boats as they pass through the locks, you can watch salmon migrate up the fish ladder (June-Sept.) from Puget Sound to Lake Washington.

Directions

To reach the East Lot and visitors center: From I-5, take exit 167 for Mercer Street toward the Seattle Center. At the end of the exit ramp, continue straight onto Mercer Street for 1.6 miles. Bear right to merge onto Elliott Avenue. In 1.9 miles, bear right for the Nickerson Street exit. Stay right on the exit ramp toward Emerson Street and merge onto Nickerson Street. In 0.2 mile, turn left onto Emerson Street at the stop sign. Drive 0.5 mile then turn right onto Gilman Avenue at the stop sign. Drive 1 mile and stay on the main road as Gilman turns into Government Way. As the road winds its way to the park entrance at 36th Avenue, continue straight onto Discovery Park Boulevard to reach the visitors center and east parking lot on the left. Restrooms are inside the visitors center (8:30am-5pm Tues.-Sun.) and also along the Loop Trail.
GPS Coordinates: 47.657729, -122.406535 / N47° 39.496' W122° 24.357'

South Lot: If the East Lot is full, head to the South Lot, where you can pick up the Loop Trail and the ADA-accessible View Point Trail. To reach the South Lot, drive to Government Way and 36th Avenue. Turn left onto 36th Avenue and continue 0.3 mile. Turn right onto Emerson Street and drive 0.4 mile. Turn right at the sign for the Discovery Park South Lot and enter the driveway.
GPS Coordinates: 47.655571, -122.410165 / N47° 39.271' W122° 24.600'

Public transit option: King County Metro Bus (www.tripplanner.kingcounty.gov) Route 33 stops at 36th Avenue and Government Way, 0.2 mile down the hill from the East Lot and the visitors center. Route 24 also stops near the South Lot (W. Emerson St. and Magnolia Blvd. W.).

11 FOSTER AND MARSH ISLANDS
Washington Park Arboretum

Best: Kid-Friendly

Distance: 2.2 miles round-trip

Duration: 1 hour

Elevation Change: 100 feet

Effort: Easy

Trail: Dirt, gravel, and bark paths

Users: Hikers; leashed dogs allowed on Foster Island, but not Marsh Island

Season: Year-round

Passes/Fees: None

Maps: USGS topographic map for Seattle North

Contact: University of Washington Botanic Gardens, www.uwbotanicgardens.org, dawn-dusk daily

---

This urban hike includes floating walkways and views of Union Bay, the Montlake Bridge, and the Cascades.

This trail through Foster and Marsh Islands can be hiked year-round, but a visit in spring and summer means the flowers are blooming, the birds are plentiful, and there's less chance of the trails being muddy and mucky from wet weather. While you will hear some traffic noise from the 520 bridge, it will not ruin the nature experience. Bring binoculars for up-close views of birds and waterfowl, and pick up a free trail brochure from the visitors center to help identify plants and sights along the walk.

Start the Hike
Begin your hike at the **Foster Island Trailhead** across Foster Island Road from the Graham Visitor Center. Notice the Empress Tree on the left, whose purple flowers bloom in spring and large brown seed pods hang like clusters of walnut shells in winter. Up ahead on the left is Duck Bay, a great place to watch colorful ducks preen and scurry about the bay.

Cross a wooden bridge onto **Foster Island,** named for Joel Foster, who donated this land. (Foster's grandson, Don Foster, was the director of exhibits for the 1962 World's Fair and an influential arts patron in Seattle.) Follow the path underneath

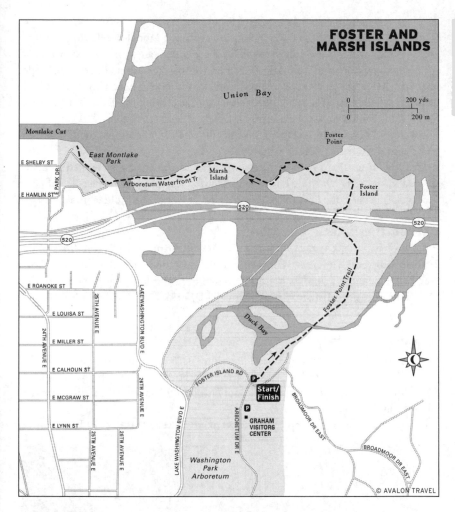

State Route 520 to the north part of the island and, in 0.5 mile, reach a sign for the Arboretum Trail. Beyond the sign, a short trail leads toward Union Bay with views of Husky Stadium to the west and peaks of the Central Cascades to the east.

At the trail sign, bear left onto the soft bark carpeting the **Arboretum Trail.** The path winds between tall grass, cattail, and hardhack, a shrub with fluffy pink flowers in summer that turn a dark russet-brown in winter. Numbered signposts along the trails identify points of interest (signposts are numbered west to east; start from the last page in the trail brochure and work your way forward).

Continue on the floating walkways to **Marsh Island.** Small spur trails lead to observation platforms that are great for catching views of rowers on Union Bay, great blue herons, and waterlilies, whose white flowers bloom in early summer.

Exiting Marsh Island, bear right to continue to **East Montlake Park,** the turn-around point at 1.1 miles. Take a break on the wooden bench and absorb views of the Montlake Bridge and Montlake Cut, a narrow passageway that's about 0.5 mile long and 30 feet deep. The Montlake Cut was completed by the U.S. Army Corp of Engineers in 1916, the last link in a chain that formed the Lake Washington Ship Canal, which transported lumber, fish, and coal from Lake Washington to Puget Sound. The Montlake Bridge was built in 1925 to connect the University District and Montlake neighborhoods.

The towering totem pole behind you is called the **Story of North Island.** Carved in the early 1900s by Chief John Dewey Wallace, it tells the story of how various spirits saved the life of an old woman in danger of dying alone in her village.

Extend the Hike

From East Montlake Park, walk the **Lake Washington Ship Canal Waterside Trail** for up-close views of the Montlake Bridge, the Montlake Cut, and Portage Bay. The trail somewhat spookily follows the Montlake Cut underneath the Montlake Bridge to finish at West Montlake Park. This detour adds 0.9 mile round-trip to the hike.

Make It a Day Trip

Visit the nearby **Seattle Japanese Garden** (1075 Lake Washington Blvd. E., 206/684-4725, www.seattlejapanesegarden.org, hours vary seasonally, $6 adults, $4 seniors, students, and disabled, free for children 5 and under) in fall to see the vibrant maples.

For a quick bite to eat, stop by the **Essential Bakery Cafe** (2719 E. Madison

Explore mild pathways and diverse plant life at the Washington Park Arboretum.

looking west to Husky Stadium from the Arboretum Trail

St., Madison, 206/328-0078, www.essentialbaking.com, 6am-7pm Mon.-Fri., 7am-6pm Sat.-Sun.) for baked goods, sandwiches, soups, and salads, as well as tea and espresso drinks.

For more substantial fare, head to **Independent Pizzeria** (4235 E. Madison St., Seattle, 206/860-6110, www.theindiepizzeria.com, 5pm-9:30pm Wed.-Sat., 5pm-8pm Sun.) for wood-fired pizza in a cozy atmosphere.

Directions

From Seattle, take I-5 north to exit 168B for State Route 520 east. Drive east on State Route 520 to the Montlake Boulevard exit. Continue straight onto Lake Washington Boulevard and, in 0.5 mile, turn left onto Foster Island Road at the stop sign. Park in one of the lots on the side of the road, or turn right onto Arboretum Drive to park at the Graham Visitor Center. ADA-accessible restrooms are located in the visitors center.

From Bellevue, head west on State Route 520 to the exit for Lake Washington Boulevard. Turn left onto 24th Avenue then left again onto Lake Washington Boulevard. Drive 0.4 mile and turn left onto Foster Island Road at a stop sign. Park in one of the lots ahead on the left, or turn right onto Arboretum Drive to park at the Graham Visitor Center. The parking lots near Foster Island tend to fill quickly on sunny weekdays and weekends; plan to arrive early.

GPS Coordinates: 47.640677, -122.294556 / N47° 38.447' W122° 17.648'

Public transit option: King County Metro Bus (www.tripplanner.kingcounty. gov) Routes 43 and 48 service the 24th Avenue East and East Calhoun Street intersection, about 0.5 mile west of the Washington Park Arboretum.

12 EVANS CREEK PRESERVE
City of Sammamish

Distance: 1.8 miles round-trip

Duration: 1 hour

Elevation Change: 200 feet

Effort: Easy

Trail: Crushed gravel and dirt paths, wooden bridges

Users: Hikers, leashed dogs

Season: Year-round

Passes/Fees: None

Maps: USGS topographic map for Redmond

Contact: City of Sammamish, www.sammamish.us, dawn-dusk daily

---

Visit a quiet, scenic preserve with rolling pathways, open fields, a canopied forest, and several wooden bridges.

Evans Creek Preserve is a great option for a quiet, restorative hour in nature or an evening stroll. There are about 2.7 miles of trails in the preserve, ranging from the mild, ADA-accessible meadow paths to steeper hillside trails on the western edge of the preserve. The scenic views are lovely: wide-open grassy meadows, forests and wetlands, and running streams connected by more than one dozen wooden bridges. Numbered signposts with trail maps are found at every trail junction, a neat feature that makes it fun and easy to explore. While this loop takes you through the Meadow and Woodland Trails, you can easily access the Hillside Trails for more mileage and elevation gain.

Start the Hike
Start from the parking lot on the **Meadow Trails,** zigzagging down the crushed gravel path and crossing a bridge over Evans Creek. Bear left to stay on the preserve perimeter toward signpost 12, and enjoy the views across the valley of the Cascade foothills. From the early 1900s to the 1990s, this land was a farm run by the Galley family. It passed down through generations until it was sold to the City of Sammamish in 2000. The Washington Trails Association, the City of Sammamish, and the local community pitched in to build the wooden bridges and the trails over a six-month period. The preserve officially opened in October 2011.

Continue on the **Woodland Trails** toward signpost 11, heading into a canopied

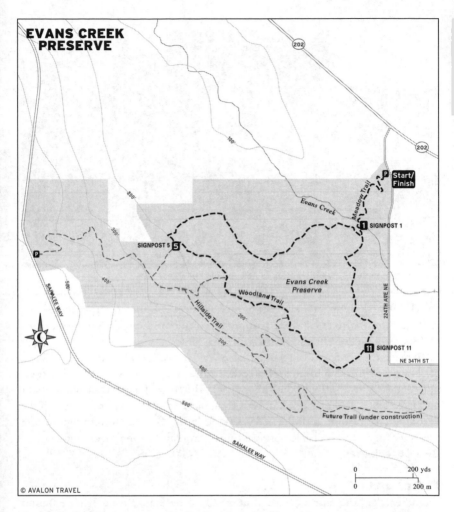

forest of red alder, western redcedar, hemlock, and big old nurse stumps with young trees growing. Arriving at **signpost 11,** bear right toward signpost 5 and pass under natural alcoves and eaves as you make your way along the moss- and fern-lined dirt path. At 1.1 miles into the hike, pass **signpost 5** and emerge in a meadow lined with tufts of blackberry shrubs, grasses, and ferns ringed by tall cottonwood and maple trees. Wind your way along the perimeter of the Woodland Trails toward **signpost 2,** rejoining the **Meadow Trails** on your way back to the trailhead.

Extend the Hike
Keep going by exploring the **Hillside Trails** along the western edge of the preserve. You can connect to this trail system via the Woodland Trails or park at the

one of several quaint wooden bridges at Evans Creek Preserve

Sahalee Way parking lot and pick up the Hillside Trails directly from there. The trails descend 325 feet from the parking lot to the Meadow Trails, so your hike will start with a descent and finish with an ascent.

To reach the upper parking lot (Sahalee Way), drive east on State Route 520 to the State Route 202/Redmond Way exit. At the end of the exit ramp, bear right onto State Route 202/Redmond Way. Stay in the center lane to continue straight on State Route 202. In 2.4 miles, turn right onto Sahalee Way and drive 1 mile. Past a sign for Evans Creek Preserve, make a sharp left at the second sign for the preserve. An ADA-accessible portable toilet is available in the parking lot.
GPS Coordinates: 47.642718, -122.055558 / N47° 38.583' W122° 03.310'

Directions

From Seattle, head east on State Route 520 to the State Route 202/Redmond Way exit. At the end of the exit ramp, bear right onto State Route 202/Redmond Way. Stay in the center lane to continue straight on State Route 202. In 3.5 miles, turn right onto 224th Avenue NE at the sign for Evans Creek Preserve. The park entrance is on the right in 0.1 mile. Restrooms are located 0.2 mile on the trail (near signpost 15).
GPS Coordinates: 47.64573, -122.040988 / N47° 38.743' W122° 02.462'

13 WILDSIDE-RED TOWN LOOP
Cougar Mountain Regional Wildland Park

Best: Easy Hikes

Distance: 2.6 miles round-trip

Duration: 1 hour 15 minutes

Elevation Change: 275 feet

Effort: Easy

Trail: Dirt paths

Users: Hikers, horseback riders, leashed dogs

Season: Year-round

Passes/Fees: None

Maps: Green Trails Map 203S for Cougar Mountain/Squak Mountain, USGS topographic map for Bellevue South

Contact: King County Parks, www.kingcounty.gov, 8am-dusk daily

---

This gentle hike explores a former coal mine, a baseball diamond, and Coal Creek, with optional side trips to two waterfalls.

A 20-minute drive from downtown Seattle, Cougar Mountain features rolling, peaceful trails, a former coal mine, and up-close views of bubbling Coal Creek. The trail system provides options to create your own loop hikes and side trips and remains mostly snow-free in winter. Bring a map to help navigate the maze-like trail junctions, and arrive early in summer—the Red Town Trailhead is popular, and the parking lot tends to fill quickly on sunny days and weekends.

One neat quirk you'll see along your hike are the prefixes in front of the trail names (such as "W1" Wildside Trail). The letters refer to a trail's relative north, south, west, or east location on Cougar Mountain. Since this hiking route is on the west side of the mountain, you'll see mostly "W" prefixes on the trail signs.

Start the Hike
At the trailhead on the **Wildside Trail,** bear right to follow the signs for the Ford Slope Mine and De Leo Wall. Cross a pedestrian bridge over Coal Creek to arrive at the **Rainbow Town Trail,** named for the multiple hues that homeowners painted their homes in the former mining town (versus nearby Red Town where the preferred color was—you guessed it—red). Bear left to explore the Ford Slope

Mine, a former coal mine that operated 1905-1926. At the information kiosk, look for the large "H" sign marking the location of a steam hoist that once pulled loaded coal cars—five at a time—up from the mine.

After exploring the Ford Slope Mine, retrace your steps on the Rainbow Town Trail back toward the **Wildside Trail.** Bear left toward De Leo Wall and enjoy the playfully undulating path flanked by mossy forest, thickets of sword fern, and red alder. In 0.5 mile, bear left at a sign for Marshall's Hill Trail; this is followed by a quick right to continue on the Wildside Trail toward De Leo Wall. The trail narrows as you hike another 0.5 mile, climb 50 feet, and pass through a quiet grove of western redcedar.

Turn left onto the **De Leo Wall Trail** and, in 200 feet, bear left again onto

a forested path along Coal Creek

Indian Trail toward the Red Town Trailhead. Hike 0.5 mile then turn right at the sign for **Marshall's Hill Trail.** Spotting a sign for the Meadow Restoration Project ahead, bear left to cross the pedestrian bridge over Coal Creek. Take time to explore the meadow and walk the small trail winding through it. Until the 1930s, the meadow used to be a baseball diamond where the community played ball. Competition among mining town baseball teams was spirited; rumor has it that local mining companies would recruit miners as much for their ball playing ability as for their mining expertise.

Pass the meadow and follow this quiet stretch of trail southeast along bubbling Coal Creek. Emerge onto the **Red Town Trail** and bear left to hike 0.75 mile toward the Red Town Trailhead. The wide, regal trail is the former main street of Red Town, now flanked by tall Douglas fir, bigleaf maple, and cottonwood. Complete your loop at the Red Town Trailhead. To learn more about the history of Cougar Mountain, read *The Authoritative Guide to the Hiking Trails of Cougar Mountain Regional Wildland Park and Surrounds* by Harvey Manning, Ralph Owen, and Charles McCrone.

Shorten the Hike

From the intersection of the Marshall's Hill Trail and Wildside Trail, hike **Marshall's Hill Trail** directly over to the Red Town Trail for a 1.6-mile loop (45 minutes) back to the trailhead.

Extend the Hike

Add 0.3 mile to your loop with a 20-minute detour to **Far Country Falls.** From

Coal Creek Falls

the intersection of the De Leo Wall Trail and Indian Trail, hike south on Indian Trail toward Far Country Trail. A signed spur trail on the right leads to a viewpoint of the waterfalls.

For a 3.5-mile hike (2 hours), extend your loop to **Coal Creek Falls.** From the intersection of the De Leo Wall Trail and Indian Trail, hike north on the Indian Trail toward the Red Town Trailhead. Take the Quarry Trail up 360 feet and bear left onto Coal Creek Falls Trail to Coal Creek Falls. Past the falls, bear left onto Cave Hole Trail and follow signs for Red Town Trailhead to complete the loop.

Directions

From Seattle, take I-90 east to exit 13 for Lakemont Boulevard. At the end of the exit ramp, turn right onto Lakemont Boulevard and drive 2.9 miles. After passing a yellow pedestrian sign at the bottom of the hill, turn left into the parking lot (marked with a blue Cougar Mountain Regional Wildland Park/Red Town Trailhead sign). This popular lot tends to fill quickly; plan to arrive by 9am on sunny weekends. Two portable toilets are available near the information kiosk.
GPS Coordinates: 47.535164, -122.128637 / N47° 32.063' W122° 07.710'

14 ANTI-AIRCRAFT PEAK
Cougar Mountain Regional Wildland Park

Best: Historical

Distance: 3.5 miles round-trip

Duration: 2 hours

Elevation Change: 675 feet

Effort: Easy/moderate

Trail: Dirt paths

Users: Hikers, horseback riders, leashed dogs

Season: Year-round

Passes/Fees: None

Maps: Green Trails Map 203S for Cougar Mountain/Squak Mountain, USGS topographic map for Bellevue South

Contact: King County Parks, www.kingcounty.gov, 8am-dusk daily

---

Explore rolling hills and historical artifacts on Cougar Mountain, with options for a picnic at Radar Park and Million Dollar View.

Anti-Aircraft Peak features gently rolling trails through a quiet forest, with options to see the Fantastic Erratic boulder and the airshaft of a former coal mine. Next to the trailhead, Radar Park offers wide-open fields, picnic tables, and historical information about the military installation that operated here in the mid-1900s. Million Dollar View provides glimpses of Lake Sammamish and a tiny Mount Baker.

Bring a map to explore both areas; although the trails are well signed, it's easy to get turned around in the maze of junctions on this side of Cougar Mountain. Since this route starts from Anti-Aircraft Peak, your hike begins with a gentle descent down Cougar Mountain and ends with an ascent back to the trailhead.

The name Cougar Mountain comes from a local landowner who felt that the name at the time, Newcastle, sounded too sooty and dirty—like the coal mining operations that had taken place on the mountain from the late 1800s to the mid-1900s. The campaign to change the name to Cougar Mountain wasn't officially accepted until the U.S. Army purchased the land in the early 1950s. The U.S. Army occupied the land from the 1950s to the 1960s, hence the name Anti-Aircraft Peak. After tireless campaigning by Harvey Manning and the Issaquah Alps Trails Club,

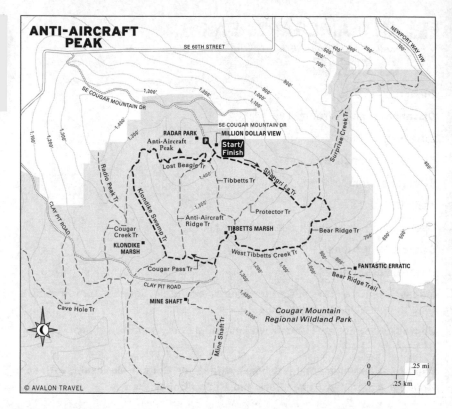

the area opened for public use in 1985 as Cougar Mountain Regional Wildland Park. In 2016, the trailhead at Anti-Aircraft Peak was renamed the Harvey Manning Trailhead in honor of Manning's stalwart contributions.

Start the Hike

Start your hike on the **Shangri-La Trail,** heading southeast toward the Fantastic Erratic. The wide, flat, gravel path slopes gently downward through a quiet forest of red alder, Douglas fir, and bigleaf maple as you make your way down the eastern slope of Cougar Mountain. After 0.9 mile, bear right onto **Bear Ridge Trail,** enjoying the views into the diverse lowland forest as you swing westward. After 0.25 mile, bear right onto the **West Tibbetts Creek Trail** to continue west. Alternatively, bear left for a short side trip to the **Fantastic Erratic,** a large rock festooned with licorice ferns that was carried to its current resting place by a glacier.

Continue on the West Tibbetts Creek Trail and listen for the gurgling sounds of West Fork Tibbetts Creek below as you climb 200 feet over the next 0.5 mile. At an impressively large western redcedar stump, turn left onto the **Tibbets Marsh Trail** and hike toward Clay Pit Road, crossing a finely crafted pedestrian bridge.

Quiet pathways wind through the forest beneath Anti-Aircraft Peak.

In 0.25 mile, arrive at the **Cougar Pass Trail.** Bear right to continue west on your loop, or turn left toward **Clay Pit Road** for a worthy side trip to the spooky, grate-covered airshaft of a former coal mine.

Hike west on the **Cougar Pass Trail** for 0.3 mile. Bear right onto the **Klondike Swamp Trail** and head north on the noticeably wider and flatter trail (it's shared with horses). In 0.6 mile, turn right onto the **Lost Beagle Trail** and head east, making your ascent back to the trailhead. The trail climbs 230 feet in 0.5 mile; take a breather as soon as the ground levels out at the top. Make three quick lefts and you're home free: Turn left onto the **Anti-Aircraft Ridge Trail,** then left onto the **Tibbetts Marsh Trail,** and left again onto the **Shangri-La Trail** to the trailhead.

Extend the Hike

While the **Fantastic Erratic** may be underwhelming to some (it basically looks like a large, fern-covered rock), it is an interesting piece of geological history. The side trip from this route is 0.8 mile round-trip with a 200-foot descent (45 minutes). From the intersection of the Bear Ridge Trail and West Tibbetts Creek Trail, head southeast on the Bear Ridge Trail to the Fantastic Erratic.

A fun detour on this route is the creepy, grate-covered airshaft of a former coal mine, located on the **Mine Shaft Trail.** This detour is 0.6 mile round-trip (20 minutes). From the junction of the Cougar Pass Trail and the Tibbetts Marsh Trail, hike the Tibbetts Marsh Trail toward Clay Pit Road. Arrive at Clay Pit Road and turn right, heading down the road to the signed Mine Shaft Trail on the left. Hopping on the trail, you'll arrive at the airshaft in 0.1 mile. A bench provides a welcome rest and a strategic spot for peering into the airshaft. Read about the history of coal mines on the interpretive sign nearby. When finished, head back up Clay Pit Road, rejoining the Tibbets Marsh Trail and Cougar Pass Trail to continue the loop.

Directions

From Seattle, head east on I-90 to exit 13 for Lakemont Boulevard. Head south on Lakemont Boulevard for 2.2 miles, then turn left onto Cougar Mountain Way. Follow the road for 1.2 miles (it turns into SE 60th St.), then bear right at a Y-intersection for Cougar Mountain Drive. Drive 1.1 miles to the parking lot and Harvey Manning

Lake Sammamish and Mount Baker from Million Dollar View

Trailhead. (The pavement ends after 0.6 mile, and the last 0.5 mile to the trailhead is gravel road.) A portable toilet is in the parking lot. Restrooms are available in nearby Radar Park (late Mar.-Oct.). Plan to arrive early on a summer weekend; this is a popular trailhead, and parking spaces fill quickly.

GPS Coordinates: 47.541029, -122.096226 / N47° 32.455' W122° 05.762'

15 SQUAK MOUNTAIN LOOP
Squak Mountain State Park, Issaquah

Distance: 6.2 miles round-trip

Duration: 4 hours

Elevation Change: 1,900 feet

Effort: Moderate

Trail: Dirt paths, rocky, gravel sections

Users: Hikers, horseback riders, leashed dogs

Season: Year-round

Passes/Fees: Discover Pass

Maps: Green Trails Map 203S for Cougar Mountain/Squak Mountain, USGS topographic maps for Maple Valley and Issaquah

Contact: Squak Mountain State Park, www.parks.state.wa.us, 6:30am-dusk daily in summer, 8am-dusk daily in winter

---

A peaceful, yet challenging hike leads to a historic fireplace and tree-tipped views of Mount Rainier.

The name "Squak" sounds like a bit of an outcast when compared to neighbors Tiger Mountain and Cougar Mountain, but there's a very meaningful connection to its past. "Squak" is an adaptation of the Lushootseed word "Isquowh." While there is disagreement over the meaning of the word, most people believe it refers to an element of nature, such as "the sound of water birds." The city of Issaquah was named Squak before adopting its current name in the late 1890s—its own creative take on the Lushootseed word.

Squak Mountain is a good choice for a quiet hiking experience among the Issaquah Alps. Exploration of Squak Mountain begins on a quiet, gently graded trail to a historic fireplace and finishes with a hilly loop to views of Mount Rainier. It is easy to get turned around on the network of trails; bring a map and prepare for mud and large puddles in the wet, winter months, as well as the possibility of snow and ice after a bout of wintry weather.

Start the Hike
From the Squak Mountain Trail sign, head north toward the May Valley Loop Trail. In 300 feet, turn right onto an access road, followed by a quick left to pick up the **May Valley Loop Trail** toward Central Peak. Hike 1.7 miles along the trail; the

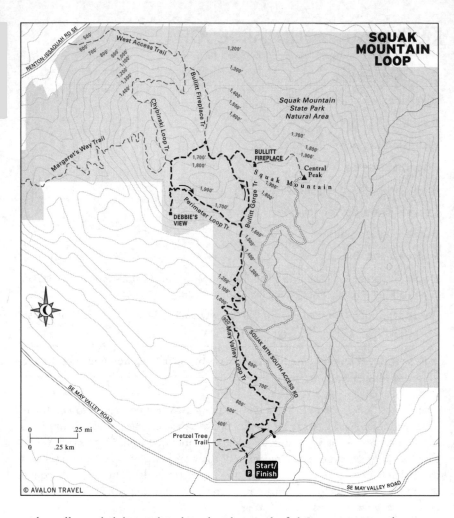

wide, well-traveled dirt path is dotted with spiny-leafed Oregon grape and a roomy forest of Douglas fir, western redcedar, and bigleaf maple. Bear left at the next two intersections toward Central Peak and listen for the gurgling sounds of Bullitt Creek and the tree-thwacking sounds of pileated woodpeckers. In early spring, white bell-like flowers of Indian plum and small pink clusters of red-flowering currant border the trail, a delicate pop of color amid the lush, green understory.

A wooden fence marks the end of horse access and the start of the **Bullitt Gorge Trail.** Zigzag through the fence and continue straight along a rocky and narrow section of trail, gaining a stiff 225 feet in 0.3 mile. Pass the Perimeter Loop Trail on the left and continue north for another 0.4 mile, enjoying a break as the trail evens out to a gentle, rolling grade. Arrive at a T-junction for the **Bullitt Fireplace**

morning sunlight at Debbie's View with Mount Rainier in the distance

Trail and turn right to head east toward Central Peak. In 0.25 mile, turn right onto a short spur trail to the impressive Bullitt Fireplace. The site was the spot of Stimson Bullitt's summer home, built in 1952 and unfortunately torn apart by vandals in the early 1970s. Bullitt donated his 590 acres of land on Squak Mountain (including the land the fireplace currently sits on) to create a public park. Squak Mountain State Park was born in 1972.

From the Bullitt Fireplace, head west on the Bullitt Fireplace Trail to retrace your steps to the intersection with the Bullitt Gorge Trail. Stay straight on the **Bullitt Fireplace Trail,** continuing west toward State Route 900. Descend 230 feet then turn left onto the **Chybinski Loop Trail** toward State Route 900. Approach your last climb of the hike—200 feet in 0.3 mile. At the top, turn left at the Debbie's View sign then make a quick right to join the **Perimeter Loop Trail.** In 0.2 mile, spot the sign for **Debbie's View** on the right and take the spur trail. In about 0.1 mile, reach a cozy bench for two with views of Mount Rainier—a perfect spot for a snack or lunch. Debbie's View is named for Debbie Anschell, a dedicated volunteer with the Issaquah Alps Trails Club who performed years of trail maintenance on Squak and Tiger Mountain.

To head back, take the spur trail from Debbie's View back to the Perimeter Loop Trail. Bear right on the trail and, in 0.4 mile, turn again onto the Bullitt Gorge Trail toward the May Valley Trailhead. In 0.3 mile, continue straight to join the May Valley Loop Trail and follow the signs for May Valley Trailhead 1.8 miles to the parking lot.

Shorten the Hike

Head directly to **Debbie's View** for a 5.2-mile round-trip hike (3.5 hours) with 1,400 feet elevation gain. From the parking lot, follow signs for May Valley Loop for 1.8 miles toward Central Peak. Continue straight onto Bullitt Gorge Trail for 0.3 mile, then turn left onto the Perimeter Loop Trail and hike 0.4 mile to the signed spur trail for Debbie's View.

The **Pretzel Tree Trail** offers a nice option for families with young children. The flat 0.3-mile trail features storyboards about the forest adventures of a young field mouse. From the parking lot, follow the signs for the Pretzel Tree Trail.

Extend the Hike

To hit **Central Peak,** the highest point on Squak Mountain, continue 0.3 mile past the Bullitt Fireplace on the Bullitt Fireplace Trail to the peak. You may see some views from small breaks in the trees, but for the most part there isn't a clear viewpoint, just a bunch of eerie radio towers.

Hike Nearby

Nearby **Margaret's Way** is a well-signed, 6.2-mile round-trip hike (4 hours) on the western side of Squak Mountain. The route has mostly forest views, with an option to connect to Debbie's View at the top. Start the hike from the Cougar Mountain-Squak Mountain Corridor parking lot and follow signs for Margaret's Way up the western side of Squak Mountain. In 3.1 miles, you'll reach an intersection with the Chybinski Loop Trail—this is the end of the Margaret's Way trail. To continue to Debbie's View, turn right onto the Chybinski Loop Trail and then turn right again at the sign for Debbie's View. Make another quick right onto the signed Perimeter Loop Trail. Hike 0.2 mile then turn right at a sign for Debbie's View and take the spur trail 0.1 mile to the bench and overlook.

To reach the trailhead, take I-90 east from Seattle to exit 15 for State Route 900 West. At the end of the exit ramp, turn right onto State Route 900 and drive 3.3 miles. Pass the sign for Squak Mountain Materials and, in 200 feet, turn left into a parking lot with a blue sign for Cougar Mountain-Squak Mountain Corridor. Leashed dogs are allowed. The parking lot is on county land; no parking pass is required.

the Bullitt Fireplace

GPS Coordinates for Margaret's Way: 47.506667, -122.086710 / N47° 30.443'
W122° 05.241'

Directions

From Seattle, head east on I-90 to exit 15 for State Route 900 West. At the end
of the exit ramp, turn right onto State Route 900 and drive 4.1 miles to May Valley Road. Turn left onto May Valley Road and continue straight for 2.3 miles.
Keep your eyes peeled for a Washington State Parks sign on your right; turn left
immediately into the parking lot with the Squak Mountain State Park sign. Two
ADA-accessible vault toilets are available at the parking lot.

GPS Coordinates: 47.481965, -122.053981 / N47° 28.912' W122° 03.255'

16 POO POO POINT
Tiger Mountain State Forest, Issaquah

Distance: 3.8 miles round-trip

Duration: 2.5 hours

Elevation Change: 1,650 feet

Effort: Moderate

Trail: Dirt paths, cobblestone steps

Users: Hikers, leashed dogs

Season: Year-round

Passes/Fees: None

Maps: Green Trails Map 204S for Tiger Mountain/Taylor Mountain, USGS topographic maps for Issaquah and Maple Valley

Contact: Washington State Department of Natural Resources, South Puget Sound Region, www.dnr.wa.gov

---

This short, challenging hike reaches views of Mount Rainier, Mount Baker, and the Olympics, with the chance to see paragliders.

The Chirico Trail to Poo Poo Point is a great bang for your hiking buck: easy access from Seattle; a great workout; views of Mount Rainier, Mount Baker, the Olympics, and the Cascades; and, if you're lucky, a chance to witness paragliders from launch sites next to the trail. Time your outing to avoid the weekend morning crowds, and bring a friendly attitude—you won't be alone on this popular hike. Practice good trail etiquette: Stay aware of hikers behind you and step aside on your downhill when encountering uphill hikers.

Start the Hike
Before you hit the trail, look toward the sky to watch for paragliders who might be landing on the field in front of you. Follow the gravel path around the perimeter of the landing field to start hiking on the **Chirico Trail,** named for Marc Chirico, the owner of Seattle Paragliding whose team completed the trail in 2000. Initially meant as a trail for paragliders to hike down when wind conditions were poor, it's since become well-liked by hikers.

Enter the forest and pause for a moment to check out the helpful kiosk with a map of the Tiger Mountain trail system. From here, a unique cobblestone path leads south along Yah-er Wall through a lush forest teeming with moss and licorice

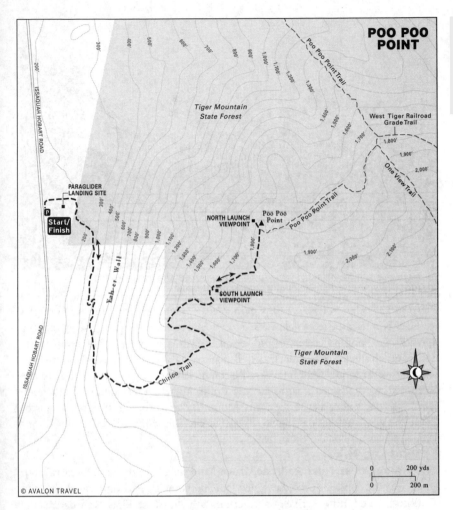

fern. Follow the trail as it slowly makes a U-turn northeast; the cobblestones melt away to reveal a dirt path lined with round, leathery salal and spiny Oregon grape. Arrive at a landing with a nice long wooden bench at 0.9 mile, a good spot for a short rest.

The trail ascends through a dry forest of western hemlock and cottonwood, then meanders through a group of red alder to a split in the trail. Follow the main trail left for a final push to a small, open field at 1.6 miles—the south launch site for paragliders and a prime viewpoint for Mount Rainier. Take a front-row seat on the nearby bench to watch paragliders pull their parachutes into the air and launch into the sky.

But this isn't it. Continue on the trail past a wooden kiosk to reach **Poo Poo**

view of Lake Sammamish and the city of Issaquah from the north launch site

Point in 1.9 miles. Why the funny name? (It's not what you're thinking.) Loggers on Tiger Mountain used to blow a steam whistle to communicate during logging operations; "Poo Poo" refers to the sound the whistle made. At the point is the north launch site for paragliders, as well as picnic tables, benches, and a restroom. Directly west is Squak Mountain, radio towers sitting atop Central Peak. To the northwest, spot Lake Sammamish, the city of Issaquah, and Issaquah High School. On a clear day you can even see a tiny Mount Baker in the distance to the north. Enjoy the views before making your way back to the trailhead.

Extend the Hike

Explore quiet **West Tiger Railroad Grade Trail** for a hike through history. From Poo Poo Point, continue onto the signed Poo Poo Point Trail toward the High Point Trailhead. In 0.5 mile, arrive at a junction with the West Tiger Railroad Grade Trail and proceed straight onto the trail. In the 1920s, a locomotive operated on this trail, transporting logs for a nearby mill. Remnants of the railroad can still be found, including railroad spikes, cables, and pieces of the track. (Please leave any railroad artifacts you might see for others to enjoy.) Wander for a bit before turning around; the trail continues for more than 3 miles and connects with trails leading to the West Tiger Peaks.

Make It a Day Trip

Stop in at the **Issaquah Visitor Center** (155 NW Gilman Blvd., Issaquah, 425/392-7024, www.discoverissaquah.com) to pick up a brochure for a self-guided walking tour and learn about events and historic sites in Issaquah. The tiny **Issaquah Depot**

Museum (78 1st Ave. NE, Issaquah, 425/392-3500, www.issaquahhistory.org, 11am-3pm Fri.-Sun.) has neat historical exhibits about communication, logging, railroad, and the mining activity that was part of Issaquah's early development.

When you're ready for a caffeine hit, head to the **Issaquah Coffee Company** (317 NW Gilman Blvd. #46, Issaquah, 425/677-7118, www.issaquahcoffee.com, 6am-7pm Mon.-Fri., 7am-7pm Sat., 8am-6pm Sun.) for Stumptown coffee, tea, pastries, and a modest sandwich selection (vegan and vegetarian options). For more substantial fare, stop in at the cozy, homey **Issaquah Cafe** (1580 NW Gilman Blvd., Issaquah, 425/391-9690, www.cafesinc.com, 6am-3pm Mon.-Sat., 7am-3pm Sun.) for breakfast, sandwiches, and a thick slab of their homemade pie. The café is quite popular and there can be a wait during busy times.

Directions

From Seattle, take I-90 east to exit 17 for Front Street. Bear right at the end of the exit ramp to merge onto Front Street. Continue straight for 2.8 miles, following the road as it turns into Issaquah-Hobart Road. Just past Seattle Paragliding, turn left into the open gravel parking lot. There are three portable toilets in the parking lot and one clivus (composting) toilet at the summit.

GPS Coordinates: 47.500243, -122.021976 / N47° 29.999' W122° 01.319'

17 WEST TIGER 3
Tiger Mountain State Forest, Issaquah

Distance: 5.3 miles round-trip

Duration: 3 hours

Elevation Change: 2,000 feet

Effort: Moderate

Trail: Dirt paths, rocky and rooty sections

Users: Hikers, leashed dogs

Season: Year-round

Passes/Fees: Discover Pass

Maps: Green Trails Map 204S for Tiger Mountain/Taylor Mountain, USGS topographic map for Fall City

Contact: Washington State Department of Natural Resources, South Puget Sound Region, www.dnr.wa.gov, 6:30am-dusk daily in summer, 8am-dusk daily in winter

---

Hiking to the summit of West Tiger 3 is challenging, but family-friendly trails are at nearby Tradition Plateau.

West Tiger 3 is a no-frills conditioning hike close to Seattle with the added bonus of ADA-accessible and kid-friendly trails in nearby Tradition Plateau. Part of the fun of Tiger Mountain is the sheer number of trails that enable hikers to stitch together all kinds of loops of varying lengths and elevations. Pick up a trail map to get a feel for hikes you can do beyond West Tiger 3.

Consider tackling the trail midweek to avoid the weekend crowds, or in winter as a warm-up for spring and summer hiking. While the trail can be hiked year-round, you may encounter snow and ice after a winter storm; check trail conditions in winter.

Start the Hike
From the **High Point Trailhead**, head left on the **Bus Trail** then left again at the **West Tiger 3 Trail** sign. From here it's a straightforward 2.5-mile climb. You'll encounter varying conditions on the trail—from clear dirt paths to rock-strewn sections—however, the trail is well signed and easy to follow. While it might be easy to navigate, you'll certainly get a workout on this route. Soon after its start, the trail ascends a challenging grade and stays that way to the summit. Pace

Barnes & Noble Booksellers #2280
401 NE Northgate Way #1100
Seattle, WA 98125
206-417-2967

STR:2280 REG:003 TRN:8381 CSHR:Maddie R

Rick Steves Best of Spain
   9781631213151   T1
   (1 @ 24.99)   24.99
Moon 75 Great Hikes Seattle
   9781631214981   T1
   (1 @ 17.99)   17.99

Subtotal   42.98
Sales Tax T1 (10.100%)   4.34
TOTAL   47.32
VISA   47.32
   Card#:   XXXXXXXXXXXX2175
   Expdate: XX/XX
   Auth: 07700C
   Entry Method: Chip Read

   Application Label: Visa Credit
   AID: a0000000031010
   TVR: 8080008000
   TSI: 6800

A MEMBER WOULD HAVE SAVED   4.30

Connect with us on Social

Facebook- @BNNorthgate
Instagram- @bnnorthgate
Twitter-   @BNNorthgate

101.46C   03/04/2018 01:49PM

CUSTOMER COPY

within 60 days of purchase, (iii) for textbooks, (iv) when the original tender is PayPal, or (v) for products purchased at Barnes & Noble College bookstores that are listed for sale in the Barnes & Noble Booksellers inventory management system.

Opened music CDs, DVDs, vinyl records, audio books may not be returned, and can be exchanged only for the same title and only if defective. NOOKs purchased from other retailers or sellers are returnable only to the retailer or seller from which they are purchased, pursuant to such retailer's or seller's return policy. Magazines, newspapers, eBooks, digital downloads, and used books are not returnable or exchangeable. Defective NOOKs may be exchanged at the store in accordance with the applicable warranty.

Returns or exchanges will not be permitted (i) after 14 days or without receipt or (ii) for product not carried by Barnes & Noble or Barnes & Noble.com.

Policy on receipt may appear in two sections.

Return Policy

With a sales receipt or Barnes & Noble.com packing slip, a full refund in the original form of payment will be issued from any Barnes & Noble Booksellers store for returns of undamaged NOOKs, new and unread books, and unopened and undamaged music CDs, DVDs, vinyl records, toys/games and audio books made within 14 days of purchase from a Barnes & Noble Booksellers store or Barnes & Noble.com with the below exceptions:

A store credit for the purchase price will be issued (i) for purchases made by check less than 7 days prior to the date of return, (ii) when a gift receipt is presented within 60 days of purchase, (iii) for textbooks, (iv) when the original tender is PayPal, or (v) for products purchased at Barnes & Noble College bookstores that are listed for sale in the Barnes & Noble Booksellers inventory management system.

Opened music CDs, DVDs, vinyl records, audio books may not be returned, and can be exchanged only for the same title and only if defective. NOOKs purchased from other retailers or sellers are returnable only to the retailer or seller from which they are purchased, pursuant to such retailer's or seller's return policy. Magazines, newspapers, eBooks, digital downloads, and used books are not returnable or exchangeable. Defective NOOKs may be exchanged at the store in accordance with the applicable warranty.

Returns or exchanges will not be permitted (i) after 14 days or without receipt or (ii) for product not carried by Barnes & Noble or Barnes & Noble.com.

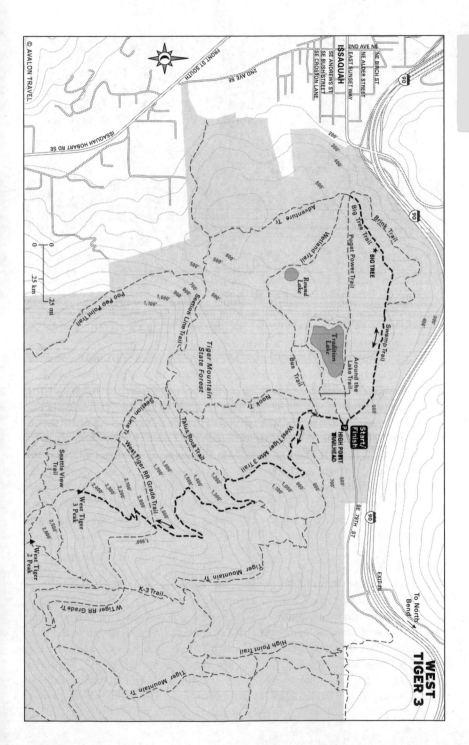

© AVALON TRAVEL

WEST TIGER 3

ISSAQUAH

2ND AVE NE
NE BIRCH ST
NE ALDER STREET
EAST SUNSET WAY
NE SUNSET WAY
SE ANDREWS ST
SE BUSH STREET
SE CROSTON LANE

FRONT ST SOUTH
2ND AVE SE
SE ANDREWS ST

ISSAQUAH HOBART RD SE

0   .25 km
0   .25 mi

Poo Poo Point Trail

Adventure Tr

Wetland Trail

Big Tree Trail

Brink Trail

BIG TREE
Puget Power Trail

Swamp Trail

Round Lake

Section Line Trail

Tiger Mountain State Forest

Tradition Lake

Around the Lake Trail

Bus Trail

Noon Tr

Talus Rock Trail

Section Line Trail

Seattle View Trail

West Tiger RR Grade Trail

West Tiger 3 Peak

West Tiger 2 Peak

K-3 Trail

W Tiger RR Grade Tr

Tiger Mountain Tr

Tiger Mountain Tr

High Point Trail

West Tiger Mtn 3 Trail

Start/Finish
HIGH POINT TRAILHEAD

SE 79TH ST

EXIT 20

To North Bend

a wide path through the forest on the West Tiger 3 trail

yourself and take small breaks as needed, enjoying the small streams and forest views along the way.

After 1 mile, pass the Talus Rock Trail on the right and continue along the slope as it peers down into the forest. Head southeast through a hall of dignified conifers, taking a breather on a break in the grade. In another 1.2 miles, pass the West Tiger Railroad Grade Trail and climb a small series of switchbacks. Upon reaching an intersection with the West Tiger Cable Line (a rough, unmaintained trail), continue straight on the main trail and press up a rubbly 0.3 mile to the summit of West Tiger 3. The views from the summit are modest; trees have grown in considerably over the years, leaving you with views of West Tiger 2 to the southeast and glimpses of the Puget Sound to the southwest. Rest and refuel on a couple of flattened rocks in the exposed clearing. When ready, head back down the West Tiger 3 Trail, keeping your eyes peeled for glimpses of the Cascades to the northeast.

Extend the Hike

Hike beyond the summit of West Tiger 3 to the summits of **West Tiger 2** and **West Tiger 1** for an extra 2.6 miles round-trip (2 hours). From the West Tiger 3 summit, head south on an unmarked trail for 0.4 mile to West Tiger 2 (no views). Past West Tiger 2, descend southwest along a gravel road. Skirt a red gate in 0.3 mile and bear left to follow a sign for West Tiger 1. Arrive at a hiker's hut after gaining a steep 300 feet in the next 0.3 mile. It's just another 0.3 mile beyond the hiker's hut to West Tiger 1. To continue, follow the ByPass Trail for 0.25 mile then bear right toward Poo Top Trail for 250 feet to the summit of West Tiger 1 (no views).

Alternatively, explore a short loop to a waterfall with large talus boulders and caves on the **Talus Rock Trail.** On your way down West Tiger 3, bear left onto the signed Talus Rock Trail. Pass a modest waterfall in 0.2 mile then, in another 0.25 mile, turn right onto the Nook Trail and right again onto the Bus Trail back to the trailhead. The loop adds 0.5 mile to your West Tiger 3 hike. On its own, this is a 2.3-mile loop (1 hour 15 minutes).

Hike Nearby

Visit the **Tradition Plateau,** located west of the High Point Trailhead, for kid-friendly and partially ADA-accessible trails. The **Around the Lake Trail** is a lovely, partially ADA-accessible 1.5-mile trail that encircles Tradition Lake. The trail links to the **Puget Power Trail** to connect back to the trailhead for a 45-minute loop hike with resting spots and interpretive signs. Download a self-guided tour from the City of Issaquah (www.issaquahwa.gov) to identify features along the trail.

The **Swamp Trail** to **Big Tree Trail** is a 1.9-mile out-and-back hike to an ancient Douglas fir tree with storyboards about a raccoon named Zoe and her adventures in the forest. Pick up the Swamp Trail from the gated gravel road next to the High Point parking lot.

Whichever trail you choose, bring a map to help navigate the maze of junctions in the Tradition Plateau.

Directions

From Seattle, take I-90 east to exit 20 for High Point Way. At the end of the exit ramp, turn right onto 270th Avenue followed by a quick right onto SE 79th Street (parallel to I-90). After 0.5 mile, drive through a gate and proceed carefully up the potholed road for 0.25 mile to the parking lot. If the lot is full, head back down the road and park alongside SE 79th Street. (Be careful to leave room for traffic to pass through, and observe any No Parking signs.) A Discover Pass is not required if parking on the road outside the gate. Two ADA-accessible vault toilets are available at the trailhead.

GPS Coordinates: 47.529239, -121.995270 / N47° 31.767' W121° 59.776'

18 NISQUALLY ESTUARY BOARDWALK TRAIL

Billy Frank Jr. Nisqually National Wildlife Refuge,
U.S. Fish and Wildlife Service

Best: Kid-Friendly

Distance: 3.9 miles round-trip

Duration: 2 hours

Elevation Change: 85 feet

Effort: Easy

Trail: Wooden boardwalks, gravel paths

Users: Hikers

Season: February-September

Passes/Fees: Entrance fee of $3 (cash or check); Interagency Annual Pass accepted

Maps: USGS topographic map for Nisqually

Contact: Billy Frank Jr. Nisqually National Wildlife Refuge, www.fws.gov, sunrise to sunset daily

---

This family-friendly hike along the Nisqually Delta has plentiful wildlife and water views.

On the southern edge of the Puget Sound sits the Nisqually National Wildlife Refuge, a protected area of freshwater marshes, saltmarshes, grasslands, woodlands, and forest that supports the habitats of more than 300 species of wildlife. Check the tides before you come: Visiting during high tide gives you a walk-on-water feel on the boardwalk trail, while a visit during low tide provides views of the expansive mudflats where birds and waterfowl forage for food.

Stop by the **visitors center** (9am-4pm Wed.-Sun.) to learn more about the history of the Nisqually Delta and to check out a pair of binoculars before heading out, enabling up-close views of wildlife. Plan to arrive early on sunny weekends, as this is a popular place for photographers, naturalists, and families.

Start the Hike

From the visitors center, start hiking on the **Twin Barns Loop Trail,** taking care as you make your way along the sometimes slippery boardwalk. Interpretive signs line the first 0.4 mile of the trail, providing insight into the freshwater wetland

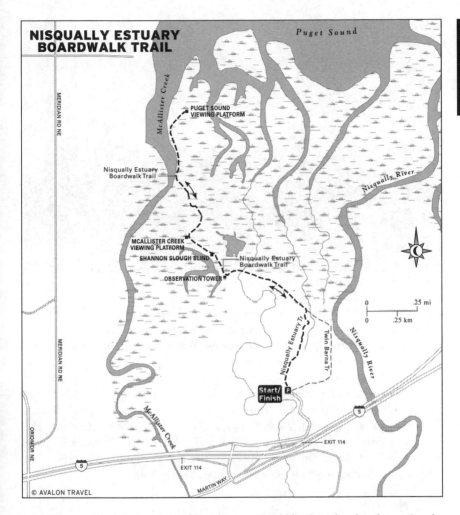

environment and the otters, bald eagles, and goldfinches that live here. On the left are two large barns, part of a farm that operated here from the late 1800s to the mid-1900s. (These barns were built in 1932 to replace the previous ones that were destroyed in a fire in 1929.) The farmland was posted for sale in 1968 and purchased by the U.S. Fish and Wildlife Service in 1974, creating the Nisqually National Wildlife Refuge.

Bear left toward the observation platform to join the **Nisqually Estuary Trail** for the next 0.5 mile. Enjoy the change of tread as you make your way along the exposed, crushed gravel path perched atop a dike. The path was constructed during the Nisqually Delta Restoration and involved breaking through a 5-mile-long dike

Walk through scenic wetlands at the refuge.

that once encircled the refuge. This enabled the tides and saltwater to flow freely into the delta, supporting the local salmon and wildlife populations.

Arrive at the **Nisqually Estuary Boardwalk Trail** and bear right onto the mile-long wooden boardwalk stretching over the Nisqually Delta. Built in 2010 and opened in February 2011, the boardwalk journeys through a temporary floodplain during high tide and expansive mudflats during low tide. Spot the occasional kayaker along McAllister Creek to the left and enjoy views of Nisqually Reach, Anderson Island, Tacoma Narrows Bridge, and the Olympics from the end of the boardwalk, your turnaround point. The last 700 feet of the Nisqually Estuary Boardwalk Trail **closes October-January** annually for hunting; plan your visit February-September to go all the way to the end of the trail.

Hike Nearby

The **Twin Barns Loop Trail** is a 1-mile ADA-accessible trail that starts next to the refuge visitors center. The trail weaves through freshwater wetlands and woodlands on a mostly flat, wooden boardwalk with viewpoints, overlooks, and interpretive signs along the way. For a nice loop option, pick up the Twin Barns Loop Trail on your return from the Nisqually Estuary Boardwalk Trail and enjoy views of the Nisqually River as you take the trail south to the visitors center.

Make It a Day Trip

Take a beachside stroll or a picnic at **Tolmie State Park** (7730 61st Ave. NE, Olympia, 360/456-6464, www.parks.state.wa.us, 8am-dusk in summer, 9am-dusk in winter, closed Mon.-Tues. mid-Sept.-mid-Apr., Discover Pass required), located 8 miles northwest of the Nisqually National Wildlife Refuge.

Directions

From Seattle, take I-5 south to exit 114 for Nisqually. At the end of the exit ramp, turn right onto Brown Farm Road at the stoplight. In 0.15 mile, bear right at the Nisqually National Wildlife Refuge sign to enter the parking lot and visitors center. Restrooms are available next to the visitors center.

GPS Coordinates: 47.072562, -122.713229 / N47° 04.383' W122° 42.813'

INTERSTATE 90

I-90 is a scenic drive through a glacially carved gorge nestled within the fertile hills of Snoqualmie Valley and rolling mountaintops of the Cascades. These trails fall within a stretch of I-90 known as the Mountains to Sound Greenway, spanning 100 miles between Seattle and Ellensburg with stunning, head-on views of Mount Rainier. Hikers enjoy easy access to hundreds of miles of trails. Climb to a mailbox-topped peak, wonder at raging waterfalls, ramble through forests or spectacular mountain scenery, and gaze at sparkling alpine lakes set among colorful meadows.

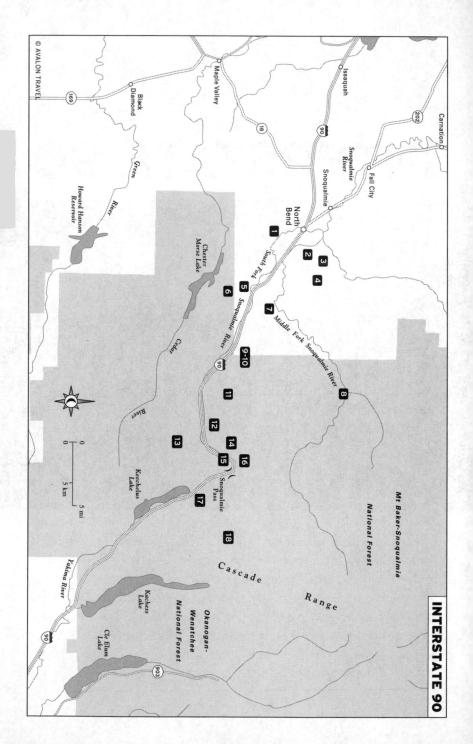

TRAIL NAME	LEVEL	DISTANCE	TIME	ELEVATION	PAGE
1 Rattlesnake Ledge	Easy/moderate	4.1 mi	2 hr	1,200 ft	116
2 Little Si	Easy/moderate	4 mi	2 hr	1,300 ft	120
3 Mount Si	Moderate/strenuous	8 mi	5 hr	3,200 ft	124
4 Teneriffe Falls	Moderate	5.8 mi	3 hr	1,475 ft	128
5 Twin Falls	Easy/moderate	2.5 mi	1.5 hr	600 ft	132
6 Mount Washington	Moderate	8.2 mi	5 hr	3,150 ft	135
7 Mailbox Peak	Strenuous	10.2 mi	7 hr	4,000 ft	139
8 Middle Fork Snoqualmie River	Easy/moderate	11.8 mi	6 hr	1,100 ft	143
9 Ira Spring Trail-Mason Lake	Moderate	7 mi	5 hr	2,400 ft	147
10 Bandera Mountain	Moderate/strenuous	6.8 mi	5 hr	3,000 ft	151
11 Talapus and Olallie Lakes	Easy/moderate	6.2 mi	3.5 hr	1,250 ft	154
12 Granite Mountain	Strenuous	8.2 mi	5 hr	3,750 ft	157
13 Annette Lake	Moderate	6.8 mi	3.5 hr	1,950 ft	161
14 Denny Creek Trail to Melakwa Lake	Easy/moderate	2.4-8.8 mi	1.5-5 hr	500-2,625 ft	164
15 Franklin Falls	Easy	2.4 mi	1 hr	375 ft	168
16 Snow Lake	Moderate	7.2 mi	4 hr	1,750 ft	172
17 Gold Creek Pond	Easy	1.2 mi	30 min	100 ft	175
18 Rachel Lake	Moderate/strenuous	7.8 mi	5 hr	2,000 ft	179

⬛ RATTLESNAKE LEDGE

Rattlesnake Mountain Scenic Area, North Bend

Distance: 4.1 miles round-trip

Duration: 2 hours

Elevation Change: 1,200 feet

Effort: Easy/moderate

Trail: Dirt paths, some rocky sections

Users: Hikers, leashed dogs

Season: Year-round

Passes/Fees: None

Maps: Green Trails Map 205S for Rattlesnake Mountain/Upper Snoqualmie Valley, USGS topographic map for North Bend

Contact: Cedar River Watershed Education Center, 19901 Cedar Falls Rd. SE, North Bend, 206/733-9421, www.seattle.gov, dawn-dusk daily

---

Rattlesnake Ledge is a moderate, easy-to-access trail with sweeping views of Rattlesnake Lake, the Cascade foothills, and the Cedar River Watershed.

While the hike to the ledge is satisfying enough, there are lots of options for further exploration—whether it's continuing north on the Rattlesnake Mountain Trail, taking a break from the crowds on the nearby Cedar Butte Trail, or visiting the **Cedar River Watershed Education Center** (hours vary Tues.-Sun.). The Education Center offers kid-friendly programs, watershed tours, interactive exhibits, guided hikes, and an entertaining rain drum garden.

Rattlesnake Ledge is typically crowded, especially on sunny spring and summer weekends. Arrive early in the morning before the Disneyland-like lines of hikers begin snaking up the trail, or consider hiking in the off-season. Although the trail is open year-round, check the conditions in winter for snow and ice.

Start the Hike

Start your hike from the parking lot, following the blue signs for the **Rattlesnake Ledge Trail.** Walk 0.25 mile past a gate along a wide, flat, dirt and gravel road, soon arriving at a large, informative kiosk and the trail sign for Rattlesnake Ledge. Ascend the moderately wide dirt path through an airy forest of Douglas fir and western hemlock tucked amid a leafy understory of salal shrubs. As you ascend,

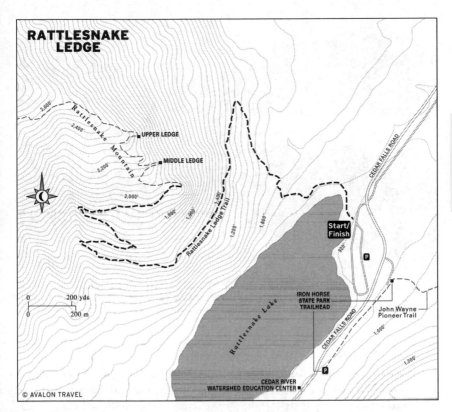

Rattlesnake Lake peeks through the trees, its size getting smaller and smaller, marking your gratifying progress toward the ledge.

In about 2 miles, arrive at a signed junction for the **Rattlesnake Mountain Trail.** Bear right to take the small spur trail to Rattlesnake Ledge. The beautiful views include sweeping vistas of the Cascade foothills, a sliver of Chester Morse Lake in the distance, and the Cedar River Watershed, which supplies two-thirds of the drinking water to the Seattle area. Take care as you explore the rocky ledge; there are steep, hazardous drop-offs, and the rocks can be slippery in wet and icy weather.

When ready, head back down the trail toward **Rattlesnake Lake.** You wouldn't know it by looking at it, but the lake was the site of a small railroad town called Moncton in the early 1900s. In 1914, a dam was built nearby in order to store drinking water and to generate electricity for the growing city of Seattle. As water collected behind the dam, it seeped underground into Moncton, slowly flooding the town in 1915 and creating Rattlesnake Lake. Today, divers can explore the remnants of Moncton at the bottom of the lake. Hikers can occasionally see it too—during the drought in 2015, the lake's water level

Rattlesnake Lake from Rattlesnake Ledge

dropped almost 29 feet, revealing the crumbling, partial foundations of the ghost town that once was.

Extend the Hike

For views beyond Rattlesnake Ledge, explore **Middle Ledge** and **Upper Ledge,** adding an extra 0.9 mile round-trip to your Rattlesnake Ledge hike. You can reach the ledges from spur trails right off the Rattlesnake Mountain Trail. From the Rattlesnake Mountain Trail sign near Rattlesnake Ledge, take the trail north toward East Peak. (Ignore the spur trail on the right.) In 0.2 mile, you'll see an obvious, unsigned spur trail for Middle Ledge and, 0.25 mile beyond that, an unsigned spur trail for Upper Ledge. Both ledges are rocky with steep, hazardous drop-offs; please take care climbing.

Hike Nearby

The **Cedar Butte Trail** in nearby Iron Horse State Park offers a quieter, less-crowded alternative to Rattlesnake Ledge. Park at the Iron Horse State Park/Cedar Falls Trailhead (Discover Pass required), 0.1 mile south of the Rattlesnake Ledge parking lot and head past the restrooms, bearing right at the information kiosks for the John Wayne Pioneer Trail. Turn left at the next two intersections and follow the signs for Iron Horse State Park. Hike east on a wide, multiuse gravel trail over Boxley Creek, then turn right onto the dirt trail signed for Cedar Butte. At a Y-junction at 0.5 mile, bear right onto the longer but gentler path to Saddle Junction beneath the summit. At the junction, head north and follow a sign (nailed to a tree) for the summit. The route is about 3.2 miles round-trip (1 hour 45 minutes).

Directions

From Seattle, head east on I-90 to exit 32 for 436th Avenue SE. At the end of the exit ramp, turn right onto 436th Avenue SE and drive 2.8 miles. Stay straight as the road turns into Cedar Falls Road. Bear right at the Rattlesnake Lake and Ledge Trail sign into the parking area. Two portable toilets (one ADA accessible) are in the picnic area next to the parking lot. Twelve portable toilets (one ADA accessible) are located 0.25 mile into the hike.

GPS Coordinates: 47.435388, -121.768346 / N47° 26.092' W121° 46.135'

2 LITTLE SI

Mount Si Natural Resources Conservation Area

Distance: 4 miles round-trip

Duration: 2 hours

Elevation Change: 1,300 feet

Effort: Easy/moderate

Trail: Dirt paths, rubbly sections, rocky outcroppings

Users: Hikers, leashed dogs

Season: Year-round

Passes/Fees: Discover Pass

Maps: Green Trails Map No. 206 for Bandera, Green Trails Map 206S for Mount Si NRCA, USGS topographic maps for North Bend and Snoqualmie

Contact: Washington State Department of Natural Resources, South Puget Sound Region, www.dnr.wa.gov

---

This short, enjoyable hike travels through a mostly shaded forest to views of the Cedar River Watershed and nearby peaks.

Little Si is a rocky knoll that sits in the shadow of Mount Si. Trail runners, families, and hikers of all abilities enjoy the trail's modest length and elevation gain to sprawling views. This is a great option for easing back into the hiking season after a winter slumber or for a quick outing when short on time. The rocky, sloping summit can get icy in the winter months—take care if hiking this time of year. The short trail is less than a 45-minute drive from Seattle. Plan to arrive early on sunny weekdays and weekends, as the main parking lot tends to fill quickly.

Start the Hike

Start your hike from the parking lot at the sign for the **Little Si Trail.** Head northwest on the rubbly, steep dirt path and in 0.2 mile follow a spur trail on the left to a viewpoint. The small pyramid-shape of Cedar Butte sits to the south with the taller Mount Washington to the southeast—a lower-elevation preview of the views from the summit. Back on the main trail, ascend north through a short, exposed boulder section; after this, the trail evens out to a gentler, rolling grade. Admire the many vine maple and bigleaf maple flanking the trail, passing signed junctions for the **Boulder Garden Loop Trail** at the 0.3-mile and 0.6-mile mark.

Large, sheer-faced boulders appear on the west side of the trail 1 mile into the

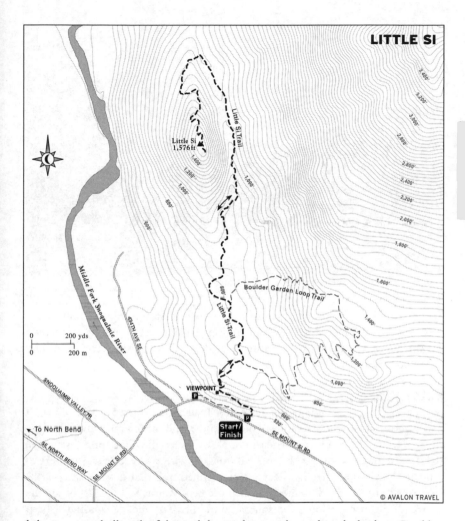

hike, a unique hallmark of the trail that is also popular with rock climbers. Boulders and the deep forest of Douglas fir and western hemlock keep you company for the next 0.5 mile along the dirt and rock path. A U-turn in the trail turns south to the summit. This final push is steep, gaining 500 feet in a rocky 0.5 mile. Social trails make navigation confusing; take your time and keep a sharp eye out, avoiding the steep ledges and drop-offs along the ridge.

After the final 0.5-mile ascent, arrive at the unusual summit—a dry, exposed rocky outcropping studded with shore pine trees and western serviceberry shrubs. The impressive views include Mount Si to the northeast, as well as Mount Washington to the southeast, Cedar Butte to the south, and Rattlesnake Ledge and Rattlesnake Mountain to the southwest. Catch glimpses of the Middle Fork

the Middle Fork Snoqualmie River as seen from Little Si

Snoqualmie River below as it winds its way northwest, joining the South Fork and North Fork Snoqualmie Rivers to continue its journey through Snoqualmie Falls. Exercise caution on the summit, as it slopes downward to steep drop-offs and slippery sections that can be hazardous.

Extend the Hike

A side trip along the **Boulder Garden Loop Trail** makes this a 5.1-mile hike (2.5 hours). From the Little Si Trailhead, head up the trail for 0.3 mile, turning right at the sign for the Boulder Garden Loop Trail. In 1 mile, look for a distinctive sign for the Boulder Garden Loop Trail (marked with white letters). Just next to it is the old Mount Si Trail, a steep, unmaintained trail that traverses the southwestern side of Mount Si to meet up with the new Mount Si Trail just below the summit. To finish the loop, continue west another 0.4 mile, descending a sharp 540 feet to the junction with the Little Si Trail. Turn right to continue on the Little Si Trail to the summit, or turn left to hike 0.6 mile back to the trailhead for a shorter, 2.3-mile loop.

Make It a Day Trip

Snoqualmie Falls is just 6 miles northwest of Little Si in the neighboring city of Snoqualmie. Take in the powerful beauty of the falls from the upper falls viewpoint located next to the main parking lot, or visit the lower falls viewpoint for an eye-level look at the falls and up-close views of the Snoqualmie River. It's a short, 1.4-mile round-trip hike (1 hour) from the upper falls viewpoint to the lower falls viewpoint, but it is a moderately steep, 240-foot elevation gain the last 0.4 mile back to the upper parking area. Alternatively, you can drive to the lower parking lot and walk 0.2 mile to the lower falls viewpoint; just follow signs for the boardwalk.

Upper (Main) Parking Lot: From the intersection of North Bend Way and Mount Si Road, head northwest on North Bend Way for 0.8 mile. At a traffic circle, take the second exit to stay on North Bend Way for 0.4 mile to Bendigo Boulevard. Turn right onto Bendigo Boulevard and drive 3.6 miles, following the road as it leaves North Bend and turns into Railroad Avenue as it passes through Snoqualmie. At the stoplight for Snoqualmie Parkway, continue straight for 0.2 mile to a traffic circle and take the third exit for State Route 202 West. The parking lot for Snoqualmie Falls is 0.2 mile ahead on the left, just past the pedestrian bridge; an overflow lot is on the opposite side of the road. Restrooms are located next to the parking lot. Parking is free and leashed dogs are welcome. The park is open dawn-dusk.

Lower Parking Lot: From the main parking area at Snoqualmie Falls, head west on State Route 202 for 1.4 miles toward Fall City. Turn left at the sign for 372nd Avenue SE and follow the road 0.2 mile to a T-intersection. Turn left onto SE Fish Hatchery Road and drive 0.4 mile to the entrance gate and parking lot. ADA-accessible restrooms are located next to the parking lot. Parking is free and leashed dogs are welcome. The park is open dawn-dusk.

Directions
From Seattle, head east on I-90 to exit 32 for 436th Avenue SE. At the end of the exit ramp, turn left onto 436th Avenue SE and drive 0.5 mile. Turn left at the stop sign onto North Bend Way and in 0.3 mile turn right onto Mount Si Road. Continue 0.5 mile then turn left at the sign for Little Si Trail into the parking lot. An overflow parking lot is located 0.1 mile west of the main parking lot (Mount Si Rd. and 434th Ave.); it is connected to the main lot and Little Si Trailhead via a 0.2-mile trail. Two ADA-accessible vault toilets are located next to the main parking lot.

GPS Coordinates: 47.486554, -121.753366 / N47° 29.206' W121° 45.203'

🖪 MOUNT SI
Mount Si Natural Resources Conservation Area
🦌 🌸 🐕

Distance: 8 miles round-trip

Duration: 5 hours

Elevation Change: 3,200 feet

Effort: Moderate/strenuous

Trail: Rocky dirt paths, wooden steps

Users: Hikers, leashed dogs

Season: April-November

Passes/Fees: Discover Pass

Maps: Green Trails Map No. 206 for Bandera, Green Trails Map 206S for Mount Si NRCA, USGS topographic maps for Mount Si and Chester Morse Lake

Contact: Washington State Department of Natural Resources, South Puget Sound Region, www.dnr.wa.gov

---

This challenging, popular hike climbs to outstanding views of Mount Rainier, the Olympics, and Snoqualmie Valley.

Trail runners, climbers training for Mount Rainier, and avid hikers all flock to Mount Si for its close proximity to Seattle, easy-to-follow trail, respectable elevation gain, and stunning views of Mount Rainier, Snoqualmie Valley, and the Olympics. Aim to arrive by 8am on weekends, as the parking lot can fill quickly, especially on sunny days. The weather on the mountaintop can be chillier and windier than at the trailhead, as well as icy and snowy in winter—pack layers.

Start the Hike
From the parking lot, follow the flat gravel trail over a bridge and through a brushy understory of vine maple and salmonberry to the **Mount Si Trail** sign. Ascend 1,350 feet in the first 1.7 miles, passing the lower junction (0.7 mile) and the upper junction (1.7 miles) with the **Talus Loop Trail.** A partial clearing with benches sits midway between the two junctions—a good place for a quick break. Enjoy the mostly shaded, sun-dappled views of towering Douglas fir, western hemlock, and cedar—a consolation to the rocky stretches of trail along your northwestern trek.

Past the second junction with the Talus Loop Trail, about 1.8 miles into the hike, arrive at **Snag Flats,** a flat section of trail where tall snags reveal evidence of a fire on Mount Si in 1910. To the left, walk the wooden boardwalk with interpretive

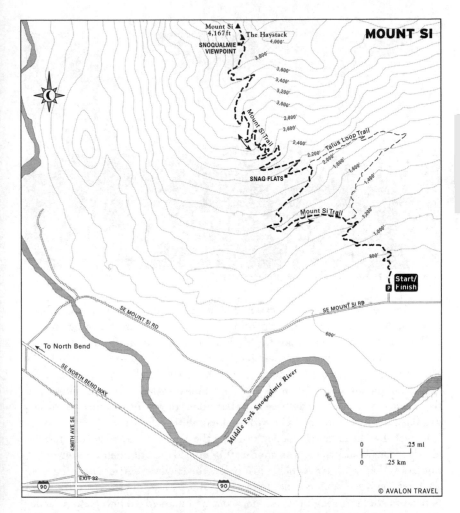

panels and check out the 350-year-old Douglas fir with scaly bark on one side (the side exposed to the fire) and rough, deeply furrowed bark on the other side (the normal bark of a Douglas fir). A bench at the end of the boardwalk makes an excellent resting spot on the way up, or a place to give your knees a break on the descent.

Continue hiking northwest past Snag Flats, ascending 1,700 feet in 2 miles. The switchbacks become tighter and more earnest as you climb, making reaching the top that much sweeter. The dirt path along this stretch is shady, well defined, and easy to follow, but becomes progressively rougher and more exposed toward the top. On a clear day, you can see Mount Rainier slowly revealing herself to the south through the trees—a motivating glimpse of the unobstructed views to come.

Mount Rainier, Rattlesnake Lake, and Rattlesnake Mountain from Mount Si

Emerge from the trail onto an exposed boulder field at the 3.8-mile mark. Most people call it a day here, and for good reason—the views are stunning and the trail is faint past this point. Look for Mailbox Peak and Mount Washington to the southeast, Mount Rainier, Rattlesnake Lake, and Rattlesnake Mountain to the south, and the Middle Fork Snoqualmie River, North Bend, and Olympics to the west. The true summit of Mount Si is 0.2 mile north, atop a rocky mast known as the Haystack; this steep scramble can be hazardous in wet, icy weather and deadly in a fall. Best leave it to the folks with rock-climbing experience.

If you're feeling adventurous upon reaching the boulder field and are comfortable hiking among boulders, press on another 0.15 mile to the **Snoqualmie Viewpoint,** a quiet overlook with two benches just below the Haystack. After emerging from the forest onto the boulder field, follow the faint path to the left then bear right to head north up through the boulders to a sign marked To Snoqualmie Valley Viewpoint/To Haystack Scramble. Climb the cement steps next to the sign and continue to veer right as you make your way around the rocks onto a dirt path. In 0.1 mile, turn left at a second sign for the Snoqualmie Valley Viewpoint and Haystack Scramble, following the dirt path to the benches. Take a well-earned break here, enjoying fewer crowds and the views to the west of North Bend and the Snoqualmie Valley.

Shorten the Hike

For a quiet, challenging hike, try the **Talus Loop Trail.** The trail shares a trailhead with Mount Si and is 3.7 miles round-trip (2 hours) with a 1,400-foot elevation gain. Start the hike from the Mount Si Trailhead and follow the trail for 0.7 mile.

Turn right at the sign for the Talus Loop Trail and hike the narrow dirt path for 1.3 miles, staying on the main path to bear left at a sign for the Talus Loop Trail. Cross the talus slope, which has open views to I-90, Mailbox Peak, McClellan Butte, and Mount Washington. In 0.25 mile, reach the junction with the Mount Si Trail. Bear left to take the Mount Si Trail 1.7 miles back to the trailhead.

Directions

From Seattle, drive east on I-90 to exit 32 for 436th Avenue SE. At the end of the exit ramp, turn left onto 436th Avenue SE and drive 0.5 mile. Turn left at the stop sign onto North Bend Way and continue 0.3 mile. Turn right onto Mount Si Road and drive 2.3 miles, turning left at the sign for Mount Si Trailhead into the parking lot. ADA-accessible restrooms are located near the start of the trail.
GPS Coordinates: 47.487334, -121.723356 / N47° 29.290' W121° 43.389

④ TENERIFFE FALLS

Mount Si Natural Resources Recreation Area, North Bend

Best: Off the Beaten Path

Distance: 5.8 miles round-trip

Duration: 3 hours

Elevation Change: 1,475 feet

Effort: Moderate

Trail: Wide dirt path with rocky, uneven switchbacks

Users: Hikers, leashed dogs

Season: March-November

Passes/Fees: Discover Pass

Maps: Green Trails Map 206 for Bandera, Green Trails Map 206S for Mount Si NRCA, USGS topographic maps for Chester Morse Lake and Mount Si

Contact: Washington State Department of Natural Resources, South Puget Sound Region, www.dnr.wa.gov

---

Teneriffe Falls packs in views of the Cascade foothills with a beautiful, plummeting waterfall.

While the first two-thirds of the hike is a gentle ascent, its character changes considerably on the last third of the hike, becoming steeper and riddled with uneven piles of rocks. Take your time along the trail and get an early start. The trail's notoriously small parking lot only fits about 10 vehicles and fills by 9:30am on weekdays and by 7am on weekends. (As of the writing of this book, the Department of Natural Resources plans a new parking lot to accommodate the growing demand.)

Start the Hike

Start your hike from the parking lot, skirting around the blue gate to head north on the wide dirt and gravel trail. The first 0.9 mile is a gentle, easy walk through a partially exposed forest of maple, cedar, Douglas fir, and hemlock. In spring, dainty purple flowers with white stripes, known as Stinky Bob geranium (for their unpleasant smell), pop up along the trail.

Bear right at the sign for **Teneriffe Falls Trail** and continue a leisurely 400-foot ascent over the next 1.1 miles. The trail narrows briefly before resuming its

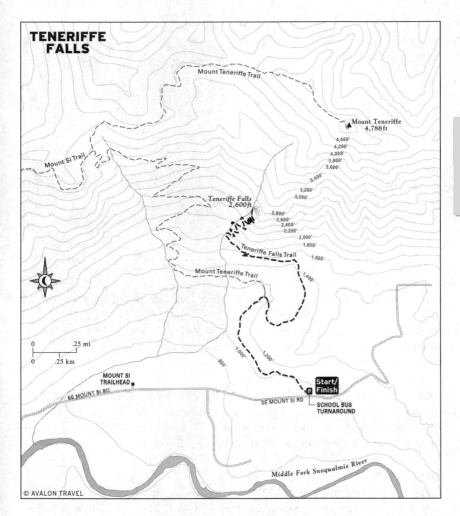

wide berth, generously lined with sword fern and salmonberry. As you climb, enjoy peeks through the trees to the south of Mount Washington—a taste of the wide-angle views to come.

Round a switchback marked with a **Teneriffe Falls Trail** sign, marking the start of the rockier and steeper part of the trail. Over the next 0.9 mile you'll gain about 800 feet in elevation, switchbacking up sunny talus slopes that are easy to roll an ankle on. Slowly pick your way through the uneven rocks, pausing to enjoy the expansive views to the south of McClellan Butte, Mount Washington, Cedar Butte, Rattlesnake Ledge, and even the snow-white tippy top of Mount Rainier on a clear day. Past these viewpoints, the switchbacks continue north through the forest; there are a couple of steep drop-offs the last 0.25 mile to the falls, so use your hands if necessary for extra balance and support.

The trail eventually peters out into a short, steep, and undeveloped dirt path to a small landing with views of **Teneriffe Falls.** The pretty upper falls fans out over the steep, rocky face, dropping 226 feet to its middle and lower tiers below. The small landing at the viewpoint is just big enough to accommodate a few people; on busy days, you may have to wait in line to enjoy the view before heading back to the trailhead.

Many hiking resources list Teneriffe Falls Trail as Teneriffe/Kamikaze Falls Trail, a nod to the falls' original name. When the Department of Natural Resources (in partnership with the Mountains to Sound Greenway Trust) finished a reroute of the trail in 2011, new signs were posted for the Teneriffe

Teneriffe Falls cascades down a steep rock face.

Falls Trail. Why the name change? Some believe it was an act of political correctness, while others think it was a practical decision—the new name is a better match with its namesake mountain. Speculation aside, Teneriffe Falls delivers as an easy-to-access, moderate hike with satisfying views.

Hike Nearby

It's possible to summit **Mount Teneriffe** from the same trailhead as Teneriffe Falls. The strenuous, 13.2-mile round-trip hike (7.5 hours) has a 4,200-foot elevation gain on its way to outstanding 360-degree views of Mailbox Peak, Mount Rainier, Mount Si, the Olympics, Mount Baker, and Glacier Peak. From the trailhead, hike up the dirt and gravel pathway for 0.9 mile. Bear left at a signed junction with the Teneriffe Falls Trail and, in 3.3 miles, arrive at an unsigned Y-junction with a wide, obvious dirt path (an unofficial trail that emerges just below the Haystack at Mount Si in 0.8 mile). Bear right to stay on the trail to Mount Teneriffe. Hike 1.5 miles then bear right again onto a dirt path for the last 0.9 mile to the exposed summit.

Directions

From Seattle, drive east on I-90 to exit 32 for 436th Avenue SE. At the end of the exit ramp, turn left onto 436th Avenue SE and continue 0.5 mile. At the stop sign, turn left onto North Bend Way and drive 0.3 mile. Turn right onto Mount Si Road and drive 3.4 miles. Turn left at a small dirt area, known as the school bus turnaround. Park close to the gate in order to leave enough room for school buses to turn around and for cars to enter and exit. Avoid parking in front of the No Parking signs 6am-5pm on school days. No facilities are available at the trailhead. **GPS Coordinates:** 47.485897, -121.700626 / N47° 29.172' W121° 42.085'

5 TWIN FALLS
Olallie State Park

Best: Waterfalls

Distance: 2.5 miles round-trip

Duration: 1.5 hours

Elevation Change: 600 feet

Effort: Easy/moderate

Trail: Dirt paths, rocky and rooty sections, wooden bridges and stairways

Users: Hikers, leashed dogs

Season: Year-round

Passes/Fees: Discover Pass

Maps: Green Trails Map 206 for Bandera, Green Trails Map 206S for Mount Si NRCA, USGS topographic map for Chester Morse Lake

Contact: Olallie State Park, www.parks.state.wa.us, 6:30am-dusk daily in summer, 8am-dusk daily in winter

---

This family-friendly hike along the South Fork Snoqualmie River leads to scenic views of Twin Falls.

A western Washington favorite, Twin Falls is a great choice in winter and early spring when the falls are raging and the nearby peaks are covered in snow. Not only is the trail a short 35-minute drive from Seattle, but it can also be accessed from two trailheads: the traditional Twin Falls Trailhead and the Homestead Valley Trailhead. The trail has a lot to offer—a lovely walk next to the river, strategic viewpoints of the lower falls, and an 80-foot wooden bridge spanning Twin Falls Gorge.

Start the Hike
From the Twin Falls Trailhead, start hiking on the **Twin Falls Trail.** The first 0.5 mile stays pleasantly close to the South Fork Snoqualmie River, winding past pink-flowered salmonberry shrubs and mossy thickets of western redcedar and Douglas fir. After ascending a short series of switchbacks, you'll soon arrive at **Bench Overlook,** about 0.7 mile into your hike. Two sturdy benches invite a short break and a preview of the lower falls in the distance.

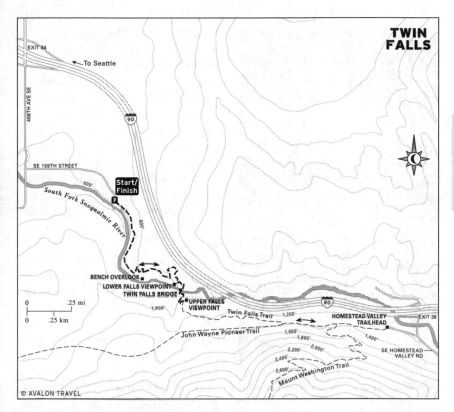

Twin Falls is a bit of a misleading name; instead of two similar waterfalls, it refers to the cascade of a falls flowing down Twin Falls Gorge. The series of falls on top are referred to as the "upper falls" and the taller, prominent waterfall on the bottom is the "lower falls." The amount of water flow varies drastically from season to season and is weather-dependent. During the drought in 2015, the falls dwindled to a trickle of 35 cubic feet per second in the summer—the capacity of a large two-door refrigerator. In wetter seasons, it can reach a raging 5,000 cubic feet per second (the capacity of 143 refrigerators).

The trail undulates for 0.4 mile. Turn right to take a wooden staircase 75 feet to the **Lower Falls Viewpoint.** Enjoy the up-close, full-length views of the 135-foot lower falls with glimpses of the Twin Falls Bridge above and the whirling rapids below. Back on the main trail, press on another 0.1 mile to the **Twin Falls Bridge** to catch views of the upper falls and the tippy top of the lower falls below. Just beyond the bridge is a better viewpoint of the upper falls—and a good turnaround point for your hike. The trail continues another 0.8 mile through the forest, winding close to the sounds of traffic on I-90, to link up with the John Wayne Pioneer Trail.

Twin Falls flows into the South Fork Snoqualmie River.

Extend the Hike

Twin Falls is also reachable via the **Homestead Valley Trailhead** off I-90 (exit 38). From the parking lot, follow signs for the Twin Falls Trail to the John Wayne Pioneer Trail. Bear right to merge onto the wide, gravel trail, ignoring unsigned spur trails on the left. In 0.4 mile, turn right at the sign for Twin Falls Trail to descend to the falls. Hike all the way to the Lower Falls Viewpoint and turn around for a 3.2-mile round-trip trek (1 hour 45 minutes).

To reach the Homestead Valley Trailhead from Seattle, head east on I-90 to exit 38 for 468th Avenue SE. At the end of the exit ramp, turn right onto Homestead Valley Road then right again at the first road on the right, signed for Olallie State Park/Homestead Valley Trailhead (also known as the Upper Twin Falls Trailhead). Stay straight to drive into the parking area. One ADA-accessible vault toilet is available in the parking area.

GPS Coordinates: 47.441450, -121.670618 / N47° 26.504' W121° 40.338

Directions

From Seattle, drive east on I-90 to exit 34 for 468th Avenue SE. At the end of the exit ramp, turn right onto 468th Avenue SE and drive 0.5 mile. Turn left onto SE 159th Street and follow the sign for Olallie State Park/Twin Falls Trailhead to the end of the road. Three ADA-accessible vault toilets are located in the parking area.

GPS Coordinates: 47.455085, -121.708084 / N47° 27.158' W121° 42.323'

6 MOUNT WASHINGTON

Olallie State Park, North Bend

Best: Mountain Views

Distance: 8.2 miles round-trip

Duration: 5 hours

Elevation Change: 3,150 feet

Effort: Moderate

Trail: Dirt, loose rock, and gravel paths

Users: Hikers, leashed dogs, horses, mountain bikers, climbers

Season: May-November

Passes/Fees: Discover Pass

Maps: Green Trails Map 206 for Bandera, Green Trails Map 206S for Mount Si NRCA, USGS topographic map for Chester Morse Lake

Contact: Olallie State Park, www.parks.state.wa.us, 6:30am-dusk daily in summer, 8am-dusk daily in winter

---

The Mount Washington trail is a worthy alternative to its more crowded neighbor, Mount Si, and boasts spectacular views of Mount Rainier, Chester Morse Lake, and the Olympics.

On the flip side, the trail is less developed than Mount Si—an unmaintained mix of rocky, rubbly sections, dirt paths, forest roads, and something in between—and there are more junctions to navigate. Bring a map, as well as sun protection and bug spray for the exposed, grassy summit area. While you will hear the dull roar of I-90 traffic for the first half of the hike, the noise fades near Washington Creek.

Start the Hike

From the parking lot, follow the signed John Wayne Pioneer Trail/Twin Falls Trail and, in 0.1 mile, merge right onto a forest road. In another 0.1 mile, merge right onto the wide, flat **John Wayne Pioneer Trail.** Continue straight, following the sign for the Twin Falls Trailhead west. In 500 feet, turn left onto an unsigned dirt trail—the start of the **Mount Washington Trail.** The trail winds through an eclectic mix of land divided among Washington State Parks, the City of Seattle (part of the Cedar River Watershed), and privately owned land. Please respect private property by staying on the trail and packing out any trash.

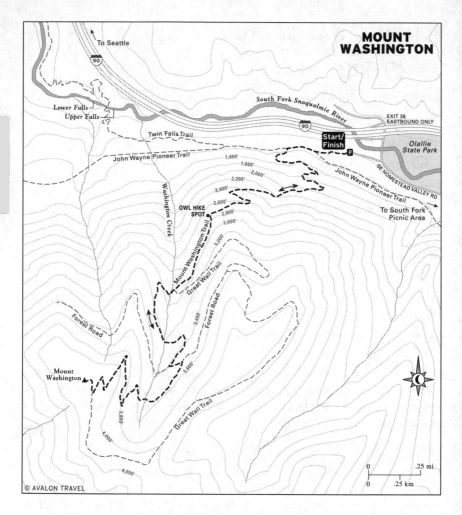

In 1.4 miles, arrive at the **Owl Hike Spot,** a small, dirt landing with views west of Cedar Butte, Rattlesnake Ledge, and Rattlesnake Mountain. After soaking in the views, hike southwest for a relatively flat 0.4 mile to a junction with the **Great Wall Trail.** Bear right at the junction, following a sign (nailed to a tree) toward Mount Washington. Hike 0.8 mile, crossing Washington Creek on a makeshift bridge of rocks, and enjoy the cool, shady forest of noble fir, hemlock, and Pacific silver fir. The trail passes through an exposed, rocky slope with views of the Cascade foothills before arriving at a junction with a forest road.

Turn left onto the dirt and gravel forest road and, in 300 feet, turn right to pick up the trail marked **Mount Washington Trail.** Hike 1.2 miles through an increasingly exposed forest, rounding a switchback with expansive views to the

views south over Chester Morse Lake to Mount Rainier just below the summit

north of Mount Si and Mount Teneriffe. Your final ascent is a steep 425 feet over the last 0.4 mile to a narrow, exposed meadow with spectacular views of Mount Rainier to the south, Chester Morse Lake and the Cedar River Watershed to the southwest, and Rattlesnake Lake, Rattlesnake Ledge, and the Olympics to the west.

Snap some pictures then follow the path another 0.1 mile past the viewpoint to the true summit, with expansive views to the north of Little Si, Mount Si, the tippy top of Mount Baker, Mount Teneriffe, the top of Glacier Peak, and Mailbox Peak. Relax on a rocky perch next to the weather station, or walk down a short distance for views south and west before returning to the trailhead.

Make It a Day Trip

Stop by the **South Fork Picnic Area** to picnic by the river and check out the modest Weeks Falls waterfall. The 1.2-mile round-trip interpretive trail begins next to the picnic tables. It is also possible to drive to the falls (a few parking spaces are available) and take an ADA-accessible trail about 300 feet to the falls.

From the intersection of the Homestead Valley parking area and Homestead Valley Road, head southeast on Homestead Valley Road for 0.6 mile and follow signs for Olallie State Park/South Fork Picnic Area. Turn left into the park; the main parking area is on the left and a parking area for oversize vehicles is down the road. To access the small parking area near the falls, continue past the main parking area and follow the road to the end (it becomes a gravel road). A cement walkway leads to the falls.

Two ADA-accessible restrooms are next to the main parking area, and an ADA-accessible restroom is located next to the cement walkway near the falls. A Discover Pass is required. Leashed dogs are permitted.

Directions

From Seattle, drive east on I-90 to the eastbound exit 38 for Olallie State Park. At the end of the exit ramp, turn right onto Homestead Valley Road. In less than 0.1 mile, turn right onto the first road on the right and follow signs for Olallie State Park/Homestead Valley Trailhead (also known as the Upper Twin Falls Trailhead). Stay straight to enter the parking area. One ADA accessible vault toilet is available in the parking area.

GPS Coordinates: 47.441450, -121.670618 / N47° 26.504' W121° 40.338

7 MAILBOX PEAK

Middle Fork Snoqualmie Natural Resources Conservation Area

Best: Strenuous

Distance: 10.2 miles round-trip

Duration: 7 hours

Elevation Change: 4,000 feet

Effort: Strenuous

Trail: Dirt and gravel paths, rocky, rubbly sections

Users: Hikers, leashed dogs

Season: May-November

Passes/Fees: Discover Pass

Maps: Department of Natural Resources Mailbox Peak Trail Map, Green Trails Map 206 for Bandera, Green Trails Map 206S for Mount Si NRCA, USGS topographic map for Chester Morse Lake

Contact: Washington State Department of Natural Resources, South Puget Sound Region, www.dnr.wa.gov

---

This grueling hike to a mailbox-topped summit rewards with views of Mount Rainier and nearby peaks.

Mailbox Peak is a popular hike among runners, climbers, hikers, and adventurers seeking the thrill of checking this inimitable peak off their list. Bring extra water and allow plenty of time to complete the trail. Consider getting an early start, especially on the weekends; the parking areas and nearby roads fill quickly due to the hike's popularity and its close proximity to Seattle.

Until September 2014, the climb up Mailbox Peak was via an eroded, steep, and unmaintained "old trail" that ascends 4,000 feet in 2.6 punishing miles. While those who "conquered" it could boast bragging rights, other hikers weren't so lucky—getting lost or tweaking an ankle and requiring more than two dozen missions by King County Search and Rescue in 2013-2015.

This hike follows the **New Mailbox Peak Trail.** Though longer and perhaps less exciting, the new trail is safer and better maintained. Hikers still get to experience the pride and accomplishment of ascending a trail with a 4,000-foot elevation gain, the fun of reaching the mailbox, awesome views at the summit, and a taste

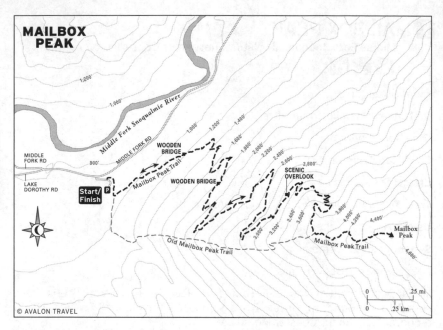

of the old trail too, as the new trail links up with the old for the last 0.6 mile to the summit.

Start the Hike

Start your hike from the parking lot next to the **Mailbox Peak Trailhead** sign. Head south up the paved road and continue straight as the road turns to gravel. Skirt a white gate and, in 375 feet, turn left at the sign for **Mailbox Peak Trail.** The well-defined trail is easy to follow as it zigzags up the west side of the mountain under a partially open canopy of red alder, Douglas fir, grand fir, and western hemlock. In spring, purple-hued bleeding heart and purplish-pink corydalis pop up near the streams, as well as pretty white trillium, yellow violet, and salmonberry shrubs.

Cross two picturesque wooden bridges (these double as a convenient marker that you're nearing the trailhead on your way back down). Past the **second bridge** (1.5 miles), continue your ascent on the northwest face of the mountain, gaining just over 2,100 feet in the next 3 miles. The trail narrows and becomes rockier, leading to a scenic overlook of the Cascade foothills at 3.5 miles—a preview of the outstanding views to come.

At 4.5 miles, reach a junction with the old trail marked **Mailbox Peak Trail** and turn left to merge onto the trail for your final push to the summit. While the trail's grade has been steady so far, this will be the steepest push—a grueling 960 feet over 0.6 mile. Reflective white diamonds drilled into the trees mark the route as you climb east; remember that the closest marker may be behind you.

the summit of Mailbox Peak with Mount Rainier to the south

In 0.1 mile, pass a large talus slope on the right then bear left to continue up a short section of uneven, protruding rocks. Emerging onto an exposed slope with windblown trees and lichen-covered rocks, zigzag up the steep, rubbly path east over the last 0.25 mile to the mailbox and summit.

At the summit (5.1 miles), take a moment to catch your breath and gaze at the outstanding views. The sticker-festooned mailbox points south toward Mount Rainier. To the west lies Cedar Butte and Rattlesnake Mountain and to the northwest Mount Si and Mount Teneriffe. Marvel at the tiny specks of cars moving in slow motion along the I-90 corridor below, and take a well-deserved break on one of the many boulders that populate the summit. Don't forget to check the mailbox before heading down and to leave a treat for another hiker to enjoy. Hikers have stumbled upon all kinds of trinkets and treats in the mailbox: stickers, whiskey, a wedding invitation, Girl Scout cookies, Clif bars, and dog treats.

Make It a Day Trip

For fantastic barbecue, stop in at **Rhodies Smokin BBQ** (30375 SE High Point Way, Preston, 425/222-6428, www.rhodiesbbq.com, 10am-8:30pm daily), a low-key restaurant just off exit 22 for Preston. Order in to dine at one of the tables inside or grab a sandwich to take with you. Their Carolina Trailboss, a roll generously stuffed with juicy meat and topped with coleslaw, is a satisfying post-hike treat.

Directions

From Seattle, drive east on I-90 to exit 34 for 468th Avenue SE. At the end of the exit ramp, turn left onto 468th Avenue SE. In 0.5 mile, turn right onto SE

Middle Fork Road and drive 0.9 mile. Arriving at a junction with Lake Dorothy Road, turn left to stay on Middle Fork Road for another 1.2 miles. Bear left at the next junction for 0.3 mile, then turn right into the parking lot. Past this lot is a second parking lot, up the paved road through the gate where ADA-accessible restrooms are available.

Middle Fork Road is undergoing a paving project scheduled to be completed in summer 2017, and until then, the road is closed weekdays (late Apr.-Oct.); however, the Mailbox Peak Trailhead is open weekends. Contact the Federal Highway Administration (www.flh.fhwa.dot.gov) for the bimonthly opening and closing schedule.

GPS Coordinates: 47.467524, -121.674571 / N47° 28.050' W121° 40.409

8 MIDDLE FORK SNOQUALMIE RIVER
Mount Baker-Snoqualmie National Forest

Distance: 11.8 miles round-trip

Duration: 6 hours

Elevation Change: 1,100 feet

Effort: Easy/moderate

Trail: Dirt and gravel paths, wooden bridges

Users: Hikers, leashed dogs, mountain bikers, horses

Season: June-October

Passes/Fees: Northwest Forest Pass

Maps: Green Trails Map 174 for Mount Si, Green Trails Map 175 for Skykomish, USGS topographic maps for Lake Philippa and Snoqualmie Lake

Contact: Mount Baker-Snoqualmie National Forest, Snoqualmie Ranger District-North Bend, www.fs.usda.gov

---

A gently rolling trail through a mossy forest features a unique cable bridge and views of the Middle Fork Snoqualmie River Valley.

This trail has a lot going for it: the finely crafted cable bridge, trailside views of the Middle Fork Snoqualmie River and Garfield Mountain, a lush lowland forest with leafy plants, and riverside campsites. It's a great option for families, trail runners, hikers, and backpackers looking for a not-too-difficult forest walk with a modest elevation gain.

The trail is open to mountain bikers on odd-numbered days June 1-October 31, and is open to horses July 15-October 31 (bikers must yield to hikers while on the trail, and both must yield to horses).

Start the Hike
From the parking lot, head south on the gravelly **Middle Fork Trail** under a tall canopy of western hemlock. Marvel at the yellow-green carpet of moss blanketing the understory and softly enveloping the tree trunks—a harbinger of moss-draped views to come. In 200 feet, arrive at the beautifully arched Gateway Bridge over the Middle Fork Snoqualmie River; pause to look upstream for views of Garfield Mountain to the northeast. Volunteers and the U.S. Forest Service built the cable bridge across the river in 1993, part of an effort by the Mountains to Sound Greenway Trust to transform and revitalize the Middle Fork area for outdoor recreation.

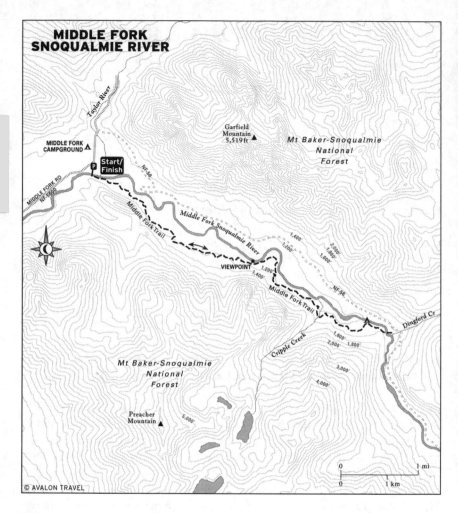

Cross the bridge and turn left at the signed **Middle Fork Trail** to hike southeast toward Dingford Creek. Hike along the river past a leafy hodgepodge of ferns, salmonberry, and thimbleberry shrubs, soaking in the views before retreating into a partially canopied forest. After 0.8 mile, look south to spot a sheer gray rock wall lined with tall trees along its spine, colorfully dubbed the Stegosaurus Butte by locals. Past the butte, the trail follows an old logging road that was used by the North Bend Timber Company in the 1920s and 1930s.

After tromping through stands of maple, cedar, and red alder, emerge to a trail-side view of the **Middle Fork Snoqualmie River** and valley in 3 miles. Enjoy the river's low, gurgling sounds over the rocky riverbed and the mesmerizing views of the valley stretching above. This is a nice spot for a break or a picnic—or a

a quiet path through mossy forest on the Middle Fork Trail

turnaround point for a shorter outing. Past the viewpoint is a washed-out bridge and a pockmarked dirt knoll, a turnaround point for horseback riders and a careful hopscotch for hikers.

As you weave between forest and river on the undulating, sometimes cobbled path, keep an eye out for hopeful anglers casting lines for cutthroat trout. Cross a well-built wooden bridge over Cripple Creek at 4.7 miles, pausing to spy Cripple Creek Falls tumble down craggy boulders to the south. Passing a spur trail to riverside **campsites** at 5.5 miles, you'll soon arrive at a signed junction for **Dingford Creek Trailhead** (5.8 miles). Bear left to descend 30 feet to the bridge over Dingford Creek. Stop for views from the bridge and a snack or lunch before heading back to the trailhead.

Shorten the Hike
A hike just to the viewpoint of the **Middle Fork Snoqualmie River** shortens this jaunt to a 6-mile round-trip trek (3 hours).

Directions
From Seattle, drive I-90 east to exit 34 for 468th Avenue SE. At the end of the exit ramp, turn left onto 468th Avenue SE. In 0.5 mile, turn right onto SE Middle Fork Road and drive 0.9 mile. Turn left at a signed junction with Lake Dorothy Road and stay on Middle Fork Road for another 1.2 miles. Bear left at the end of the road to continue on Middle Fork Road. Drive 9.3 miles to the signed Middle

Fork Trailhead and parking area on the right. A vault toilet is available at the trailhead.

Middle Fork Road is undergoing a paving project scheduled to be completed in summer 2017, and until then, the road is closed weekdays (late Apr.-Oct.); however, the Mailbox Peak Trailhead is open weekends. Contact the Federal Highway Administration (www.flh.fhwa.dot.gov) for the bimonthly opening and closing schedule. **GPS Coordinates:** 47.547977, -121.537217 / N47° 32.863' W121° 32.220'

Gateway Bridge over the Middle Fork Snoqualmie River

9 IRA SPRING TRAIL-MASON LAKE

Mount Baker-Snoqualmie National Forest

Best: Lakes

Distance: 7 miles round-trip

Duration: 5 hours

Elevation Change: 2,400 feet

Effort: Moderate

Trail: Dirt and gravel paths, creek crossing

Users: Hikers, leashed dogs

Season: May-October

Passes/Fees: Northwest Forest Pass

Maps: Green Trails Map 206 for Bandera, Green Trails Map 207S for Snoqualmie Pass Gateway, USGS topographic map for Bandera

Contact: Mount Baker-Snoqualmie National Forest, Snoqualmie Ranger District-North Bend, www.fs.usda.gov

---

The Ira Spring Trail is a lovely hike to Mason Lake with views of Mount Rainier, McClellan Butte, and Mount Defiance.

This trail honors the memory of Ira Spring, a prolific photographer, author, conservationist, trail advocate, and a board member of the Washington Trails Association. When Spring passed away in 2003, he left a lasting legacy with the creation of the Spring Family Trust for Trails, a nonprofit organization that provides grants for trail projects (such as the log bridge over Mason Creek on this trail). For more about Ira Spring, check out "Memories of Ira," a tribute published by the *Washington Trails Magazine* in their June 2003 issue (www.wta.org).

Trailhead parking can fill by 8am on a sunny weekend; consider arriving early on weekends or hiking the trail midweek. The Ira Spring Trail shares the starting point for the Bandera Mountain Trail, which branches off from Ira Spring Trail after 2.8 miles. You can easily extend this hike with a trip to Mount Defiance, Island Lake, or Bandera Mountain.

Start the Hike

Start your hike at the **Ira Spring Trail kiosk** next to the parking area. Ascend the wide, gentle path through a canopied forest of cedar, hemlock, maple, and alder.

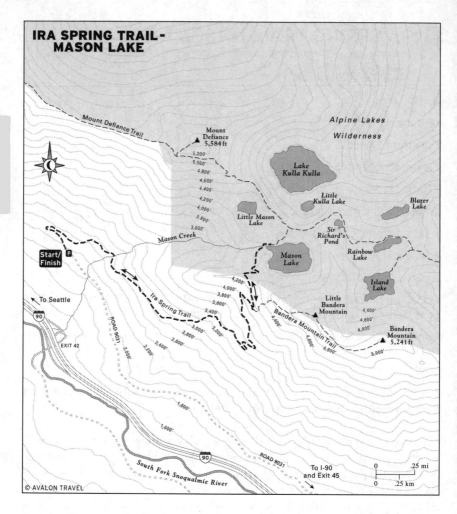

IRA SPRING TRAIL-
MASON LAKE

Mount Defiance Trail

Alpine Lakes
Wilderness

Mount
Defiance
5,584 ft

5,200'
5,000'
4,800'
4,600'
4,400'
4,200'
4,000'
3,800'
3,600'

Lake
Kulla Kulla

Little
Kulla Lake

Blazer
Lake

Little Mason
Lake

Sir
Richard's
Pond

Rainbow
Lake

Mason Creek

Mason
Lake

Start/
Finish

To Seattle

90

Ira Spring Trail

ROAD 9031

EXIT 42

4,200'
4,000'
3,800'
3,400'
3,200'
3,000'
2,800'
2,600'
2,400'
2,200'
2,000'
1,800'

Island
Lake

Little
Bandera
Mountain

Bandera Mountain Trail

4,400'
4,600'
4,800'
5,000'

Bandera
Mountain
5,241 ft

1,600'

90

ROAD 9031

South Fork Snoqualmie River

To I-90
and Exit 45

0   .25 mi
0   .25 km

© AVALON TRAVEL

In 0.8 mile, cross a log bridge over Mason Creek, with its waterfall-like features. Built in 2015, the bridge was made possible in part by a grant from the Spring Family Trust for Trails. (The crossing was once a bit tricky for hikers to navigate due to the dipped creek bed, slippery rocks, and rushing creek water in spring.)

Traverse a series of south-facing talus slopes to a signed junction for **Mason Lake** and **Bandera Mountain** at 2.8 miles. As you hike southeast, the trail's grade becomes steeper, gaining 1,650 feet over 2 miles. Take small breaks and stop for intermittent views across the valley to the sharp, pointy peak of McClellan Butte. Scampering chipmunks dart in and out among the rocky slopes while a shy grouse occasionally bleats a soft *whoomp whoomp* from the forest.

Turn left at the signed junction toward **Mason Lake** and follow the path as it

trailside view of Mason Lake

cuts through a boulder field to descend 145 feet to the lake at 3.5 miles. Winding north through the boulder field, enjoy views of Mount Rainier to the south as well as Mount Defiance overhead to the northwest. Arrive at Mason Lake and cross an outlet on a lily pad-like arrangement of rocks, enjoying the quiet lake basin. The trail winds around the north edge of the lake and has lots of rocky perches for relaxing and enjoying a snack before heading back to the trailhead.

Extend the Hike

Hiking to spectacular, 360-degree views on **Mount Defiance** adds 3.2 miles round-trip (2 hours) to this hike. Take the Ira Spring Trail along the north side of Mason Lake for 0.2 mile, following the signs marked Main Trail to a signed junction with the Mount Defiance Trail. Turn left at the junction and follow the trail 1.2 miles to a rocky spur trail on the right marked with a cairn. Scramble the 0.2 mile to a small summit area, using your hands for balance and support if needed.

To hike to a series of lakes, head to **Sir Richard's Pond, Rainbow Lake,** and **Island Lake** for a 3.4-mile round-trip addition (2 hours) to your Mason Lake hike. Continue as above to the signed junction with the Mount Defiance Trail. Turn right for Island Lake and follow the trail past Sir Richard's Pond and Rainbow Lake. Reach a signed junction for Island Lake in 1.1 miles and turn right to the lake in 0.4 mile.

Yet another popular two-for-one option is to tackle **Bandera Mountain** for a 1.2-mile round-trip add-on (1.5 hours) to the Mason Lake hike. From the signed junction for Mason Lake and Bandera Mountain, head northeast up the steep, rocky trail. Continue east along a ridgeline of boulders to a small dirt landing; this is the false summit of Bandera Mountain (called Little Bandera) and your turnaround point.

Directions

From Seattle, drive I-90 east to exit 45 for Forest Road 9030. At the end of the exit ramp, turn left onto Forest Road 9030 and follow the road as it curves south. The pavement ends in 0.4 mile; the rest of the drive is on a dirt and gravel road that can have stretches of potholes. Continue 0.4 mile and bear left at the sign for Ira Spring Trail 1038 to continue on Forest Road 9031 for 3 miles to the parking area. A vault toilet is available near the trailhead.

GPS Coordinates: 47.424688, -121.583346 / N47° 25.485' W121° 35.015'

10 BANDERA MOUNTAIN
Mount Baker-Snoqualmie National Forest

Best: Strenuous

Distance: 6.8 miles round-trip

Duration: 5 hours

Elevation Change: 3,000 feet

Effort: Moderate/strenuous

Trail: Dirt and gravel paths, scrambling

Users: Hikers, leashed dogs

Season: May-October

Passes/Fees: Northwest Forest Pass

Maps: Green Trails Map 206 for Bandera, Green Trails Map 207S for Snoqualmie Pass Gateway, USGS topographic map for Bandera

Contact: Mount Baker-Snoqualmie National Forest, Snoqualmie Ranger District-North Bend, www.fs.usda.gov

---

Scramble up a waterfall of boulders to stunning views of Mount Rainier with an option to visit nearby Mason Lake.

Bandera Mountain is one of a handful of hikes along I-90 where you may feel as though you're literally climbing a mountain. Tire-size, uneven boulders protrude from the western ridgeline of Bandera, often requiring the use of hands for support and balance. This boulder challenge makes the victory of the summit all the sweeter with a reward of full-on views of Mount Rainier, McClellan Butte, and the Olympics. Bring plenty of water and sun protection; the trail is exposed the last mile to Little Bandera, the turnaround point. The parking area can fill by 8am on a sunny weekend; arrive early on weekends or hike the trail midweek.

Start the Hike
Start your hike at the **Ira Spring Trail kiosk** next to the parking area. Ascend the wide dirt trail through a forest of vine maple on the first 1.1 miles. Wander past streams and over a well-crafted log bridge spanning waterfall-like Mason Creek that was built in 2015. The trail gains 575 feet through this section, a good warm-up for the climb to come. Past a sign for the Alpine Lakes Wilderness, the trail begins

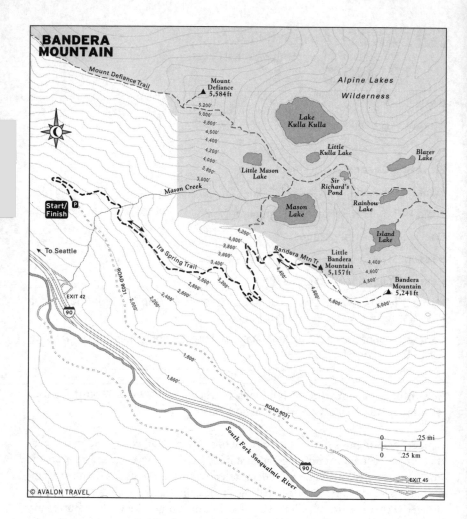

BANDERA MOUNTAIN

Alpine Lakes Wilderness

a grueling ascent, switchbacking 1,400 feet up the south face of the mountain to a signed junction for Mason Lake and Bandera Mountain at 2.8 miles.

At the junction, bear right toward **Bandera Mountain.** The next 0.25 mile is a thigh-burning, 450-foot elevation gain up a waterfall of large, uneven boulders interspersed with narrow dirt passageways. After huffing your way up the steep slope, bear right at a junction to follow the trail east as the grade eases through a partially shaded forest. Beyond the forest, a ridgeline of boulders runs along the western side of the mountain; at one point there is a wide boulder field where it feels like the trail disappears. Climb about 35 feet and then turn right to cross the field, picking up the dirt path on the other side. As you climb, take a moment to enjoy the views northwest: Mason Lake can be seen below and Mount Defiance above.

looking south toward Mount Rainier from the false summit of Bandera Mountain

Arrive at the false summit, known as **Little Bandera Mountain,** in 3.4 miles. From the small dirt landing, take in the fantastic views across the valley of Mount Rainier, McClellan Butte, and the Olympics. Most hikers call it a day at Little Bandera. The true summit is 0.8 mile east on a steeply undulating, unmaintained trail with no views; it sits less than 90 feet higher than Little Bandera. Best to leave it to those with route-finding skills.

Extend the Hike

Extend your hike with a side trip to **Mason Lake,** an additional 1.4 miles round-trip (45 minutes). From the signed junction for Mason Lake and Bandera Mountain, head north toward Mason Lake for 0.7 mile and descend 145 feet through the forest to the lake.

Directions

From Seattle, drive I-90 east to exit 45 for Forest Road 9030. At the end of the exit ramp, turn left onto Forest Road 9030 and follow the road as it curves south. The pavement ends in 0.4 mile; the rest of the drive is on a dirt and gravel road that can have stretches of potholes. After another 0.4 mile, bear left at the sign for Ira Spring Trail 1038 to continue on Forest Road 9031 for 3 miles to the parking area. A vault toilet is available near the trailhead.

GPS Coordinates: 47.424688, -121.583346 / N47° 25.485' W121° 35.015'

11 TALAPUS AND OLALLIE LAKES
Mount Baker-Snoqualmie National Forest

Distance: 6.2 miles round-trip

Duration: 3.5 hours

Elevation Change: 1,250 feet

Effort: Easy/moderate

Trail: Root-strewn dirt paths, wooden boardwalks

Users: Hikers, leashed dogs

Season: May-October

Passes/Fees: Northwest Forest Pass

Maps: Green Trails Map 206 for Bandera, Green Trails Map 207S for Snoqualmie Pass Gateway, USGS topographic map for Bandera

Contact: Mount Baker-Snoqualmie National Forest, Snoqualmie Ranger District-North Bend, www.fs.usda.gov

---

This family-friendly hike passes through a shady forest to two lakes with rushing creekside views.

The trail to Talapus and Olallie Lakes is perfect for a half-day hike. In addition to the lakes, there are a fun series of boardwalks, fine views of rushing Talapus Creek, and wildflowers that line the trail in spring and summer. The trail can be marshy with shallow mud pools; wear shoes or boots that you can muck up. The trail is popular and parking can fill quickly on weekdays and weekends. Plan to arrive early on sunny spring and summer days, or swing by in the afternoon when the morning crowds are returning.

Start the Hike
From the parking lot, head north on the **Talapus Lake Trail.** Enjoy the shady canopy of western hemlock and Douglas fir as the trail alternates between rocky dirt paths and wooden boardwalks. Climb gentle switchbacks through second-growth forest and listen for the sounds of Talapus Creek to the east, which slowly comes into view in 1 mile. Views of the rushing mini-rapids continue as you hike north on the wooden boardwalks (which can become slippery in wet and icy weather).

Bear right at a sign for Pratt and **Talapus Lakes,** crossing a bridge over Talapus Creek. Reach the southern end of Talapus Lake at 1.7 miles and take a short spur trail on the left. Grab a seat on a log and enjoy the modest views down the length

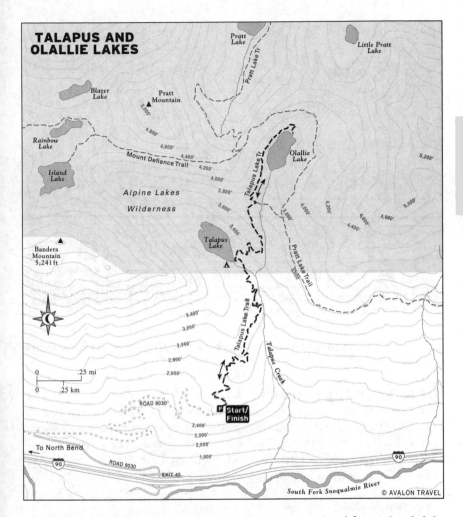

TALAPUS AND OLALLIE LAKES

Pratt Lake

Little Pratt Lake

Blazer Lake

Pratt Mountain

5,000'

4,800'

4,600'

4,400'

Rainbow Lake

Mount Defiance Trail

4,200'

4,000'

Island Lake

3,800'

Alpine Lakes

3,600'

Wilderness

3,400'

Bandera Mountain 5,241 ft

Talapus Lake

Olallie Lake

5,200'

Talapus Lake Tr

5,000'

4,600'

4,400'

4,800'

4,200'

Pratt Lake Trail

3,800'

3,600'

Talapus Lake Trail

3,400'

3,200'

3,000'

2,800'

2,600'

Talapus Creek

0 — .25 mi

0 — .25 km

ROAD 9030

P Start/ Finish

2,400'

2,200'

2,000'

1,800'

To North Bend

90

ROAD 9030

EXIT 45

90

South Fork Snoqualmie River

© AVALON TRAVEL

of this quiet, tree-ringed lake. From here, you can turn around for a 3.4-mile hike (2.5 hours) or hike 1.4 miles farther to Olallie Lake.

Continue on toward Olallie Lake, following the trail north to a sign for **Olallie Lake** and Pratt Lake. Bear right at the sign and head east for 0.3 mile on the root-filled trail to a creek. Veer left at the creek to hike north for 0.4 mile to the signed Pratt Lake junction at 2.4 miles. There are many social trails between Talapus Lake and the Pratt Lake junction, making it easy to get turned around; take your time and bring a trail map and compass to help you navigate.

Turn left at the Pratt Lake junction and hike 0.7 mile north to **Olallie Lake** at 3.1 miles. Enjoy the huckleberries, beargrass, mountain hemlock, and Pacific silver fir that line the trail, spotting Olallie Lake as it peeks through the trees to

Driftwood gathers near the outlet of Talapus Lake.

the east. Pick a campsite or a clearing near the lake to enjoy a snack and water views before heading back to the trailhead.

Get Away for the Weekend
Turn your hike into an overnight stay by camping at Talapus Lake or Olallie Lake. Designated campsites (first-come, first-served, year-round) are available on the southeastern side of Talapus Lake and on the western and northern sides of Olallie Lake. Campfires are strictly prohibited (bring a camp stove), and practice Leave No Trace principles. Spur trails lead to a pit toilet at both lakes.

Directions
From Seattle, drive east on I-90 to exit 45 for Forest Road 9030. At the end of the exit ramp, turn left onto Forest Road 9030 and pass under I-90. In 0.8 mile, turn right at the sign for Talapus Lake Trail 1039 to stay on Forest Road 9030. Drive 2.3 miles to the parking area and trailhead. An ADA-accessible vault toilet is located near the trailhead.

GPS Coordinates: 47.401135, -121.518443 / N47° 24.078' W121° 31.100'

12 GRANITE MOUNTAIN

Mount Baker-Snoqualmie National Forest, Alpine Lakes Wilderness

Best: Berry Picking

Distance: 8.2 miles round-trip

Duration: 5 hours

Elevation Change: 3,750 feet

Effort: Strenuous

Trail: Dirt and rock paths

Users: Hikers, leashed dogs

Season: July-October

Passes/Fees: Northwest Forest Pass

Maps: Green Trails Map 207 for Snoqualmie Pass, Green Trails Map 207S for Snoqualmie Pass Gateway, USGS topographic map for Snoqualmie Pass

Contact: Mount Baker-Snoqualmie National Forest, Snoqualmie Ranger District-North Bend, www.fs.usda.gov

---

This sharp, scenic climb leads to a functioning fire lookout with stellar views of the Snoqualmie Pass area and prominent Cascade peaks from the summit.

From its rocky perch just west of Snoqualmie Pass, Granite Mountain offers spectacular 360-degree views of the I-90 corridor and Alpine Lakes Wilderness. All this mountain goodness comes at a price, however—a strenuous, grunt-worthy climb zigzagging across avalanche chutes on the south face of the mountain.

Time this trail in summer for ample huckleberry picking, wildflower viewing, and the chance to peek inside the operational fire lookout at the summit. (According to Seattle Mountain Rescue, the winter route bypasses the main avalanche chutes and can be dangerous and subject to avalanches.) Pack plenty of water, sun protection, and warm layers too—seasonal streams tend to dry out in the summer, and the trail is exposed, chilly, and windy on the upper part of the mountain.

Start the Hike

Start your hike at the Pratt Lake Trailhead on the **Pratt Lake Trail.** Fill out a free Alpine Lakes Wilderness permit, then hike north on a series of shallow wooden steps up the dirt trail, enjoying the tall canopy of Douglas fir, western hemlock,

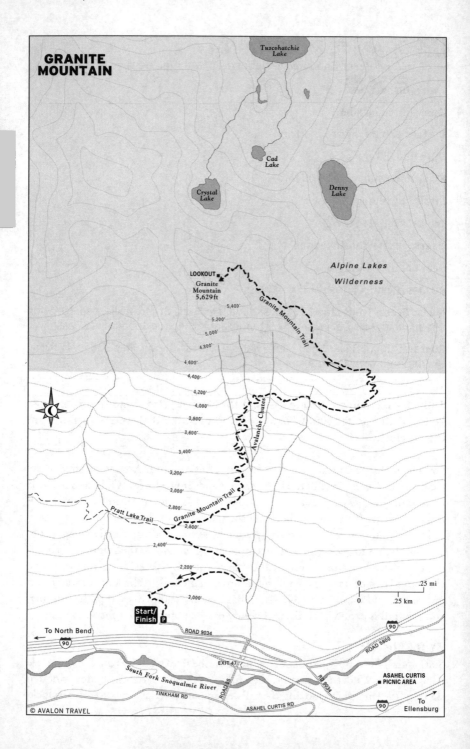

Granite Mountain Lookout and Mount Rainier

and red alder that stretch to the sky above, a kaleidoscope of limbs and leaves. In just over 0.6 mile, reach a wide-open gully with a treeless view north to Granite Mountain—an avalanche chute you'll pass through farther along on the trail.

Arrive at a signed junction at 1.1 miles and bear right to head northeast on the **Granite Mountain Trail.** Winding along the boulder-strewn path, marvel at frog-foot-shaped vanilla leaf sprinkled next to the trail as well as plentiful, star-shaped vine maple that turn a bright, beautiful red-orange in fall. The switchbacks become tighter and more frequent as you seemingly head straight up the mountain, climbing more than 1,800 feet in the next 1.6 miles.

After passing through avalanche chutes, enter a sunny, sprawling meadow at 2.7 miles. Traverse east, pausing for a moment to enjoy the views along I-90 and the top of Mount Rainier as it slowly emerges above the horizon to the south. Wind past pockets of noble fir, following the trail northwest through a passage lined with huckleberries. If you're hiking when the berries are ripe (typically mid-Aug.), pick a few for a quick snack while admiring Granite Mountain Lookout perched overhead.

Reach a garden of large boulders and small ponds at the base of a ridge at 3.25 miles. Bear left to head northwest up a ridge for 300 feet. Bear right at splits in the trail to follow the rocky path around the ridge and into a basin on the north side of the mountain. The lookout sits perched like a tiny toy along the ridge, framed by grassy meadows and windblown mountain hemlock. Ascend a steep 500 feet in the next 0.6 mile and head south on your final approach to the lookout.

Arrive at **Granite Mountain Lookout** at 4.1 miles and revel in your accomplishment! Check to see whether the lookout is staffed (typically on summer weekends). If it's locked, no problem—enjoy the astounding views of Mount Adams and Mount

Rainier to the south, the Olympics, Bandera Mountain, and Mount Defiance to the west, Mount Baker, Kaleetan Peak, Chair Peak, and Glacier Peak to the north, Mount Stuart to the east, and Keechelus Lake to the southeast. Scramble among the uneven boulders, carefully picking your way to the north edge of the boulder field for a sterling view of Crystal Lake and Tuscohatchie Lake below. Grab a boulder to set up shop and enjoy your snack or lunch before heading back to the trailhead.

Hike Nearby

Explore the **Pratt Lake Trail** for a 12.4-mile round-trip hike (7 hours) to Pratt Lake. From the Pratt Lake Trailhead, head west for 1.1 miles to the junction with the Granite Mountain Trail. Bear left to stay on the Pratt Lake Trail for another 2 miles to a signed junction for Talapus Lake. Continue straight toward Pratt Lake for 1.2 miles, then bear right at a signed junction with Island Lake. Descend 775 feet in the next 1.9 miles to the north end of Pratt Lake, where the trail reaches the water's edge (elevation you'll need to regain on your hike back to the trailhead). Campsites are available here, as well as at nearby Lower Tuscohatchie Lake (a worthy destination if you've got gas left in the tank). To reach Tuscohatchie Lake, head east from Pratt Lake toward Melakwa Lake for 0.6 mile; this adds 1.2 miles round-trip to your Pratt Lake hike.

Directions

From Seattle, drive I-90 west to exit 47 for Denny Creek and Asahel Curtis. At the end of the exit ramp, turn left to cross the interstate. At a T-intersection, turn left and follow signs for Granite Mountain Lookout and Pratt Lake Trail. Drive 0.3 mile to the parking area. A vault toilet is available next to the trailhead.
GPS Coordinates: 47.397819, -121.486542 / N47° 23.874' W121° 29.211'

13 ANNETTE LAKE

Mount Baker-Snoqualmie National Forest, Snoqualmie Pass

Distance: 6.8 miles round-trip

Duration: 3.5 hours

Elevation Change: 1,950 feet

Effort: Moderate

Trail: Dirt paths with rocks, exposed roots, stream crossings

Users: Hikers, leashed dogs, mountain bikers, horses

Season: June-mid-November

Passes/Fees: Northwest Forest Pass

Maps: Green Trails Map 207 for Snoqualmie Pass, USGS topographic maps for Snoqualmie Pass and Lost Lake

Contact: Mount Baker-Snoqualmie National Forest, Snoqualmie Ranger District-North Bend, www.fs.usda.gov

---

This moderate hike parallels Humpback Creek, leading to a crisp, clear lake in the shadow of Abiel Peak.

Annette Lake is a great trail for beginner hikers to use as a "bridge" to more challenging hikes along I-90. The hike features mini-waterfalls, pretty wildflowers in spring and summer, towering Douglas fir, western redcedar, and western hemlock, and of course, the cool, clear waters of Annette Lake waiting at the end of the trail.

Annette Lake is named for Annette Wiestling Platt, an avid outdoorswoman who hiked to the lake on May 17, 1913. She wrote a wonderful story about her adventure with her friend, her friend's father, and another gentleman who accompanied them on the hike. Her friend's father submitted Annette's name in consideration for the naming of the lake. The U.S. Geological Survey officially adopted the name in 1918 and it's been known as Annette Lake ever since. For more about Annette's story and those of other regional explorers, check out *The Mountaineer,* 1980, vol. 75, no. 8 (www.mountaineers.org).

Start the Hike

From the information kiosk, follow the sign for **Annette Lake.** The first 0.9 mile gains a mild 500 feet on the moderately wide trail. Almost immediately, you're treated to views of Humpback Creek from a sturdy wooden bridge; its rushing mini-cascades are a scenic start (and finish) to your hike. Beyond the creek, the airy forest is filled with lowland conifers and is dotted with trillium in spring. Wind through an exposed slope, with skittering and crackling power lines overhead, to an intersection with the John Wayne Pioneer Trail. At this point, you may be asking yourself why anyone would think this hike was challenging. But wait—there are switchbacks and elevation gains to come.

Arriving at the wide, gravelly John Wayne Pioneer Trail, admire a pretty waterfall to the east then take a quick jog west to pick up the signed **Annette Lake Trail.** The next 0.5 mile is where you'll see the main elevation gain— 1,100 feet over a series of switchbacks. This section is also home to some neat trail features, such as a thick fallen log repurposed into a one-armed bridge with steps carved into its stump. Take small breaks to admire the pretty miniwaterfalls and creeks you pass by, as well as the Pacific silver fir, named for the silvery-blue patina beneath its shiny green needles.

After the last turn on the long switchbacks, the trail flattens out noticeably for the next 1 mile, gaining 250 feet before dropping slightly to **Annette Lake.** Continue your southward trek, crossing a series of talus slopes that may be avalanche prone when snow is present. Arriving at Annette Lake, enjoy the sight of the calm, clear lake nestled beneath Silver Peak to the east and Abiel Peak to the south. There are some clear, shallow areas by the water's edge that are great for cooling your feet in on a hot day. If you're a keen angler, bring a fishing rod to try your hand at catching the small- to medium-sized rainbow trout that populate the lake.

Hike Nearby

The **Asahel Curtis Nature Trail** is a family-friendly, 0.75-mile interpretive loop located next to the Annette Lake Trail. The trail is named for Asahel Curtis, a

looking south across Annette Lake toward Abiel Peak

prolific Pacific Northwest photographer and outdoorsman who was one of the founding members of The Mountaineers. Pick up a pamphlet from the trail box on the information kiosk to learn more about Asahel Curtis and the natural features on the trail. Several benches are spaced throughout the trail for quick, easy breaks.

Directions

From Seattle, drive I-90 west to exit 47 for Denny Creek and Asahel Curtis. Turn right at the end of the exit ramp and drive 0.1 mile to a T-intersection. Turn left onto Forest Road 5590 and follow the sign for Annette Lake. The parking area is 0.4 mile ahead on the right. A vault toilet is available in the parking lot.

GPS Coordinates: 47.392770, -121.474116 / N47° 23.566' W121° 28.438

14 DENNY CREEK TRAIL TO MELAKWA LAKE
Mount Baker-Snoqualmie National Forest

Best: Kid-Friendly

Distance: 2.4-8.8 miles round-trip

Duration: 1.5-5 hours

Elevation Change: 500-2,625 feet

Effort: Easy/moderate

Trail: Dirt and boulder-strewn paths

Users: Hikers, leashed dogs

Season: July-October

Passes/Fees: Northwest Forest Pass

Maps: Green Trails Map 207 for Snoqualmie Pass, Green Trail Map 207S for Snoqualmie Pass Gateway, USGS topographic map for Snoqualmie Pass

Contact: Mount Baker-Snoqualmie National Forest, Snoqualmie Ranger District-North Bend, www.fs.usda.gov

---

Less than an hour's drive east of Seattle, the Denny Creek Trail to Melakwa Lake is a scenic, family-friendly romp with the option to visit waterfalls.

This popular trail is a Seattle family favorite for picnicking and frolicking at the natural waterslide. Plan to arrive early (the small parking lot can fill quickly), and visit in summer when water levels for Denny Creek are safe to cross, or come in early fall for a cool outing among fall foliage. Bring bug spray to ward off the persistent mosquitoes in early summer.

Start the Hike
Start your hike on the **Denny Creek Trail** next to the parking area. Fill out the Alpine Lakes Wilderness day-use permit in the wooden box and head north on a dirt path interspersed with wooden bridges and staircases under a mossy tree canopy. Cross a sturdy pedestrian bridge over Denny Creek, with beautiful views of the creek flowing south along the rocky creek bed. Passing underneath the westbound I-90 viaduct, leave the sounds of traffic behind as you ascend deeply into the forest.

In 1.2 miles, arrive at the **Denny Creek waterslide.** (As Denny Creek streams south over thick slabs of boulders and shallow pools, it forms a natural waterslide.)

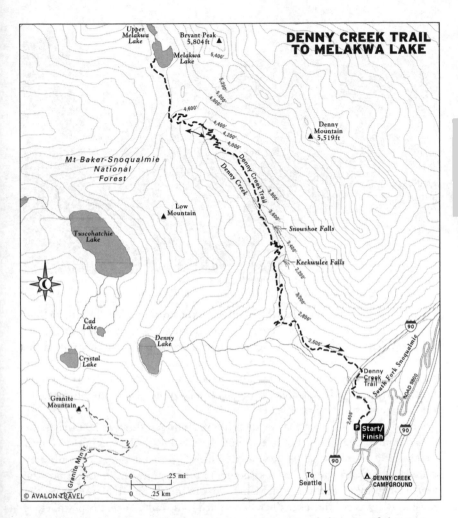

Take care exploring the boulders—they can be wet and slippery. If this is your destination for the day, enjoy a picnic and a quick break near the water, a cool treat on a hot summer day. The water can be quite cold and runs quickly, especially in winter and spring when lingering snow melts. There is no bridge crossing Denny Creek, so if you continue past you will be hopscotching over rocks that can be icy and submerged in water. Signs along the trail warn hikers that crossing is impassable and unsafe in high water; please heed the signs and use caution.

If continuing, cross Denny Creek toward the **Main Trail** sign, heading northwest to Hemlock Pass. The trail is considerably rougher and more challenging from here to Melakwa Lake, gaining the bulk of the hike's elevation on large, uneven rocks packed into the dirt trail. After switchbacking up an exposed, brushy slope,

Mountain heather lines the basin around Melakwa Lake.

stop for views of Keekwulee Falls at 1.9 miles to the northeast. Just beyond, a brief break in the grade offers welcome relief. Arrive at another crossing for Denny Creek at 2.5 miles, hopscotching across the wide creek to pick up the trail on the other side. Emerge on the slope of a picturesque valley brightened with patches of tall bluebell in early summer. Although the trail is quite rocky, you're on the right track. Crossing a series of talus slopes (avalanche prone when snow is present), continue northwest along the valley.

Ascend 750 feet on a series of switchbacks to **Hemlock Pass** at 3.9 miles—the highest point of the hike at 4,600 feet. From Hemlock Pass, the rough, eroded trail descends 150 feet to **Melakwa Lake** at 4.4 miles. Cross an outlet to a day-use area and take a break on one of the rocks before returning to the trailhead. Enjoy the view of Bryant Peak to the east and Chair Peak to the northeast, looming over the translucent waters of the lake. There is a signed spur trail to a nearby pit toilet, as well as designated campsites if you're keen to turn your hike into an overnight stay.

Shorten the Hike

If you've already visited the Denny Creek waterslide, but don't want to hike as far as Melakwa Lake, **Keekwulee Falls** is a worthwhile destination for a 3.8-mile round-trip hike (2.5 hours).

Extend the Hike

A visit to **Upper Melakwa Lake** adds 0.4-mile round-trip to your Melakwa Lake hike. From the day-use area at Melakwa Lake, look for a primitive, unmaintained trail on the western edge of the lake. Follow the trail 0.2 mile north to Upper

view of Bryant Peak over Melakwa Lake

Melakwa Lake. Keep a sharp eye out for falling rocks and step carefully along the rocky slope.

Directions

From Seattle, drive east on I-90 to exit 47 for Denny Creek/Asahel Curtis. At the end of the exit ramp, turn left onto Forest Road 55 and drive over the overpass. At a T-intersection, turn right onto Forest Road 9034 and follow the sign for Denny Creek Road. In 0.2 mile, turn left onto Forest Road 58, following the sign for Denny Creek Road. Drive 2.3 miles, passing the Denny Creek Campground on your left. Turn left onto Forest Road 5830 and follow the sign for Denny Creek Trail 1014 for 0.2 mile to the Denny Creek Trailhead. Two vault toilets are at the trailhead; one is ADA-accessible.

If the small parking lot is full, try parking at a parking lot 0.1 mile north of the turn-off for the Denny Creek Trail on Forest Road 58. It is a 0.4-mile walk from the overflow lot to the trailhead via a path next to the lot; this adds an extra 0.8 mile round-trip to your hike. Please use caution crossing Forest Road 58 to reach the trailhead.

GPS Coordinates: 47.415315, -121.443338 / N47° 24.925' W121° 26.598'

15 FRANKLIN FALLS
Mount Baker-Snoqualmie National Forest

Best: Waterfalls, Kid-Friendly

Distance: 2.4 miles round-trip

Duration: 1 hour

Elevation Change: 375 feet

Effort: Easy

Trail: Dirt paths, wooden and rock steps

Users: Hikers, leashed dogs

Season: April-November

Passes/Fees: Northwest Forest Pass

Maps: Green Trails Map 207 for Snoqualmie Pass, Green Trails Map 207S for Snoqualmie Pass Gateway, USGS topographic map for Snoqualmie Pass

Contact: Mount Baker-Snoqualmie National Forest, Snoqualmie Ranger District-North Bend, www.fs.usda.gov

---

A gentle hike through a partially canopied forest along the South Fork Snoqualmie River leads to a gorgeous waterfall.

Franklin Falls is one of the most popular hikes in the Snoqualmie Pass area. This gentle, shady trail along the South Fork Snoqualmie River ends at beautiful, 70-foot Franklin Falls. The short distance, mild elevation gain, and spectacular falls make this a great option for families and beginner hikers. Visit in late spring when the trail has shed its winter coat and the falls are raging, or in early fall when the water flow has quieted and you can get close to the falls without getting doused in a misty shower.

The trail is very popular. Avoid holiday weekends and visit midweek or early in the day on weekends to get a head start on the foot traffic. It's possible to easily extend your day with a visit to Annette Lake or the Asahel Curtis Nature Trail; both start from the same trailhead, less than a 4-mile drive from the Franklin Falls Trailhead.

Start the Hike
From the main parking lot, hike 0.2 mile on a path next to the lot. Carefully cross Forest Road 58 to the brown **Franklin Falls Trail** sign marking the start

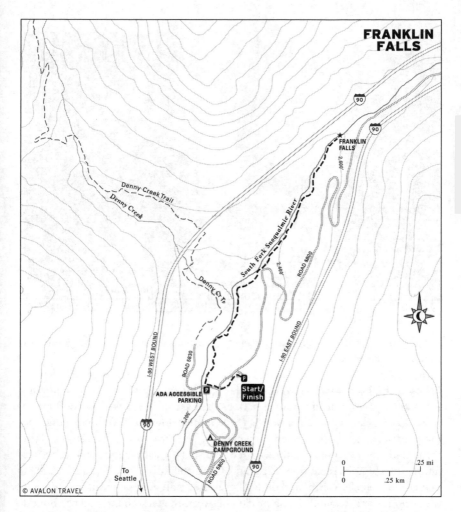

of the trail. Right from the start, you're treated to the rushing, roaring sounds of the South Fork Snoqualmie River, a constant, mellow companion as you hike the well-groomed dirt and gravel path to the falls. Hike among tall, thick western redcedar, western hemlock, and red alder that rise next to the trail in a partial canopy with huckleberry shrubs, trillium, skunk cabbage, and the dreaded devil's club making up the damp, yellow-green understory.

As you ascend a series of shallow wooden staircases, take time to pause at small viewpoints along the trail that showcase views of the clear river and its cascades. The viewpoints, as well as footbridges and trail reroutes, were completed in 2015 thanks to the work of more than 350 volunteers from the Washington Trails

misty view at Franklin Falls

Association. Give these folks a silent tip of your hat as you enjoy these wonderful trail improvements.

At 1.2 miles, descend 50 feet on rock staircases to a wide, staggering view of **Franklin Falls.** A small viewing area is great for taking pictures and enjoying a snack, or press on to the plunge pool at the base of the falls for a cool, misty shower and a close view. Take care as you scramble down to the plunge pool; the rough path can be slippery when wet and icy in wintry weather. The 70-foot falls are actually the third tier of a three-tiered waterfall—the first and second tiers are unfortunately not visible from the trail. Above the falls to the west is a viaduct that carries vehicles westbound on I-90 over the small gorge—Franklin Falls has the curious distinction of sitting nestled between the westbound and eastbound lanes of I-90. Take a seat on a rock, watch the falls, and snap a few photos before heading back to the trailhead.

Extend the Hike

Combine a visit to Franklin Falls with a 0.75-mile hike on the **Asahel Curtis Nature Trail** or a 6.8-mile hike (3.5 hours) to **Annette Lake.** Both trails are accessed from the Annette Lake Trailhead, less than a 4-mile drive from the Franklin Falls Trailhead. To get there, drive back to the I-90 overpass and turn left to follow the signs for Tinkham Road for 0.1 mile past the off-ramp. At a T-intersection, turn left onto Forest Road 5590 and follow the sign for Annette Lake. The parking area is 0.4 mile ahead on the right. There is a vault toilet in the parking lot.

Snowshoe in Winter

Franklin Falls is a popular winter destination for picturesque snowy scenes along the trail and at the falls. While the off-ramp for exit 47 is plowed, often the forest roads leading to the trailhead are not and can have deep snow, ice, and tree blockages. Drive slowly, follow posted signs, and leave room for other vehicles to turn around and get by. You may need to park away from the trailhead and hike along the road to reach the trail. In winter, pack warm clothes, plenty of water, and traction devices such as microspikes, or wear snowshoes.

Call the North Bend ranger station to check road and trail conditions before making the drive and visit midweek, early in the morning, or late in the afternoon—this tends to be a popular winter destination.

Directions

From Seattle, take I-90 east to exit 47 for Denny Creek/Asahel Curtis. At the end of the exit ramp, turn left onto Forest Road 55 and drive over the overpass. At a T-intersection, turn right onto Forest Road 9034 and follow signs for the Franklin Falls Trail. In 0.2 mile, turn left and follow signs for the Franklin Falls Trail onto Forest Road 58. Drive 2.3 miles, passing the Denny Creek Campground on your left.

For ADA-accessible parking, turn left at the sign for Denny Creek Trail 1014 onto Forest Road 5830. The small parking area is across from the trailhead for Franklin Falls. For all other vehicles, continue north for 0.1 mile past the sign for Denny Creek Trail on Forest Road 58 to a parking lot. Hike 0.2 mile to the trailhead via a path next to the lot (use caution crossing Forest Rd. 58). Two ADA-accessible vault toilets are located next to the trailhead.

GPS Coordinates:

Main parking lot: 47.413912, -121.440442 / N47° 24.806' W121° 26.397
Trailhead and ADA-accessible parking: 47.413072, -121.442677 / N47° 24.797' W121° 26.559'

16 SNOW LAKE
Mount Baker-Snoqualmie National Forest,
Alpine Lakes Wilderness, Snoqualmie Pass

Best: Lakes

Distance: 7.2 miles round-trip

Duration: 4 hours

Elevation Change: 1,750 feet

Effort: Moderate

Trail: Rocky paths

Users: Hikers, leashed dogs

Season: July-October

Passes/Fees: Northwest Forest Pass

Maps: Green Trails Map 207 for Snoqualmie Pass, Green Trails Map 207S for Snoqualmie Pass Gateway, USGS topographic map for Snoqualmie Pass

Contact: Mount Baker-Snoqualmie National Forest, Snoqualmie Ranger District-North Bend, www.fs.usda.gov

---

This scenic hike to an alpine lake surrounded by peaks and valleys has the option to continue to Gem Lake.

Snow Lake is the quintessential Seattle-area hike—a not-too-difficult trek to a striking blue lake surrounded by peaks in the Alpine Lakes Wilderness. This hike is extremely popular; avoid summer weekends or plan to arrive at the parking lot near sunrise for solitude on your way to the lake. Snow on the trail (typically into July) means there is high avalanche danger—do not attempt the trail in these conditions. Bring hiking poles to help you navigate the rocky, uneven trail.

Start the Hike
From the parking lot, cross the road to the **Snow Lake Trail** entrance in 85 feet. Fill out the Alpine Lakes Wilderness permit, then hike north up a series of wooden stairs through a lush forest of tall Pacific silver fir and mountain hemlock. The grade soon evens out as you pass through open-air talus slopes. From the start, you'll understand why the trail is so popular: Views of Chair Peak stand out along a mountainous ridge to the northwest, the sounds of the South Fork Snoqualmie River flow musically to the southwest, and wildflowers pepper the trail in summer.

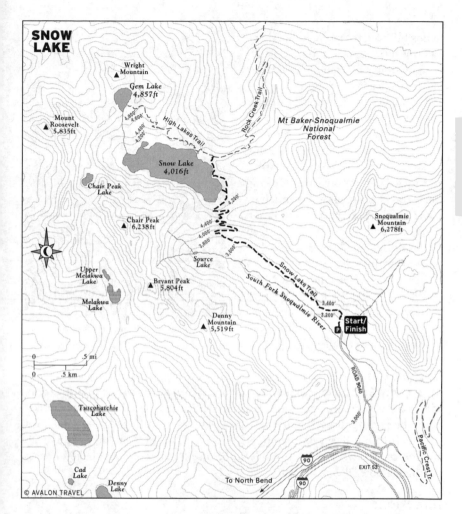

In 1.75 miles, bear right at a signed junction for **Source Lake.** Ascend 500 feet north on a series of switchbacks—the steepest part of the hike. In 0.5 mile, reach the saddle at 4,400 feet and bear right past a sign for the Alpine Lakes Wilderness, beginning your descent to the lake basin. Many people (especially those with youngsters in tow) choose to hike to the first switchback with a lovely view of the lake and turn around there. For more panoramic, up-close views, continue down the trail for 0.7 mile, descending 325 feet to a spur trail down to the lake.

About 3 miles into your hike, you'll arrive at the lake basin. Follow the Lake Access signs to descend 59 feet on a short, 0.2-mile spur trail to **Snow Lake.** The lake's blue-green water lines the shallow, transparent shoreline; see if you can spot the stony ruins of a cabin built in the 1930s. The majestic setting includes rolling hillsides, the peaks of the Alpine Lakes Wilderness, and tufts of fanciful beargrass and white mountain-heather in nearby meadows in spring.

Explore the spur trail then head back on the trail to continue north along the lake's eastern flank. Follow the **Main Trail** sign across a rocky inlet, passing a trail to campsites. In 0.3 mile, arrive at a rocky outcropping overlooking the lake—a great place for lunch or a snack. (Heed the posted restoration signs here and be careful not to step on the already fragile vegetation.) The trail officially ends in 0.2 mile at an intersection with the High Lakes Trail and Rock Creek Trail. (Rock Creek Trail is a longer, backdoor entrance to Snow Lake from the Middle Fork Snoqualmie River Valley).

Mount Roosevelt from Snow Lake

Extend the Hike

Make pretty **Gem Lake** your destination for a 10.4-mile round-trip hike (6 hours), adding 3.2 miles round-trip and 950 feet in elevation gain to the Snow Lake hike. From the signed intersection of the Snow Lake Trail and High Lakes Trail, turn left and hike northwest on the High Lakes Trail toward Gem Lake. The rocky and sometimes tricky-to-spot trail leads across an outlet of Snow Lake to reach the small alpine lake in 1.6 miles.

Directions

From Seattle, take I-90 east to exit 52 for West Summit. At the end of the exit ramp, turn left under the overpass and follow signs for Alpental Road. In 0.1 mile, turn right onto Alpental Road 9040 at the brown sign for Snow Lake Trailhead. In 1.2 miles, turn left into the large Alpental Ski Area parking lot. From the parking lot, walk north along Alpental Road for 85 feet to the signed trailhead on the right side of the road. Vault toilets are located on the left side of the road.

GPS Coordinates: 47.445405, -121.423528 / N47° 26.705' W121° 25.415'

17 GOLD CREEK POND

Mount Baker-Snoqualmie National Forest, Snoqualmie Pass

Best: Easy Hikes

Distance: 1.2 miles round-trip

Duration: 30 minutes

Elevation Change: 100 feet

Effort: Easy

Trail: Paved path, wooden boardwalks

Users: Hikers, leashed dogs

Season: May-October

Passes/Fees: Northwest Forest Pass

Maps: Green Trails Map 207 for Snoqualmie Pass, Green Trails Map 207S for Snoqualmie Pass Gateway, USGS topographic maps for Snoqualmie Pass and Chikamin Peak

Contact: Mount Baker-Snoqualmie National Forest, Snoqualmie Ranger District-North Bend, www.fs.usda.gov

---

This family-friendly hike around a large pond nestled in the scenic Gold Creek Valley is also popular with beginning snowshoers.

Gold Creek Pond is a lovely, ADA-accessible loop around a picturesque pond at the start of Gold Creek Valley. The trail is a great option for families with strollers, beginner hikers, and those looking for a quick nature fix. Visit in the fall when the leaves turn bright crimson and gold and kokanee salmon spawn in the creek, or in the winter for a beginner snowshoe. Whatever the season, this trail provides the serenity of mountain and water views, coupled with benches and picnic tables for easy enjoyment. Be prepared for company—this can be a popular hike on sunny weekends and in the winter. Leave your bike, fishing pole, and swim trunks at home; cycling, fishing, and swimming are prohibited at the pond.

Start the Hike

From the parking lot, head west on the paved trail to the signed **Gold Creek Pond Loop.** Although the western hemlock, Douglas fir, and vine maple are plentiful, the hike is pretty exposed—a hat, sunscreen, and plenty of water will come in

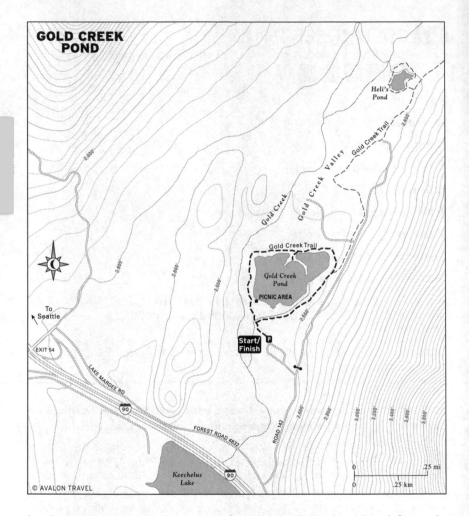

handy. In 0.1 mile, reach the junction for Gold Creek Pond and bear left or right to start the 1-mile loop—it's your choice. To the left is a scenic picnic area; to the right is a series of wooden boardwalks and a signed junction with the Gold Creek Trail. Halfway around the pond, explore a spur trail that leads to the water and a couple of benches that are perfect for quiet reflection or a quick break. Enjoy the views of Chikamin Peak and Alta Mountain to the north, with Mount Catherine standing out to the southwest.

In the late 1970s and early 1980s, what is now Gold Creek Pond used to be a gravel pit. Cranes dug gravel and sand used to pave parts of I-90 near Snoqualmie Pass. After the pit closed in 1983, the Washington State Department of Transportation and U.S. Forest Service turned it into a habitat for fish and wildlife. Today,

Gaze north along the Gold Creek Valley to Chikamin Peak and Alta Mountain.

beavers, Canada geese, ducks, osprey, salmon, and chattering birds call Gold Creek and Gold Creek Pond home.

Extend the Hike

Add 2.2 miles round-trip (1 hour) to your hike with a visit to **Hell's Pond**, a small pond with a grassy loop trail and views of Chikamin Peak and Alta Mountain. From the east side of Gold Creek Pond, follow signs for Gold Creek Trail north, merging onto a wide gravel road that winds through a private community. (Please respect private property and practice Leave No Trace principles.) Continue following signs for Gold Creek Trail along the gravel road. In 0.9 mile, look left for a wooden kiosk that marks Heli's Pond. The narrow, inconspicuous loop around the pond starts from the Danger! Deep Water sign. Heed posted signs on the kiosk and do not go on the pond in winter.

Snowshoe in Winter

Gold Creek Pond is a popular beginner snowshoe in winter. The snowshoe trail begins 0.6 mile south of the Gold Creek Pond parking lot (intersection of Forest Rd. 4832 and Gold Creek Rd. 142) for a 2.4-mile round-trip winter walk (2 hours). A Sno-Park Permit (www.parks.state.wa.us, Nov.-Apr., $20 daily pass, $40 seasonal pass) is required when parking on Forest Road 4832. A Northwest Forest Pass is not required. Forest Road 4832 can be crusted with ice and snow in winter; drive slowly and be prepared for winter conditions. Consider visiting midweek, early in the morning, or in the late afternoon as parking along the narrow road can fill quickly.

If you plan to snowshoe beyond Heli's Pond on the Gold Creek Trail, note that there are talus slopes that can be avalanche prone. Only proceed if you have proper training in avalanche safety and snow travel.

Directions

From Seattle, take I-90 east to exit 54 for Hyak. At the end of the exit ramp, turn left onto State Route 906. In 0.2 mile, turn right onto Forest Road 4832 at the sign for Gold Creek. In 0.9 mile, turn left onto Gold Creek Road 142 (some maps list this as Road 144). In 0.4 mile, turn left at the Gold Creek Pond Picnic Area for the parking lot. An ADA-accessible vault toilet is available next to the trailhead.
GPS Coordinates: 47.396527, -121.379380 / N47° 23.808' W121° 22.766'

18 RACHEL LAKE

Okanogan-Wenatchee National Forest, Alpine Lakes Wilderness

Best: Off the Beaten Path

Distance: 7.8 miles round-trip

Duration: 5 hours

Elevation Change: 2,000 feet

Effort: Moderate/strenuous

Trail: Dirt paths, steep rocks, roots

Users: Hikers, leashed dogs

Season: June-October

Passes/Fees: Northwest Forest Pass

Maps: Green Trails Map 207 for Snoqualmie Pass, Green Trails Map 207S for Snoqualmie Pass Gateway, USGS topographic map for Snoqualmie Pass

Contact: Okanogan-Wenatchee National Forest, Cle Elum Ranger District, www.fs.usda.gov

---

This popular hike along Box Canyon Creek travels to a sparkling lake with options to explore Rampart Ridge and Alta Mountain.

Sitting just east of Snoqualmie Pass below Rampart Ridge, Rachel Lake has a little bit of everything—mountain views, gurgling creeks, small waterfalls, and trailside berry picking. The trail leads to a quietly lapping lake cradled beneath a picturesque cirque and has a dual personality: The pleasant ramble through Box Canyon morphs into a mean, slippery scramble the last 1.1 miles to the lake. Bring hiking poles to help navigate the rocky tread and bug spray to keep ferocious insects at bay in summer. Camp at Rachel Lake, Lila Lake, or Rampart Lakes to explore the area thoroughly.

Start the Hike

From the parking lot, cross Forest Road 4930 to pick up the **Rachel Lake Trail.** At the trailhead kiosk, fill out a free Alpine Lakes Wilderness permit (one per party). You may notice signs regarding crowd control and preservation: Rachel Lake is one of the most popular hikes in the Cle Elum Ranger District and is also used as a gateway to nearby Rampart Ridge, Rampart Lakes, Lila Lake, and Alta Mountain.

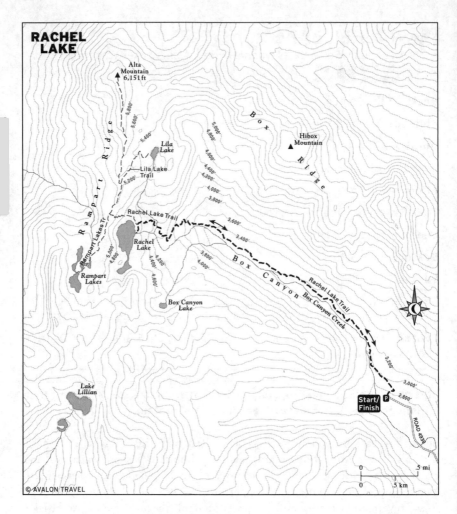

Help preserve this area by observing Alpine Lakes Wilderness regulations (limit group size to 12 hikers, including dogs) and practice Leave No Trace principles.

Ascend northwest on the **Rachel Lake Trail** through an airy forest of hemlock, cedar, and vine maple. While mostly clear, the trail has a worn-in feel, with packed dirt, exposed rocks and roots, and social trails around downed trees. Pass a sign for the Alpine Lakes Wilderness in 0.4 mile and enjoy the churning pools and rapids of Box Canyon Creek below. The sidewalls of the canyon rise steeply to the southwest and northeast, giving the hike a subterranean feel as you cross over small streams and wind through thick, shrubby meadows of devil's club and thimbleberry.

Emerge briefly into an open, tree-lined valley with a view of **Hibox Mountain**

view of Rachel Lake from Rampart Ridge

to the northeast at 1.9 miles. Head back into the forest and carefully cross a wide stream on a makeshift pile of timber and rocks, pausing to enjoy the modest, cascading waterfalls. The crossing at 2.7 miles marks the start of your steep ascent to Rachel Lake. There's no nice way to say it: The trail gets mean and stays that way for the next 1.1 miles, gaining a lung-busting 1,200 feet up thick roots and rough, uneven boulders to the lake.

Cresting a ridge, arrive at **Rachel Lake** at 3.8 miles. At a four-way junction (turning clockwise), the trail behind to the south leads to campsites near the lake, the path straight ahead to the west leads to shady, rocky perches overlooking the lake, a sign to your right marked Trail leads north to Rampart Ridge, and a sign on the right marked Toilet travels northeast to a pit toilet. Pick the lakeside route (straight ahead) to enjoy a snack or lunch before returning to the trailhead. To continue to Rampart Ridge, follow the Trail sign at the four-way junction to hike the north side of Rachel Lake, gaining 450 feet in a little over 0.4 mile to the ridge.

Extend the Hike

Add on a trip to **Rampart Lakes** (10 miles round-trip, 6 hours), **Lila Lake** (10.5 miles round-trip, 6.5 hours), or **Alta Mountain** (11.5 miles round-trip, 8.5 hours) to extend your day. To reach any of the three destinations from Rachel Lake, follow the Trail sign at the four-way junction to hike around the north side of the lake for 0.4 mile. At Rampart Ridge and a signed T-junction, you have the option to bear left for Rampart Lakes or right for Lila Lake and Alta Mountain. Bearing left, hike 0.7 mile southwest to Rampart Lakes. Bearing right, hike 0.3 mile northeast to a Y-junction (sometimes marked with a cairn) and bear right to continue northeast for 0.7 mile to Lila Lake. Alternatively, bear left to continue north, gaining more than 1,100 feet in the next 1.1 miles to the summit of Alta Mountain. While not a technical climb, the trail to Alta Mountain is exposed, with sharp drop-offs and rock scrambles—please be careful. Bring a map (there are many social trails at the lakes, making it easy to get turned around) and sun protection as there is little shade on Rampart Ridge. Snow can linger on Rampart Ridge and Alta Mountain until mid-July, creating slippery and hazardous conditions; wait until midsummer (or better yet early fall) to explore the area.

Lila Lake, an optional hike from Rachel Lake.

Getaway for the Weekend
Camp at Rachel Lake, Rampart Lakes, or Lila Lake to explore scenic Rampart Ridge and the surrounding lakes. Campsites are first-come, first-served; rangers ask that you camp in established campsites to help preserve the natural area. Fill out an Alpine Lakes Wilderness permit at the trailhead and practice Leave No Trace principles. Campsites here are popular, so get an early start to nab a good site.

Directions
From Seattle, take I-90 east to exit 62 for Stampede Pass and Lake Kachess. At the end of the exit ramp, turn left onto Kachess Lake Road. Drive 5.1 miles northeast toward the Kachess Campground (the road turns into Forest Rd. 49). Arrive at a T-junction next to the campground and turn left for Trail No. 1313 where the pavement ends. Drive 0.4 mile then bear right at a Y-junction onto Forest Road 4930. Drive 3.5 miles on the potholed road to the parking area and trailhead.
GPS Coordinates: 47.400773, -121.283568 / N47° 24.049' W121° 17.015'

HIGHWAY 2

Highway 2, also known as the Stevens Pass Scenic
Highway, abounds with hiking opportunities. With the Wild Sky Wilderness and
Henry M. Jackson Wilderness to the north and the Alpine Lakes Wilderness to
the south, the area features hundreds of lakes tucked into pockets of the central
Cascades, scenic mountain views, fire lookouts, easy access to the Pacific Crest
Trail, and historic remnants of the Great Northern Railway. In addition to hiking,
the highway serves as a gateway to fishing, tubing, kayaking, and whitewater
rafting along the Skykomish and Wenatchee Rivers. Skiers, snowboarders, and
snowshoers will find a winter playground at the Stevens Pass Ski Resort, while
those looking for an overnight stay have their pick of cozy bed-and-breakfasts
in nearby Leavenworth.

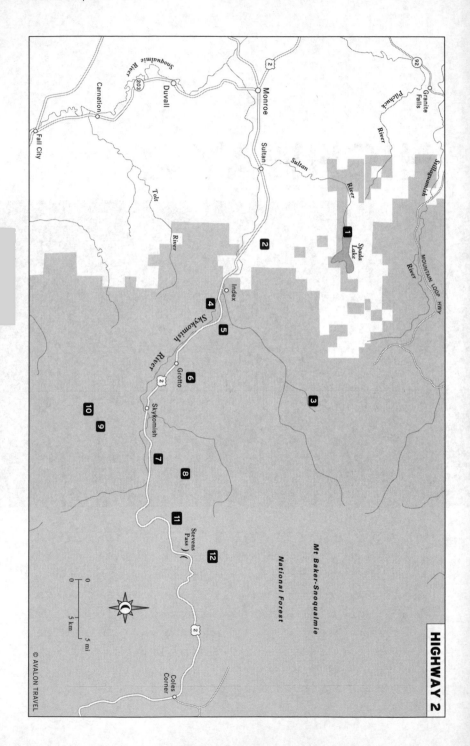

HIGHWAY 2

© AVALON TRAVEL

TRAIL NAME	LEVEL	DISTANCE	TIME	ELEVATION	PAGE
1 Spada Lake Overlook	Easy/moderate	5.6 mi	3.5 hr	990 ft	186
2 Woody Trail to Wallace Falls	Easy/moderate	5 mi	3 hr	1,300 ft	190
3 Blanca Lake	Strenuous	11.8 mi	7 hr	3,900 ft	194
4 Lake Serene	Moderate	8.2 mi	4 hr	2,350 ft	198
5 Heybrook Lookout	Moderate	2.1 mi	1.5 hr	980 ft	202
6 Barclay Lake	Easy	4.3 mi	2.5 hr	300 ft	206
7 Beckler Peak	Moderate	7.7 mi	4 hr	2,300 ft	209
8 Johnson Ridge-Scorpion Mountain	Moderate/strenuous	7.8 mi	5.5 hr	2,600 ft	213
9 West Fork Foss Lakes	Easy/strenuous	3.4-14.8 mi	2-10 hr	500-3,960 ft	217
10 Lake Dorothy	Easy/moderate	3.3 mi	2 hr	850 ft	221
11 Wellington Ghost Town-Windy Point	Easy	5.6 mi	3 hr	300 ft	225
12 Lake Valhalla	Moderate	6.5 mi	3.5 hr	1,400 ft	230

1 SPADA LAKE OVERLOOK
Culmback Dam Recreation Site, Gateway Trailhead, Sultan

Distance: 5.6 miles round-trip

Duration: 3.5 hours

Elevation Change: 990 feet

Effort: Easy/moderate

Trail: Gravel path

Users: Hikers, leashed dogs, mountain bikers, Snohomish County PUD

Season: Mid-April-October

Passes/Fees: Free; registration required at Olney Pass

Maps: Green Trails Map 111SX for Mountain Loop Highway, USGS topographic map for Wallace Lake

Contact: Snohomish County Public Utility District (PUD), www.snopud.com, dawn-dusk daily

---

Spada Lake Overlook provides a panoramic viewpoint of Spada Lake nestled within nearby peaks of the Cascades.

Visit in spring while waiting for high-elevation trails to clear, or in summer when berries line the trail, ripe for picking. You may see friendly Snohomish County PUD workers and the occasional PUD vehicle on this trail; access to the Gateway Trailhead can change depending on weather, road conditions, and repair work. Contact the Snohomish County PUD before you go to ensure access is open. Please protect the quality of the reservoir water and the health of local wildlife by following posted guidelines.

Start the Hike
Start your hike from the **Gateway Trailhead.** Skirt around the yellow gate and head northwest on the gravel service road toward **Culmback Dam.** Well-signed kiosks explain the history of the dam and the creation of the Spada Lake Reservoir, while picnic tables offer a break with a view. On the lake, red buoys form a semicircle (called a log boom) to keep boats from getting too close to the dam and spillway. On the west side of the dam, water from the reservoir fans out into the Sultan River below. In September, officials increase the water flow into the river and regulate its temperature to ensure that spawning salmon have enough cool water to get upstream. Pretty neat, right?

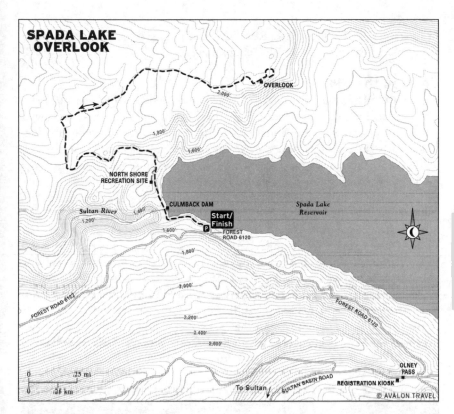

SPADA LAKE OVERLOOK

OVERLOOK

2,000'

1,800'

1,200'

1,600'

NORTH SHORE
RECREATION SITE

Sultan River

1,400'

CULMBACK DAM

1,200'

1,600'

Start/
Finish
P
FOREST
ROAD 6120

Spada Lake
Reservoir

1,800'

2,000'

FOREST ROAD 6122

2,200'

FOREST ROAD 6120

2,400'

2,600'

OLNEY
PASS

0   .25 mi
0   .06 km

To Sultan   SULTAN BASIN ROAD   REGISTRATION KIOSK

© AVALON TRAVEL

Cross the dam and follow the gravel service road for 2.6 undulating miles. Tall, beautiful western hemlock, Douglas fir, and red alder stand protectively along this secluded section of the trail; in summer, salmonberries, red huckleberries, thimbleberries, and blackberries provide a trailside snack. As the road descends 150 feet northwest, it may feel like you're heading in the wrong direction, but at the 1.5-mile mark the trail bottoms out and swings east, climbing 600 feet to an overlook.

At the top of the hill, bear right at a Y-junction and head east up a paved road for 0.2 mile to the **overlook.** Truth be told, there isn't much to the overlook—it has the feel of an overgrown cul-de-sac with a chain-link fence along the ledge. The area used to be a recreation site, but was decommissioned in 2011. No matter—the views are still gorgeous and there is plenty to see.

Take in the expansive views of Spada Lake Reservoir stretching to the south ringed by Prospect Peak and Mount Stickney to the southeast and Del Campo Peak and Red Mountain to the east. The easternmost point of the overlook is a particularly pretty spot where purple foxglove and sunny patches of yellow goldenrod sway in the breeze. Below to the southwest is **Culmback Dam,** built in 1965 to create the Spada Lake Reservoir, which supplies roughly 80 percent of the drinking water to Snohomish County residents.

Shorten the Hike

Explore **Culmback Dam** for a flat, 0.8-mile round-trip hike with beautiful views of Spada Lake and Bald Mountain. From the Gateway Trailhead, hike northwest on the gravel service road to Culmback Dam. If you're keen to explore further, follow the service road past the dam to the North Shore Recreation Site, which adds another 0.6 mile round-trip and 150 feet of elevation gain. The site has a modest viewpoint with picnic tables and a vault toilet nearby.

Hike Nearby

A quiet, shady adventure to the Sultan River is a great option on a hot day. The **Sultan River Canyon Trail** (4 miles round-trip) descends sharply to the river—500 feet in 0.75 mile—but is broken up by numerous switchbacks. Start by walking 200 feet from the Gateway Trailhead to Forest Road 6122 (signed for Sultan River Canyon Trail). Hike southwest along Forest Road 6122 for 1.1 miles, then turn right at the signed junction for Sultan River Canyon Trail and descend 0.9 mile to the river. Enjoy a good splash in the cool water, taking care with young children near the river. Leashed dogs are allowed. While mountain bikes are allowed on Forest Road 6122, they are not permitted on the Sultan River Canyon Trail.

Spada Lake from Spada Lake Overlook

Directions

From Seattle, take I-5 north to exit 194 toward Snohomish and Wenatchee. Merge onto U.S. Highway 2 East and drive 1.9 miles, bearing right at the split in the highway to continue on U.S. Highway 2 East to Sultan.

From Bellevue or the east side of Lake Washington, head north on I-405 to exit 23 for State Route 522 East toward Woodinville. Drive 12.7 miles on State Route 522 East, taking the exit for U.S. Highway 2 East toward Wenatchee. Merge onto U.S. Highway 2 East in Monroe, continuing east for 8 miles to Sultan.

Drive past milepost 23 and turn left in 0.2 mile onto Sultan Basin Road. Drive 13.2 miles on Sultan Basin Road (the pavement ends at 10.3 miles) to a registration kiosk on the right side of the road. Fill out the visitor registration form (keep the yellow receipt on your dash) and in 350 feet, turn left at a Y-junction toward Culmback Dam Road and the Gateway Trailhead. Drive 1.5 miles to the parking area at the end of the road. Two restrooms are located next to Culmback Dam (0.25 mile from the parking area), and there is a vault toilet at the North Shore Recreation Site.

GPS Coordinates: 47.973433, -121.682115 / N47° 58.397' W121° 40.897'

② WOODY TRAIL TO WALLACE FALLS
Wallace Falls State Park, Gold Bar

Best: Waterfalls

Distance: 5 miles round-trip

Duration: 3 hours

Elevation Change: 1,300 feet

Effort: Easy/moderate

Trail: Dirt and gravel paths, some rocky sections, wooden steps and bridges

Users: Hikers, mountain bikers, leashed dogs

Season: Year-round

Passes/Fees: Discover Pass

Maps: Green Trails Map 142 for Index, USGS topographic maps for Gold Bar and Wallace Lake.

Contact: Wallace Falls State Park, www.parks.state.wa.us, 8am-dusk daily

---

Enjoy this family-friendly hike to a series of waterfalls with views of the Skykomish River Valley, central Cascades, and Olympics.

Wallace Falls State Park may be best known for its waterfalls, but what makes it a great place to hike are the well-signed junctions, interpretive signs, scenic overlooks with mountain and valley views, and proximity to the Wallace River. Save this hike for winter and early spring when the waterfall and river flows are at their peak. The trail can get muddy and wet in these seasons; wear shoes you don't mind getting dirty. The park and trail are generally busy year-round, so it's a good bet to arrive early in the day, especially on sunny weekends.

Start the Hike
From the trailhead in the parking lot, head east on an open gravel path lined with Himalayan blackberry and salmonberry shrubs. You'll walk under power lines in this section, and their skittering, crackling sounds are an oddly urban start to this otherwise forested hike. While mountain bikers are allowed on this section of the trail, the continuing Woody Trail is hiker-only.

Pause at an interpretive sign in 0.3 mile for views of Mount Baring, Mount Index, and Mount Persis, then enter the forest. Listen to the sound of the Wallace River in the distance and enjoy the cocooned feel among the red alder, Douglas fir, and

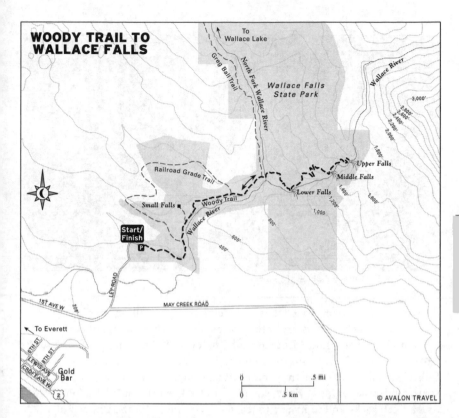

hemlock lining the dirt trail. Reach a signed intersection at 0.4 mile then bear
right to join the **Woody Trail.** (The Railroad Grade Trail to the left also reaches
the falls, but adds an additional mile each way and is open to mountain bikers.)
Zigzagging through a wooden fence, enjoy your first views of the Wallace River
as you descend the trail.

A spur trail to **Small Falls** appears on the left at 0.5 mile; this pretty waterfall is worth the trip if you have time. Half-mile markers near the trail offer
a helpful way to gauge your progress as you hike. Another neat feature is the
short set of stairs that lead down to the bank of the Wallace River, offering
a way to see the river up close. Enjoy the view then continue west along the
undulating trail, passing a collection of Douglas firs riddled with holes from
pileated woodpeckers.

Arriving at a signed junction with the Greg Ball Trail at 1.4 miles, bear right to
stay on the **Woody Trail** toward the Lower Falls. Descend the trail to a wooden
bridge over the North Fork Wallace River and pause to take in the spacious views
north and south. At 0.25 mile past the bridge, partial views of the Skykomish River
Valley and Olympics open to the southwest. **Lower Falls** (1.7 miles) is just east of

Middle Falls in Wallace Falls State Park

the viewpoint, a modest waterfall with a view of Middle Falls in the distance. The nearby picnic shelter offers a spot for a break, or shelter in wet weather.

From Lower Falls, hike east to ascend 230 feet in 0.3 mile to 265-foot **Middle Falls** (2 miles)—the showstopper in the series of waterfalls that comprise Wallace Falls. Snap a few pictures of the photogenic falls from a nearby bench, then press on another 0.5 mile to **Upper Falls,** stopping to check out the valley overlook ahead. Ascend 470 rocky and rooty feet to reach the viewpoint for the **Upper Falls** (2.5 miles), your turnaround point.

Shorten the Hike

Hike to **Small Falls** (1 mile round-trip, 45 minutes), **Lower Falls** (3.5 miles round-trip, 2 hours), or **Middle Falls** (4 miles round-trip, 2.5 hours) for a shorter outing.

Hike Nearby

For a longer and quieter alternative to the crowds at Wallace Falls, head to Wallace Lake and Jay Lake for an 11.6-mile round-trip hike (6 hours). From the intersection of the **Greg Ball Trail** and Woody Trail, bear left to take the Greg Ball Trail toward Wallace Lake. In 2 miles, turn right onto a DNR road and hike 0.1 mile to pick up the signed trail to **Wallace Lake** ahead on the left. Follow the rocky trail for 0.6 mile to the southern end of Wallace Lake. To continue to Jay Lake, head left to follow a wide trail for 0.7 mile around the west side of Wallace Lake. At the northern end of the lake, cross an inlet and follow the sign for Jay Lake; it's another mile to the lake. There is a composting toilet at the lake.

Get Away for the Weekend

Spend the weekend in one of five quaint cabins at **Wallace Falls State Park** (888/226-7688, www.parks.state.wa.us, fees vary seasonally). Cabins can accommodate up to five guests; each has a bunk bed and full-size futon. Two cabins have two rooms; Cabins 3 and 4 are pet-friendly. Two cabins are equipped with ADA-accessible ramps. Restrooms with showers are located outside the cabins. Bring your own bed linens.

If you don't want to cook, **Rico's Pizza** (40709 State Rte. 2, Gold Bar, 360/793-3333, www.eatricospizza.com, 3pm-9pm Mon.-Thurs., noon-10pm Fri.-Sat., noon-9pm Sun.) delivers to Wallace Falls State Park.

Directions

From Seattle, drive north on I-5 to exit 194 toward Snohomish and Wenatchee. Merge onto U.S. Highway 2 East and drive 1.9 miles, bearing right at the split in the highway to continue on U.S. Highway 2 East to Gold Bar.

From Bellevue or the east side of Lake Washington, drive north on I-405 to exit 23 for State Route 522 East toward Woodinville. Drive 12.7 miles on State Route 522 East, taking the exit for U.S. Highway 2 East toward Wenatchee. Merge onto U.S. Highway 2 East in Monroe, continuing 13 miles to Gold Bar.

Once in Gold Bar, look for a brown sign for Wallace Falls State Park on the right. In 0.25 mile, turn left onto 1st Street. Drive for 0.3 mile then turn right onto 1st Avenue West. Continue driving 1 mile as the road becomes May Creek Road and then Ley Road. Bear left at Camp Huston and follow the sign for Wallace Falls State Park to the parking lot. Restrooms are in the parking lot, and there is a composting toilet near the intersection of the Greg Ball Trail and Woody Trail. **GPS Coordinates:** 47.867062, -121.678457 / N47° 52.016' W121° 40.659'

3 BLANCA LAKE

Mount Baker-Snoqualmie National Forest, Henry
M. Jackson Wilderness, Skykomish

🦌 🌸 🐕

Best: Strenuous

Distance: 11.8 miles round-trip

Duration: 7 hours

Elevation Change: 3,900 feet

Effort: Strenuous

Trail: Dirt path, sections of rocks and roots

Users: Hikers, leashed dogs

Season: July-October

Passes/Fees: Northwest Forest Pass

Maps: Green Trails Map 143 for Monte Cristo, USGS topographic map for Blanca Lake

Contact: Mount Baker-Snoqualmie National Forest, Skykomish Ranger District, www.fs.usda.gov

---

This challenging hike climbs to a picturesque basin anchored by the stunning turquoise-green waters of Blanca Lake.

Nestled in a rugged basin between Mountain Loop Highway to the north and U.S. Highway 2 to the south lies Blanca Lake. The lake's stunning color and picturesque lake basin, combined with healthy word-of-mouth, means this trail sees a heavy stream of hiker traffic despite the challenging, strenuous climb. Visit during the week if you can, or head out early on the weekend to get a jump start on the boisterous crowds that gather at the lake on summer weekends. Please treat the trail with care and observe posted signs; the trail has taken a beating over the years and could use a little TLC.

While Blanca Lake is typically a 7.6-mile round-trip hike, the temporary closure of Forest Road 63 adds an extra 4.2 miles round-trip to the original hike distance. Forest Road 63 is scheduled to reopen in 2018.

Start the Hike

Start your hike from the intersection of Forest Roads 63 and 65, skirting a gate to head northeast on Forest Road 63. The wide gravel road offers a gentle ascent

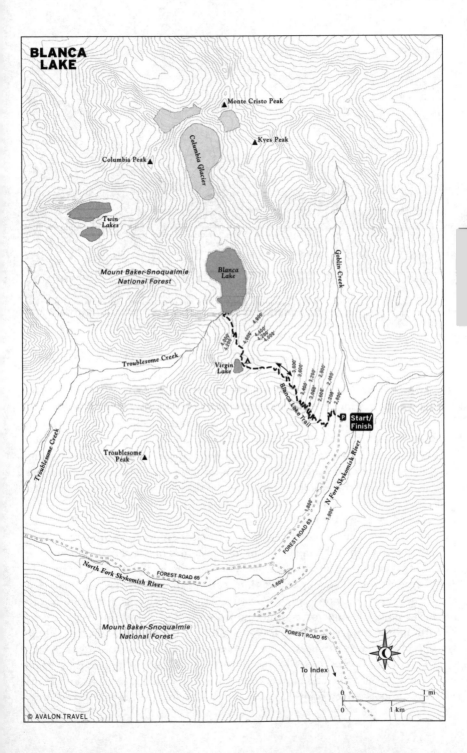

looking north over Blanca Lake toward Columbia Glacier

with easy-to-follow paths around the damaged portions of the road. In 2 miles, veer left at a split in the road and follow the sign for Blanca Lake to the trailhead.

Arriving at the trailhead for **Blanca Lake Trail,** stop at the information kiosk and fill out a registration card. Set out on the dirt path into a shady forest of Douglas fir, hemlock, and cedar. After a brief, flat section, the trail climbs northwest up a steep series of switchbacks, gaining more than 1,500 feet in the next 1.7 miles. While the trail is easy to follow, there are lots of exposed rocks and roots flowing in and out of the path that, in addition to the challenging grade, can make progress a bit slow. Take breaks, stopping to enjoy the thick conifers, and keep your eyes peeled for pinecone scales that litter the forest floor—signs that they have been ransacked by Douglas squirrels.

The trail straightens out but continues its relentless grade, gaining more than 1,000 feet in the next 1.1 miles. Thankfully, plentiful huckleberry shrubs line the trail as you continue toward the ridge, offering a sweet treat when they ripen in mid-August. Reach a rocky **overlook** toward the top of the ridge and marvel at Glacier Peak to the northeast, visible on a clear day. After catching your breath and snapping a few photos, continue northwest on the rocky trail.

Round the border of **Virgin Lake,** admiring the tree-lined reflection along its perimeter, and descend a sharp 600 feet in 0.75 mile to Blanca Lake. Take care on this section of the trail—the sharp, rocky pathway is notorious for being slick and slippery when it's raining. Arriving at Blanca Lake, pause to admire the bright turquoise-green color that seems to glow against the rugged, mottled-gray backdrop of Columbia Peak, Monte Cristo Peak, and Kyes Peak to the north. Spot Columbia Glacier resting in a shallow pocket between Columbia Peak and Monte Cristo Peak, its meltwaters carrying fine sediment into Blanca Lake, which creates the turquoise-green color. Take a seat on one of the pieces of driftwood and enjoy a break before heading back to the trailhead.

Get Away for the Weekend

Overnight at one of the campsites next to **Virgin Lake** or along the ridgeline. Campsites are first-come, first-served and there is no fee; just fill out a self-issue permit at the trailhead. Campfires are permitted in established campfire rings only. Pit toilets are available at Virgin Lake and Blanca Lake. Camping is closed within 200 feet of the shoreline of Blanca Lake (including all former campsites at the lake) to help restore the area.

Directions

From Seattle, drive north on I-5 to exit 194 toward Snohomish and Wenatchee. Merge onto U.S. Highway 2 East and drive 1.9 miles, bearing right at the split in the highway to continue on U.S. Highway 2 East to Skykomish.

From Bellevue or the east side of Lake Washington, drive north on I-405 to exit 23 for State Route 522 East toward Woodinville. Drive 12.7 miles on State Route 522 East, then take the exit for U.S. Highway 2 East toward Wenatchee. Merge onto U.S. Highway 2 East in Monroe and continue 34 miles to Skykomish.

Pass milepost 49 on U.S. Highway 2 and in 0.4 mile turn left onto Beckler Road. Drive 6.9 miles (the pavement ends at 6.8 miles) to arrive at an intersection. Stay straight onto Forest Road 65 and drive 5.6 miles. At a five-way intersection, take the second road on the left to stay on Forest Road 65 toward Forest Road 63/ Blanca Lake. Drive 2.2 miles to Forest Road 63.

As of 2016, **Forest Road 63 is closed** due to washouts. Until it reopens in 2018, park at the junction of Forest Roads 63 and 65 and hike 2.1 miles on Forest Road 63 to the trailhead. Display your Northwest Forest Pass in your vehicle before you head out; even though you are parked along the road, this is a temporary trailhead and cars not displaying the pass will be ticketed. The vault toilet at the original trailhead will be locked and closed, so plan to use the portable toilet at the temporary trailhead.

GPS Coordinates: 47.890480, -121.332247 / N47° 53.431' W121° 19.939'

4 LAKE SERENE

Mount Baker-Snoqualmie National Forest, Index

Best: Lakes, Waterfalls

Distance: 8.2 miles round-trip

Duration: 4 hours

Elevation Change: 2,350 feet

Effort: Moderate

Trail: Dirt paths, rocky stretches, wooden stairs

Users: Hikers, leashed dogs

Season: May-October

Passes/Fees: Northwest Forest Pass

Maps: Green Trails Map 142 for Index, USGS topographic map for Index

Contact: Skykomish Ranger District, www.fs.usda.gov

A rocky, yet rewarding hike to a stunning lake with a side trip to a powerful, veiled waterfall.

Nestled in the shadow of Mount Index, Lake Serene is a beautiful, tranquil day hike with the two-for-one option of seeing Bridal Veil Falls. The trail is not quite as easy as its name suggests—the second half of the trail is steep and often jumbled with rocks. Still, its high scenic value and the easy 60-mile drive from Seattle make it a very popular hike.

To snag a parking spot, plan to arrive at the trailhead by 8am on a weekend—earlier in the summer high season. Prepare for a misty shower at Bridal Veil Falls and bring a rain jacket or poncho and a plastic bag for your camera or pack to keep items dry.

Fall is a beautiful time to hike this trail; as the leaves turn, their colors mellow into dusky green, marigold, and auburn hues. In the winter months, the trail is often covered in snow, ice, and water. Check trail conditions before planning a winter trip.

Start the Hike

From the **Lake Serene Trailhead** next to the parking lot, ascend 600 feet in 1.7 miles to a junction for Bridal Veil Falls. The first half of the hike is a gentle warm-up on a wide dirt and gravel trail, a former logging road. Tall red alder, western

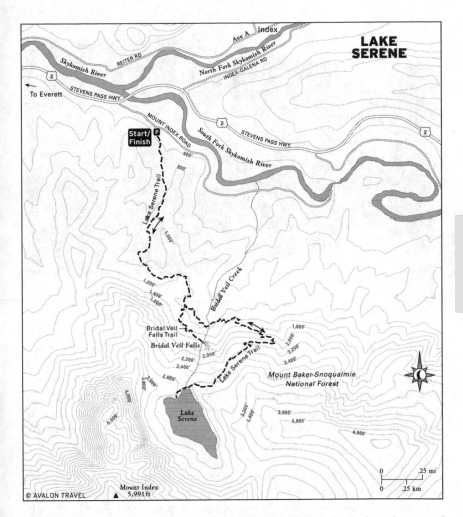

hemlock, and bigleaf maple line the trail, which is filled with a lush understory of sword fern, lady fern, vine maple, salmonberry, and the occasional elderberry. In spring, purple bleeding heart, white, three-petaled trillium, and the crinkly white flowers of thimbleberry shrubs offer pops of color along with leafy greenery. After 1.3 miles, listen for the whooshing sounds of Bridal Veil Falls in the distance and catch a glimpse of the falls in another 0.25 mile.

Arriving at the signed junction for **Bridal Veil Falls,** bear right on the 0.5-mile spur trail to the falls. The moderately steep trail gains 350 feet in 0.5 mile up a series of wooden stairways and rocky paths. View the raging, misty falls from behind a wooden fence (those wet rocks are slippery) and enjoy scenic vistas of Skykomish Valley and Heybrook Mountain to the northeast.

reflections in Lake Serene

Return to the trail junction for **Lake Serene** and hike east, wending your way southwest over the next 1.9 miles to climb 1,300 feet to the lake. After crossing a wooden bridge over Bridal Veil Creek you'll pass a sheer rock face with several small, miniature cascading waterfalls. Past the falls a rocky path awaits—a careful climb that alternates between steep, ladderlike staircases and rubbly, rock-strewn trail. Still, there are neat facets to this trail as mossy boulders, thick Douglas fir and Sitka spruce, and deep-green, elongated deer fern spill from the mountainside. Emerge onto an exposed slope after 1.1 miles with views across the Skykomish Valley and a peek at the South Fork Skykomish River below. In 0.4 mile, pass a signed trail to a pit toilet and continue southwest to the lake.

Arrive at Lake Serene at 4.6 miles. Cross the one-armed pedestrian bridge over Bridal Veil Creek and follow the sign for Lunch Rock. A small bench on the left offers a nice respite, but stay on the trail heading west to Lunch Rock, a smooth, wide boulder that slopes somewhat steeply toward the lake. Break here before heading back, and enjoy the calm, peaceful waters of Lake Serene and the cathedral-like peaks of Mount Index reflected below. While a restoration effort is under way at Lake Serene, camping and campfires are not permitted within 0.25 mile of the lake.

Shorten the Hike

Skip the hike to Bridal Veil Falls and stick to **Lake Serene** for a 7.2-mile round-trip hike (4 hours) with a 2,000-foot elevation gain. Too steep? Then take the trail to Bridal Veil Falls instead for a 4.4-mile round-trip hike (2.5 hours) with only a 950-foot elevation gain.

Directions

From Seattle, drive north on I-5 to exit 194 toward Snohomish and Wenatchee. Merge onto U.S. Highway 2 East and drive 1.9 miles, bearing right at the split in the highway to continue on U.S. Highway 2 East past Sultan and Gold Bar.

From Bellevue or the east side of Lake Washington, drive north on I-405 to exit 23 for State Route 522 East toward Woodinville. Drive 12.7 miles on State Route 522 East, taking the exit for U.S. Highway 2 East toward Wenatchee. Merge onto U.S. Highway 2 East in Monroe, continuing past Sultan and Gold Bar.

Drive past milepost 35 and turn right onto Mount Index Road in 0.1 mile. Continue 0.2 mile then bear right at a

Bridal Veil Falls

Y-junction to reach the parking area. Two ADA-accessible restrooms are located next to the parking lot and a pit toilet is near the lake.

GPS Coordinates: 47.809254, -121.573998 / N47° 48.546' W121° 34.443'

5 HEYBROOK LOOKOUT

Mount Baker-Snoqualmie National Forest, Index

Best: Mountain Views

Distance: 2.1 miles round-trip

Duration: 1.5 hours

Elevation Change: 980 feet

Effort: Moderate

Trail: Dirt paths, wooden stairs

Users: Hikers, leashed dogs

Season: March-November

Passes/Fees: None

Maps: Green Trails Map 142 for Index, Green Trails Map 176S for Alpine Lakes West-Stevens Pass, USGS topographic map for Index

Contact: Mount Baker-Snoqualmie National Forest, Skykomish Ranger District, www.fs.usda.gov

---

A short, sharp hike to a former fire lookout rewards with fantastic views of the central Cascades.

Heybrook Lookout is a great hike for active kids, out-of-town visitors up for a challenge, and family members looking for a short day hike with fantastic views. Don't let the short distance fool you, though; the quick elevation gain will get your heart pumping. The hike is also a great option to add onto shorter hikes along U.S. Highway 2 (such as Bridal Veil Falls).

Start the Hike
From the west side of the parking area, look for an information kiosk and start hiking east on the **Heybrook Lookout Trail.** The dirt and gravel trail is steep at times—gaining more than 800 feet as you hike northeast. At least it's shady with moss-draped trees, a second-growth forest that has flourished since a clear-cut in the 1920s. The easy-to-follow trail is rough in spots with several rocky and root-strewn stretches. Take mini-breaks as needed.

Arrive at the bottom of the **lookout** in about 1 mile. While you can rest at the picnic table here, fantastic views await above. Climb seven flights of stairs to enjoy

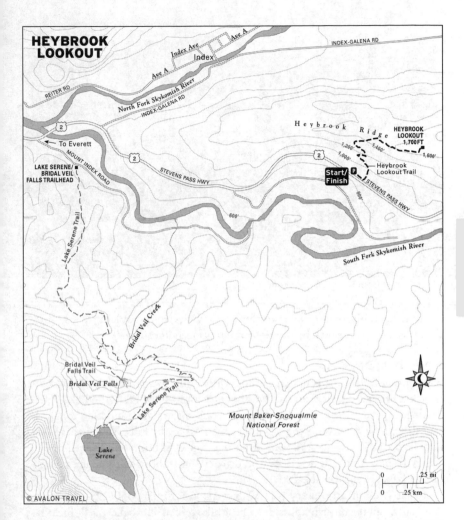

magnificent views across the valley of Mount Persis, Mount Index, and Bridal Veil Falls to the southwest and Philadelphia Mountain to the south.

The lookout hut atop the 70-foot tower was built by the Everett Mountaineers Lookout and Trail Maintenance Committee. The eight-year restoration project was completed in 2002 and involved tearing down the old hut, constructing a new one in the Skykomish Ranger Station's parking lot, and then transporting the pieces to the site. The pieces were hefted up the tower and reassembled. Contact **Everett Mountaineers** (www.everettmountaineers.org) for more information and to learn about volunteering for lookout and trail maintenance projects. The lookout is for day-use only; overnight camping is not permitted.

Mount Index from Heybrook Lookout

The lookout is usually locked, so take in your views from the platform just below, then fuel up with a snack before returning to the trailhead.

Make It a Day Trip

Bag another trail while you're in the area with a hike to nearby **Bridal Veil Falls** (4.4 miles round-trip, 2.5 hours, 950-foot elevation gain). From the Lake Serene Trailhead, hike 1.7 miles on Lake Serene Trail to the signed junction for Bridal Veil Falls. Bear right onto the 0.5-mile spur trail to the falls. To get there from the Heybrook Lookout Trailhead, drive west on U.S. Highway 2 for 2.4 miles. Turn left onto Mount Index Road and drive 0.2 mile, bearing right at a junction for the Lake Serene Trailhead.

Stop at **The Sultan Bakery** (711 W. Stevens Ave., Sultan, 360/793-7996, 6am-7pm daily, call to confirm hours) for a post-hike refuel. The bakery sells breakfast sandwiches, soups, burgers, and wraps in addition to cookies, bars, pies, and éclairs. Take your sandwich to go or enjoy lunch in their friendly seating area.

Directions

From Seattle, drive north on I-5 to exit 194 toward Snohomish and Wenatchee. Merge onto U.S. Highway 2 East and drive 1.9 miles, bearing right at the split to continue on U.S. Highway 2 East past Index.

From Bellevue or the east side of Lake Washington, drive north on I-405 to exit 23 for State Route 522 East toward Woodinville. Head 12.7 miles on State Route 522 East, taking the exit for U.S. Highway 2 East toward Wenatchee. Merge onto U.S. Highway 2 East in Monroe, continuing past Index.

After passing Index and milepost 37, turn left in 0.5 mile to park in the parking area on the north side of the highway past the Mount Baker-Snoqualmie National Forest sign.

GPS Coordinates: 47.808314, -121.535085 / N47° 48.502' W121° 32.108'

Heybrook Lookout

6 BARCLAY LAKE

Mount Baker-Snoqualmie National Forest, Baring

🦌 🌿 🐕 👫

Distance: 4.3 miles round-trip

Duration: 2.5 hours

Elevation Change: 300 feet

Effort: Easy

Trail: Dirt path, wooden bridge

Users: Hikers, leashed dogs

Season: April-November

Passes/Fees: Northwest Forest Pass

Maps: Green Trails Map 143 for Monte Cristo, Green Trails Map 176S for Alpine Lakes West/Stevens Pass, USGS topographic map for Baring

Contact: Mount Baker-Snoqualmie National Forest, Skykomish Ranger District, www.fs.usda.gov

---

An easy, rolling hike to the north shore of Barclay Lake includes scenic views of Baring Mountain.

Barclay Lake is a great choice for children, beginning hikers, first-time backpackers, and anglers. The modest dirt path to the lake is easy to follow, with several campsites available along the lake's north shore. Due to the trail's popularity, visit in late spring or early fall, or try to come midweek in summer.

Start the Hike

Start your hike from the parking lot by following the **Trail** sign. In 200 feet descend into a partially canopied forest to arrive at the information kiosk for Barclay Lake. Fill out the register with your hiking information, then continue heading southeast on a narrow dirt path for 1.1 miles. Enjoy the quiet, roomy forest of western hemlock, Douglas fir, and red alder carpeted with a lush understory of deer fern, lady fern, and red elderberry. Unique wooden planks begin to appear on either side of the trail, guiding you past a couple of small creeks with mini-waterfalls to a bridge over Barclay Creek.

Cross the long, one-armed **wooden bridge** over the gurgling creek and hike 0.5 mile southeast to the lake. Bleeding heart, trillium, salmonberry, and yellow violet pop up along the trail in spring. Cross a shallow, uneven talus slope before

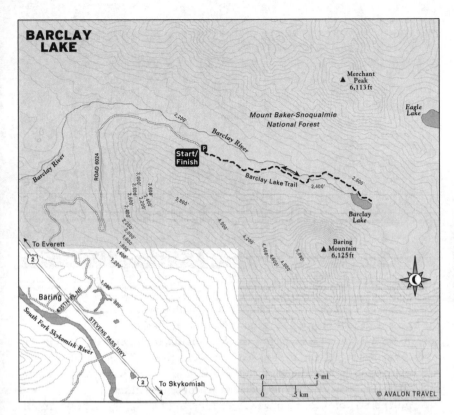

descending 40 feet to the western edge of Barclay Lake. The clear, elongated lake is dominated by proud, imposing Baring Mountain to the southwest.

Hike along the north rim of the lake for 0.5 mile, passing several small campsite clearings and little alcoves with tiny beaches—great spots for a break. Anglers can stop here to fish for rainbow trout before heading back to the trailhead.

Get Away for the Weekend

Spend the night at one of several established campsites along the north shore of Barclay Lake. The **first-come, first-served campsites** are open year-round; however, the trail is usually only accessible April-November. Campsites tend to fill quickly on summer weekends; arrive early, camp during the week, or come in the late spring or early fall to secure a spot. Two small spur trails (signed Toilet) near the campsites lead to pit toilets.

Directions

From Seattle, drive north on I-5 to exit 194 toward Snohomish and Wenatchee.

bridge crossing at Barclay Creek

Merge onto U.S. Highway 2 East and drive 1.9 miles, bearing right at the split in the highway to continue on U.S. Highway 2 East to Baring.

From Bellevue or the east side of Lake Washington, drive north on I-405 to exit 23 for State Route 522 East toward Woodinville. Drive 12.7 miles on State Route 522 East, taking the exit for U.S. Highway 2 East toward Wenatchee. Merge onto U.S. Highway 2 East in Monroe and drive 27 miles to Baring.

At milepost 41 on U.S. Highway 2, an Entering Baring sign appears. In 0.1 mile, turn left onto 635th Place NE. Drive over the train tracks and continue straight on the narrow, gravel road. In 0.2 mile, bear left as the road turns into Forest Road 6024. Drive 4 miles to the trailhead (watch out for potholes). A vault toilet is at the trailhead.

GPS Coordinates: 47.792527, -121.459296 / N47° 47.540' W121° 27.547'

7 BECKLER PEAK

Mount-Baker Snoqualmie National Forest, Skykomish

Distance: 7.7 miles round-trip

Duration: 4 hours

Elevation Change: 2,300 feet

Effort: Moderate

Trail: Dirt path

Users: Hikers, leashed dogs

Season: Late June-October

Passes/Fees: None

Maps: Green Trails Map 175 for Skykomish, Green Trails Map 176S for Alpine Lakes West-Stevens Pass, USGS topographic map for Skykomish

Contact: Mount Baker-Snoqualmie National Forest, Skykomish Ranger District, www.fs.usda.gov

---

A straightforward and steadily graded trail through a diverse forest leads to expansive, 360-degree mountain views at the summit.

Challenging, yet not too difficult, Beckler Peak Trail is a great middle-of-the-road hike to mountain and valley views. With a consistent grade and doable mileage, this is a great one to keep in your back pocket and use as a "bridge hike" for more challenging 3,000- and 4,000-foot elevation gains.

The memorial trailhead is named in honor of Jennifer Dunn, a prominent Republican in Washington State. Dunn was the first woman to chair Washington State's Republican Party in 1981, and she served in the U.S. House of Representatives 1993-2005, cosponsoring the bill that created the Wild Sky Wilderness that borders Beckler Peak Trail to the north. Dunn passed away in 2007 after decades of service.

Start the Hike

From the parking lot, head north on the **Beckler Peak Trail,** a former logging road. The trail is clear and easy to follow, passing several pretty streams and mini-waterfalls under a canopy of hemlock, alder, maple, and cottonwood. Pretty red columbine, lavender bleeding heart, and whisker-like petals of youth-on-age line the trail in spring. Carefully cross a washout at 0.6 mile; the trail drops abruptly

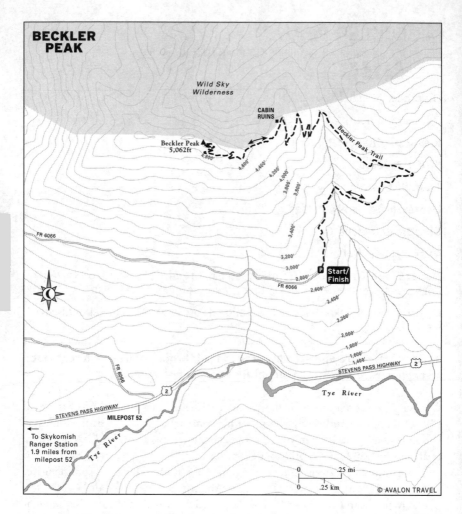

down a couple of feet to a stream, and you may need to use your hands or trekking poles to cross to the other side.

Follow the trail as it veers west for 1.25 miles, gaining 300 feet over the next 0.5 mile. At a break in the trees, look south to see the peaks in the Alpine Lakes Wilderness. Past this **viewpoint,** the trail's grade gentles out through tall, beautiful stands of Douglas fir and hemlock. The next 2 miles offer teasing views of the rising mountains as you switchback up on a clear dirt path. Just below the summit, ascend a stone staircase that leads to a rocky outcropping with views northeast—a preview of the summit views to come.

Arrive at **East Becker Peak** at 3.8 miles, a small, rocky outcropping with 360-degree views. From the east summit, take in the view of West Becker Peak,

West Beckler Peak from East Beckler Peak

Baring Mountain, Mount Index, and Eagle Rock to the west, Glacier Peak to the north, Mount Fernow to the east, and the peaks of the Alpine Lakes Wilderness to the south. The Tye River and the town of Skykomish are visible to the southwest—you may even see mountain goats roaming the rocky terrain. Take care as you enjoy the summit; the north side of the small, rocky summit drops off steeply.

Hike Nearby

Just 4 miles east on U.S. Highway 2 is **Deception Falls Picnic Area,** home to a pretty, moss-draped hike with wonderful viewpoints of Deception Creek, Deception Falls, and the Tye River. The 0.5-mile loop trail is partially ADA accessible. To get there, head east on U.S. Highway 2 from Forest Road 6066. Pass milepost 56 and in 0.6 mile turn left into the signed parking area. No parking pass is required, leashed dogs are allowed, and there are vault toilets next to the parking lot.

Directions

From Seattle, drive north on I-5 to exit 194 toward Snohomish and Wenatchee. Merge onto U.S. Highway 2 East and drive 1.9 miles, bearing right at the split in the highway to continue on U.S. Highway 2 East and continue 34 miles to Skykomish.

From Bellevue or the east side of Lake Washington, drive north on I-405 to exit 23 for State Route 522 East toward Woodinville. Drive 12.7 miles on State Route 522 East and take the exit for U.S. Highway 2 East toward Wenatchee. Merge onto U.S. Highway 2 East in Monroe and continue 34 miles to Skykomish.

Just east of milepost 52, turn left onto Forest Road 6066 at an unmarked opening in the guardrails. Drive 1.9 miles on the dirt and potholed road to a Y-junction.

Bear right uphill and continue on Forest Road 6066 for 4.8 miles to the Jennifer Dunn Trailhead. The narrow road makes it challenging to pass other vehicles, and its steep edges can erode—please drive carefully. An ADA-accessible vault toilet is available at the trailhead.

GPS Coordinates: 47.724096, -121.266838 / N47° 43.464' W121° 15.995'

8 JOHNSON RIDGE-SCORPION MOUNTAIN

Mount Baker-Snoqualmie National Forest,
Wild Sky Wilderness, Skykomish

Best: Berry Picking

Distance: 7.8 miles round-trip

Duration: 5.5 hours

Elevation Change: 2,600 feet

Effort: Moderate/strenuous

Trail: Dirt and gravel paths

Users: Hikers, leashed dogs

Season: Late June-October

Passes/Fees: None

Maps: Green Trails Map 143 for Monte Cristo, Green Trails Map 144 for Benchmark Mountain, Green Trails Map 176S for Alpine Lakes West, USGS topographic maps for Evergreen Mountain and Captain Point

Contact: Mount Baker-Snoqualmie National Forest, Skykomish Ranger District, www.fs.usda.gov

---

This undulating ridgeline hike leads through forest to magnificent views with an option to visit Joan Lake.

Johnson Ridge Trail tours a shady ridgeline with panoramic mountain views from Scorpion Mountain. This trail has a kind of camel hump in the middle—Sunrise Mountain—that you'll have to ascend on the way back. Summer is a great time to visit, when the fields around Scorpion Mountain burst with wildflowers and berries ripe for picking. Bring plenty of water; while the hike is mostly shaded, there are no water sources on the trail until Joan Lake (a 0.4-mile, 400-foot descent beyond Scorpion Mountain). Bug spray will come in handy too—as insects can be persistent in the summer.

Start the Hike

From the parking area, follow **Johnson Ridge Trail 1067** east on the narrow, rocky path. The trail gets down to business straightaway, gaining more than 600 feet in the first 0.75 mile. Take small breaks at the mini-landings to catch your breath and enjoy the forest's pointy edges of Sitka alder leaves, J-shaped needles of noble fir, and mouse tail-like prongs sticking out from Douglas fir cones. Once

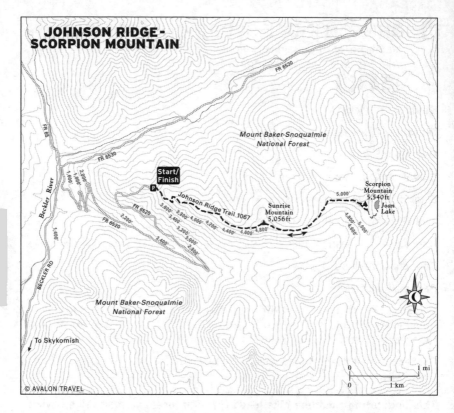

JOHNSON RIDGE-SCORPION MOUNTAIN

you've conquered this steep section, the trail gentles out into a pleasant, sun-dappled forest of tall hemlock painted in light green lichen. Pass the Wild Sky Wilderness boundary at 1.3 miles, enjoying the blueberry and huckleberry shrubs that line the trail—a sweet treat when they ripen in summer.

Soon you'll arrive at the camel hump—**Sunrise Mountain.** Sharply climb 330 feet to the summit (2.1 miles) then descend the other side as you continue east along the trail. The views from the rocky and exposed forest opening are modest, but on a clear day you can spot the pointed outline of Sloan Peak as well as Glacier Peak to the north. When you're ready to press on, follow the trail as it descends steeply along the ridge.

After a brief break in the grade, begin your final ascent, gaining a steep 800 feet to Scorpion Mountain. Enjoy the magnificent mountain views to the north and south as the forest gives way to an open, exposed ridgeline with fields of wildflowers on the slope in summer. At 3.8 miles, bear left at a **junction** to reach the summit of Scorpion Mountain, or bear right and follow the trail as it descends an open meadow to the southeast. The trails reconnect to make a loop, so either direction works—but the left route is the most direct way to the summit.

Columbia Peak, Kyes Peak, Sloan Peak, and Glacier Peak from the Johnson Ridge Trail

Follow the trail through forest as it ascends the summit of **Scorpion Mountain** at 3.9 miles. The panoramic views are breathtaking—Columbia Peak, Kyes Peak, Sloan Peak, and Glacier Peak to the north, Mount Howard and Rock Mountain to the east, Sherpa Peak and Mount Stuart to the southeast, and Mount Daniel, Mount Hinman, and Mount Fernow to the south. Enjoy a break, along with the views, on one of the shallow rocks. Turn around here or descend 0.1 mile to view Joan Lake before looping to the west to return to the trailhead.

Extend the Hike

Visit pretty **Joan Lake** for an extra 0.8-mile round-trip. From the summit of Scorpion Mountain, follow the trail east as it descends 400 feet in 0.4 mile to the lake below. Did you bring your fishing rod? According to the Department of Fish and Wildlife, the lake contains eastern brook trout 6-8 inches in size. Consider casting around for a bite.

Directions

From Seattle, drive north on I-5 to exit 194 toward Snohomish and Wenatchee. Merge onto U.S. Highway 2 East and drive 1.9 miles, bearing right at the split in the highway to continue on U.S. Highway 2 East to Skykomish.

From Bellevue or the east side of Lake Washington, drive north on I-405 to exit 23 for State Route 522 East toward Woodinville. Drive 12.7 miles on State Route 522 East and take the exit for U.S. Highway 2 East toward Wenatchee. Merge onto U.S. Highway 2 East in Monroe, continuing 34 miles to Skykomish.

After passing milepost 49, turn left onto Beckler Road in 0.4 mile. Drive 6.9 miles (the pavement ends at 6.8 miles) and arrive at a three-way intersection. Make a sharp right (as if you're making a U-turn) onto Forest Road 6520. Drive 2.6 miles then bear left at a Y-junction to stay on Forest Road 6520. Drive 4.1 miles to the end of the road and the trailhead. A small parking area has room for about six cars. There are no toilet facilities.

GPS Coordinates: 47.796561, -121.262586 / N47° 47.470' W121° 11.811'

9 WEST FORK FOSS LAKES

Mount Baker-Snoqualmie National Forest,
Alpine Lakes Wilderness, Skykomish

Distance: 3.4-14.8 miles round-trip

Duration: 2-10 hours

Elevation Change: 500-3,960 feet

Effort: Easy-strenuous

Trail: Dirt and gravel paths, uneven rocky stretches, wooden bridges

Users: Hikers, leashed dogs

Season: July-October

Passes/Fees: Northwest Forest Pass

Maps: Green Trails Map 175 for Skykomish, Green Trails Map 176S for Alpine Lakes West, USGS topographic maps for Skykomish and Big Snow Mountain

Contact: Mount Baker-Snoqualmie National Forest, Skykomish Ranger District, www.fs.usda.gov

---

Hike to a series of serene, high-elevation lakes set within the rugged, picturesque Alpine Lakes Wilderness.

A collection of five high-elevation lakes in the Alpine Lakes Wilderness provide ample opportunities to mix and match a variety of hiking and backpacking destinations. In addition to the spectacular scenery, this hike boasts views of the rolling West Fork River Valley and nearby peaks, waterfalls, stands of old-growth forest, and plentiful berry picking in summer. Unsurprisingly, the hike and campgrounds are popular on summer weekends, and parking can fill quickly at the trailhead. For a quieter outing, arrive early or visit during the week.

Start the Hike

At the trailhead kiosk next to the parking lot, fill out a free permit for the Alpine Lakes Wilderness and read through the trail information. When ready, head southwest on a gravel path under the lush, partially shaded canopy of hemlock, maple, and cedar. Passing a sign for the Alpine Lakes Wilderness, enjoy the pleasant walk past salmonberry shrubs, moss-covered rocks, and nurse logs teeming with plant life. At 0.9 mile, cross a narrow but sturdy wooden bridge over the **West Fork Foss River.** A gigantic tree shortly appears—marvel at the impressive size and try to wrap your arms around its mammoth diameter before pressing on.

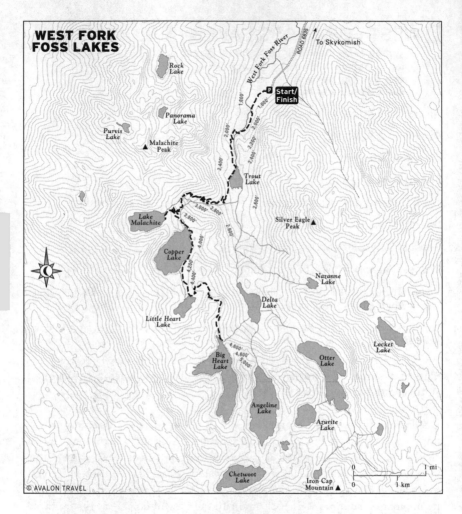

A trailside kiosk announces your arrival to **Trout Lake** at 1.7 mile. The kiosk includes a helpful map of campsite locations near the lake, and a signed day-use area offers a great option for a lakeside break. If your destination lies farther ahead, press on, weaving in and out of a shrubby understory of vine maple and thimbleberry. The trail is rough, steep, and uneven as you continue southwest, gaining a thigh-burning 1,900 feet in the next 2.3 miles. Take small breaks and enjoy views of a large waterfall to the south and Silver Eagle Peak across the valley to the east, and listen for the "eep! eep!" squeaks from pikas darting in and out of rocky crevasses.

At a signed junction for Copper Lake and Malachite Lake at 3.9 miles, bear right for a worthy side trip to **Malachite Lake** (4.1 miles). The 0.4-mile round-trip trail

Copper Lake

climbs steeply up a rough stretch of boulders and may be difficult for children. Your efforts are rewarded, however, with views of the translucent, blue-green lake set in the shadow of a steep cirque. Explore for a bit, then head back to the trail junction with Copper Lake and follow the sign toward the lake. The creek-side views keep you company, and the plentiful blueberries and huckleberries lining the trail provide a delicious snack in August.

Bear left to cross an outlet on a makeshift rock bridge, emerging at the northern tip of **Copper Lake** at 4.6 miles. Pause for a moment to admire the lake's length in the glacially carved basin encircling its cobalt-blue waters. Continue hiking south along the eastern border of the lake for further trailside views, drinking in the quiet lapping sound of the shore. Pass a boulder field and continue to the southern end of the lake at 5.3 miles, a good turnaround point. Many folks choose to set up camp at one of the nearby sites and make a trip to Little Heart and Big Heart Lakes the next day.

Continuing on, leave Copper Lake and hike south through open forest for 0.6 mile to **Little Heart Lake** (5.9 miles). Take in the sights and sounds of the outlet as it flows north from Little Heart Lake to Copper Lake. Pass by Little Heart Lake (partially hidden behind trees along the trail) and weave east then south along the rough trail toward Big Heart Lake. Over the next mile, keep your eyes peeled for views of Glacier Peak to the north as you ascend 700 feet to the apex of your hike at 4,900 feet. You'll gradually descend 350 feet over the next 0.7 mile—elevation you'll have to gain on the way back—to arrive at the outlet of **Big Heart Lake** at 7.6 miles. Soak in the southward views of mountain ridges lining the lake and its coves before heading back to the trailhead or setting up camp.

Shorten the Hike
Customize this hike to suit your interests by visiting one or several of the lakes according to the round-trip mileage and elevation gain: Trout Lake (3.4 miles, 500 feet), Malachite Lake (8.2 miles, 2,500 feet), Copper Lake (8.4 miles, 2,500 feet), Little Heart Lake (11 miles, 2,750 feet), or Big Heart Lake (14.4 miles, 3,800 feet). The mileage and elevation for Copper Lake, Little Heart Lake, and Big Heart Lake does not include the side trip to Malachite Lake, which adds an additional 0.4 mile round-trip and 160 feet of elevation gain.

Get Away for the Weekend
Several established **campsites** near the lakes offer the opportunity to extend your time in the Alpine Lakes Wilderness. Campsites are first-come, first-served, and campfires are not allowed. Fill out an Alpine Lakes Wilderness permit at the trailhead and observe Leave No Trace principles during your stay.

Directions
From Seattle, drive north on I-5 to exit 194 toward Snohomish and Wenatchee. Merge onto U.S. Highway 2 East and drive 1.9 miles, bearing right at the split in the highway to continue on U.S. Highway 2 East to Skykomish.

From Bellevue or the east side of Lake Washington, drive north on I-405 to exit 23 for State Route 522 East toward Woodinville. Drive 12.7 miles on State Route 522 East, then take the exit for U.S. Highway 2 East toward Wenatchee. Merge onto U.S. Highway 2 East in Monroe and continue 34 miles to Skykomish.

At 0.5 mile past milepost 50 and the Skykomish Ranger Station, turn right onto Foss River Road. In 1.1 miles, bear right to stay on the main road and follow signs for Forest Road 68. Drive 3.6 miles, passing the Necklace Valley Trailhead, and turn left at the signs for Forest Road 6835 and West Fork Foss Trail No. 1064. Drive 1.8 miles on Forest Road 6835 to the parking area. An ADA-accessible vault toilet is available next to the trailhead.

GPS Coordinates: 47.634819, -121.303902 / N47° 38.078' W121° 18.233'

10 LAKE DOROTHY
Mount Baker-Snoqualmie National Forest, Skykomish

Best: Berry Picking

Distance: 3.3 miles round-trip

Duration: 2 hours

Elevation Change: 850 feet

Effort: Easy/moderate

Trail: Rocky, dirt paths, wooden steps and bridges

Users: Hikers, leashed dogs

Season: June-October

Passes/Fees: Northwest Forest Pass

Maps: Green Trails Map 175 for Skykomish, Green Trails Map 176S for Alpine Lakes Wilderness-Stevens Pass, USGS topographic map for Snoqualmie Lake

Contact: Mount Baker-Snoqualmie National Forest, Skykomish Ranger District, www.fs.usda.gov

---

Hike to a large, scenic lake in the Alpine Lakes Wilderness and explore additional lakes along the trail.

This pleasant forest hike leads to an expansive view of tree-ringed Lake Dorothy and its surrounding cliffs. It's a great choice for berry picking, fishing, and camping, with the option to continue to Bear Lake, Deer Lake, and Snoqualmie Lake. Get an early start if you plan to camp at Lake Dorothy in summer—the campsites here are popular and fill quickly.

Exploring beyond Lake Dorothy requires crossing a wide inlet at the lake's south end. High water levels are common in spring; bring hiking poles to help wade across or wait until summer when the water recedes.

Start the Hike
From the parking lot, head south on the **Lake Dorothy Trail.** (If hiking May 15-Nov. 15, fill out an Alpine Lakes Wilderness permit and review trail updates on the kiosk.) The dirt trail beckons past shady cedar and hemlock lush with pockets of deer fern, vanilla leaf, and little Oregon beaked moss. Listen for the sound of the East Fork Miller River flowing below to the southwest as you climb shallow wooden stairs and passageways. At a wide wooden bridge in 0.75 mile, enjoy the

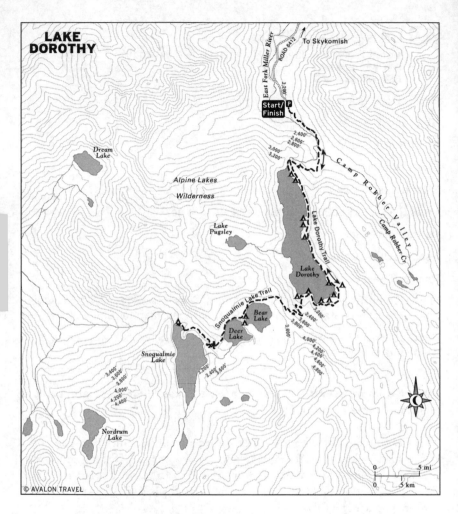

sight of Camp Robber Creek rushing in waterfall-like rapids over large rock slabs; the creek eventually merges with the East Fork Miller River downstream.

Continue south past the bridge on a series of wooden stairs, steps, and boardwalks, gaining a heart-pounding 500 feet in the next 0.8 mile to **Lake Dorothy.** Plentiful blueberries line the trail and make a great snack when they ripen in mid-August. Arrive at a signed junction for the **Outlet Spur** at 1.55 miles, where a helpful map with campsite and toilet locations around Lake Dorothy is usually posted. Stay straight to explore the 0.2-mile round-trip spur trail, which leads to beautiful views south down the length of the lake. Snap a few photos and enjoy a snack or lunch break before heading back to the trailhead. If you have your fishing rod, try catching cutthroat trout from the lakeside alcoves.

Lake Dorothy

Extend the Hike

Hiking along the east edge of **Lake Dorothy** adds another 4 miles round-trip to the trek. The trail leads to an inlet with scenic viewpoints of the islands in the lake. There are campsites near the lake, but the trail stays perched above it. The trail becomes rough and rocky as you make your way to the south end of the lake and the inlet crossing (7.3 miles round-trip). From the inlet, it's another 2 miles to **Bear Lake** (11.3 miles round-trip), a lovely destination for a longer hike. The trail climbs about 800 feet in elevation, then drops 200 feet to the lake.

Deer Lake (12.1 miles round-trip) sits just 0.4 mile beyond Bear Lake. If you're feeling hardy, descend 500 feet in 1.3 miles from Deer Lake to **Snoqualmie Lake** (14.7 miles round-trip), where a campsite and a small, sandy beach sit on the north end of the lake.

Get Away for the Weekend

Campsites at Lake Dorothy, Bear Lake, Deer Lake, and Snoqualmie Lake provide time to explore this series of lakes. All campsites are first-come, first-served. Campfires are not allowed at Lake Dorothy (camp stoves are okay), but are permitted in established campfire rings at Bear Lake, Deer Lake, and Snoqualmie Lake.

Directions

From Seattle, drive north on I-5 to exit 194 toward Snohomish and Wenatchee.

Merge onto U.S. Highway 2 East and drive 1.9 miles, bearing right at the split in the highway to continue on U.S. Highway 2 East past Index and Baring.

From Bellevue or the east side of Lake Washington, drive north on I-405 to exit 23 for State Route 522 East toward Woodinville. Drive 12.7 miles on State Route 522 East and take the exit for U.S. Highway 2 East toward Wenatchee. Merge onto U.S. Highway 2 East in Monroe and continue east for 31 miles past Index and Baring.

Once you've passed Index and Baring, look for milepost 45. In 0.8 mile, turn right onto Old Cascade Highway (signed for Money Creek Campground). Continue past a Road Closed sign. Drive south for 0.9 mile, following the road as it veers left past train tracks. Turn right onto Miller River Road (the road turns into Forest Rd. 6412) and drive 9.1 miles to the parking area at the end. The pavement ends in 0.1 mile, becoming a gravel surface with some potholes for the rest of the drive. An ADA-accessible vault toilet is available at the trailhead.

GPS Coordinates: 47.608880, -121.386113 / N47° 36.527' W121° 23.165'

11 WELLINGTON GHOST TOWN-WINDY POINT

Mount Baker-Snoqualmie National Forest, Stevens Pass

Best: Historical

Distance: 5.6 miles round-trip

Duration: 3 hours

Elevation Change: 300 feet

Effort: Easy

Trail: Dirt and crushed-gravel paths, wooden bridges

Users: Hikers, leashed dogs

Season: July-October

Passes/Fees: Northwest Forest Pass

Maps: Green Trails Map 176 for Stevens Pass, Green Trails Map 176S for Alpine Lakes West-Stevens Pass, USGS topographic map for Scenic

Contact: Mount Baker-Snoqualmie National Forest, Skykomish Ranger District, www.fs.usda.gov

---

This gentle hike passes a concrete snowshed and tunnel-ghosts of the Great Northern Railway that once trundled through Windy Mountain.

The Wellington Ghost Town, located at Stevens Pass, provides an extraordinary look back at the worst avalanche disaster in the history of the United States. Spooky snowsheds, railroad artifacts, and interpretive signs bring to life the story of the March 1, 1910, disaster in which two Great Northern Railway trains—stranded in severe snowstorms—were swept down Windy Mountain in an early morning avalanche.

Wellington sits on the eastern end of the Iron Goat Trail, a path that retraces the original 1893-1929 route of the Great Northern Railway on Windy Mountain. While two other trailheads access the Iron Goat Trail, the Wellington trailhead provides a family-friendly and partially ADA-accessible option with quiet surroundings and helpful interpretive signs. It also offers the chance to walk through a 0.5-mile-long concrete snowshed—a spooky, visceral experience that drives home the history of the Great Northern Railway at the turn of the 20th century. The Wellington trailhead typically melts out later than the other trailheads; check road conditions online if you're looking to visit earlier in the season.

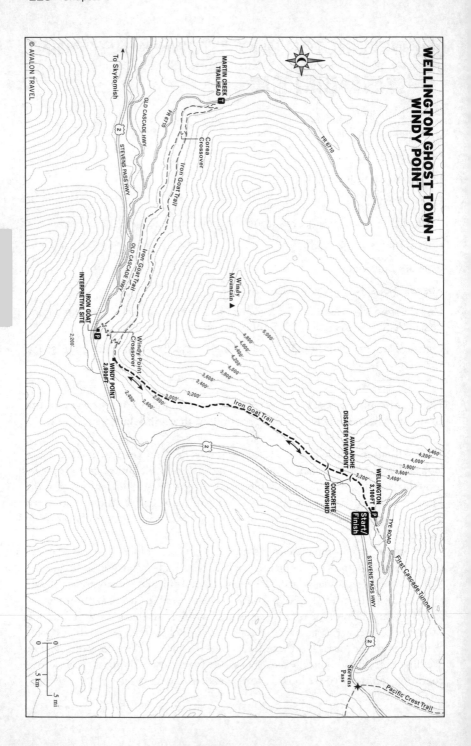

WELLINGTON GHOST TOWN - WINDY POINT

To Skykomish

MARTIN CREEK TRAILHEAD

FR 6710

OLD CASCADE HWY

STEVENS PASS HWY

Corea Crossover

Iron Goat Trail

FR 6710

© AVALON TRAVEL

IRON GOAT INTERPRETIVE SITE

Iron Goat Trail

OLD CASCADE HWY

Windy Mountain ▲

5,000'
4,800'
4,600'
4,400'
4,200'
4,000'
3,800'
3,600'
3,400'
3,200'
3,000'
2,800'
2,600'
2,400'

WINDY POINT 2,800FT

Windy Point Crossover

Iron Goat Trail

2,200'

AVALANCHE DISASTER VIEWPOINT

CONCRETE SNOWSHED

WELLINGTON 3,100FT

Start/Finish

TYE ROAD

STEVENS PASS HWY

First Cascade Tunnel

4,400'
4,200'
4,000'
3,900'
3,600'
3,400'
3,200'

Stevens Pass

Pacific Crest Trail

0 — 5 km
0 — .5 mi

a concrete snowshed built in 1911

Start the Hike

From the parking lot, turn right at the information kiosk onto the **Iron Goat Trail** and head toward the all-concrete snowshed. The trail descends gently as you hike to Windy Point, so expect a slight uphill incline on your return to the trailhead. The informative interpretive signs at the start of the trail provide the background on the railroad activity in Wellington. After crossing a wooden bridge, enter the towering, 0.5-mile-long concrete snowshed, built in 1911 after the Wellington disaster. Are you spooked yet? I was!

About halfway through the tunnel, look for a wooden walkway on the left that leads to the **Avalanche Disaster Viewpoint** at 0.3 mile. Interpretive panels illustrate the timeline of events leading to the avalanche, and nearby benches provide an opportunity for a short rest. When ready, continue on the trail southwest through the concrete snowshed to emerge onto a dirt pathway lined with brushy wildflowers in summer. At 0.65 mile, the trail narrows and may be difficult for those with strollers or wheelchairs. Turn around here for a 1.3-mile round-trip hike or continue southwest another 2.1 miles to Windy Point.

Continuing southwest on the **Iron Goat Trail,** pass a white post marked 1712 at 1.2 miles. Located throughout the trail, these tall mileposts are replicas of those used by the Great Northern Railway to indicate the railroad mileage from St. Paul, Minnesota (Great Northern's headquarters) to the marked point. Beyond the milepost is a pretty waterfall and plentiful thimbleberry shrubs. Arrive at the Windy Point Tunnel at 2.75 miles and peek inside to read the interpretive sign tucked in its damp, tomb-like belly. When finished, follow the narrow concrete walkway beside the tunnel to the overlook.

Windy Point Overlook, at 2.8 miles, is a nice spot for a rest and a snack. Level, rocky patches offer a great perch for views of Cowboy Mountain to the northeast, Spark Plug Mountain to the south, and the Second Cascade Tunnel in the valley below. About 250 feet west of the overlook is a signed spur trail to a pit toilet overlooking the valley. To return to the trailhead, turn around and gradually ascend the trail.

Shorten the Hike

To visit **Wellington Ghost Town,** hike to the end of the concrete snowshed and back for a 1.3-mile round-trip trek (1 hour).

Extend the Hike

Visit the **First Cascade Tunnel** to add 0.5 mile round-trip to your hike. From the information kiosk in the parking lot, head left toward the gravel path. Explore the footings of the former coal tower, the remains of a work pit used by rail mechanics, and the First Cascade Tunnel, closed to hikers as of the writing of this book.

Hike Nearby

The **Iron Goat Interpretive Site,** located about 7 miles west of Stevens Pass, offers great hiking options. At the trailhead is historical information about the Iron Goat Trail, suggested hiking routes, and a red caboose that was built in 1951 in St. Cloud, Minnesota. Follow the signs to the Twin Tunnels for a 2.5-mile round-trip hike (1.5 hours), or make a clockwise loop past the Twin Tunnels for a 5.6-mile round-trip hike (3 hours).

To follow the loop hike, head west from the Iron Goat Interpretive Site on the lower grade toward the Martin Creek Trailhead. In 2.2 miles, turn right at the signed Corea Crossover, heading north for 0.2 mile. At the top of the crossover, turn right onto the upper grade for 2.5 miles and head east. Turn right at the Windy Point Crossover to descend a steep 0.7 mile back to the Iron Goat Interpretive Site.

To get to Iron Goat Interpretive Site, take U.S. Highway 2 East past milepost 58 and, in 0.2 mile, turn left for the Iron Goat Interpretive Site. Bear right into the parking area. No parking pass is required, leashed dogs are allowed, and there are ADA-accessible vault toilets next to the information kiosks. The site is generally open May-early November, depending on weather conditions. The trailhead doubles as a rest stop for tourists, so parking may be limited in high season.
GPS Coordinates: 47.711354, -121.161789 / N47° 42.690' W121° 09.707'

Directions

From Seattle, drive north on I-5 to exit 194 toward Snohomish and Wenatchee.

Merge onto U.S. Highway 2 East and drive 1.9 miles, bearing right at the split in the highway to continue on U.S. Highway 2 East to Stevens Pass.

From Bellevue or the east side of Lake Washington, drive north on I-405 to exit 23 for State Route 522 East toward Woodinville. Drive 12.7 miles on State Route 522 East, then take the exit for U.S. Highway 2 East toward Wenatchee. Merge onto U.S. Highway 2 East in Monroe, continuing 50 miles to Stevens Pass.

Pass milepost 64 on U.S. Highway 2 and look for unmarked Tye Road on the north side of the highway in 0.3 mile (but do not turn, as visibility is limited). Continue to Stevens Pass and use one of the parking areas there to turn around, now heading west on U.S. Highway 2. In 0.2 mile, make a sharp right onto unsigned Tye Road, which is located beneath a speed limit sign. Drive 2.8 miles on the rough gravel road and watch for potholes. Turn right onto an unpaved road with a stop sign and drive 0.3 mile. Bear left into the parking area. ADA-accessible parking is available, and two ADA-accessible vault toilets are next to the parking area.

GPS Coordinates: 47.747252, -121.127309 / N47° 44.829' W121° 07.660'

12 LAKE VALHALLA

Okanogan-Wenatchee National Forest,
Henry M. Jackson Wilderness, Stevens Pass

Best: Off the Beaten Path, Lakes

Distance: 6.5 miles round-trip

Duration: 3.5 hours

Elevation Change: 1,400 feet

Effort: Moderate

Trail: Dirt paths

Users: Hikers, horses, leashed dogs

Season: Mid-June-October

Passes/Fees: None

Maps: Green Trails Map 144 for Benchmark Mountain, Green Trails Map 176S for Alpine Lakes West-Stevens Pass, USGS topographic map for Labyrinth Mountain

Contact: Okanogan-Wenatchee National Forest, Wenatchee River Ranger District, www.fs.usda.gov

---

Hike to the quietly lapping shores of Lake Valhalla with an optional side trip to stunning views from Mount McCausland.

Just east of Stevens Pass, Lake Valhalla packs the one-two punch of an alpine lake with a side trip to a bird's-eye view of the lake from above. Visit the trail in summer for ripe blueberries and huckleberries, or in fall for the exquisite foliage. Bring your bug spray in early summer to combat the mosquitoes and a light jacket to wear once you get to the lake. Sitting at over 4,000 feet, the lake can be breezy and cool even in the summer. For a quieter experience, arrive early on summer and early fall weekends—the trail is popular and sees steady hiker traffic.

Start the Hike

Start your hike from the parking lot, heading northwest on the **Smithbrook Trail** for 1.2 miles. The thick, shrubby forest is lined with Sitka mountain-ash, blueberry, and huckleberry shrubs, their blazing leaves a deep red, magenta, burnt orange, and ripe yellow in the fall. Listen for the sounds of Smith Brook trickling nearby as you wind north, entering the Henry M. Jackson Wilderness. While easy to follow, the trail can be rough, rocky, and muddy in some stretches;

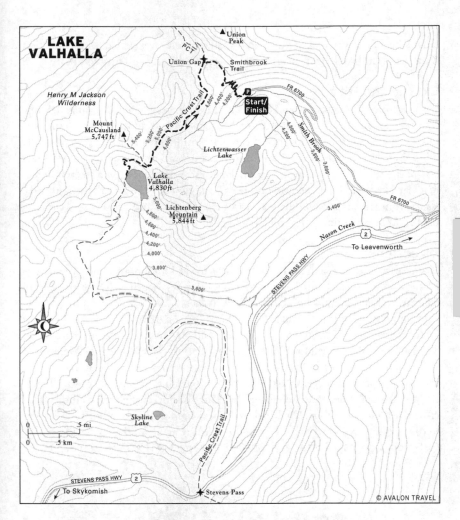

agile puddle-hopping skills will come in handy, as will shoes with good traction. Climb a moderate 625 feet as you switchback up the hillside to a junction with the Pacific Crest Trail (PCT).

Turn left at the Pacific Crest Trail—marked by a **Smithbrook Trail No. 1059** sign nailed to a tree—and continue southwest for 1.5 miles. The mild trail climbs gently, winding along a scenic hillside with views of Mount Lichtenberg across the valley to the south. Descend 275 feet in the last 0.5 mile to **Lake Valhalla,** peeking at the lake and the sandy beach on its northwest shore. Upon arrival at the lake basin head south, passing a signed spur trail to a pit toilet and campsites, and make your way down to the beach. Take a seat on one of the beached logs and gaze at the sheer face of Lichtenberg Mountain to the southwest rising above the quiet lake. When you're ready to head back, keep your eyes peeled for the junction with the Smithbrook Trail that returns to the trailhead—it's easy to miss.

Extend the Hike

For stunning views above Lake Valhalla and Lichtenberg Mountain, hike 0.9 mile (round-trip) to the summit of Mount McCausland. It adds an extra half hour to your hike and is located right off the main trail. Following the Lake Valhalla hike, keep your eyes peeled for an unsigned spur trail to the right about 150 feet before the trail starts to descend to the lake. Hike northwest for a steep 620 feet to a flattened area near the top, and take your time to navigate the social trails. Aside from its stiff incline, the trail can be overgrown and brushy, so wear long pants and bring hiking poles to help you climb.

Directions

From Seattle, drive north on I-5 to exit 194 toward Snohomish and Wenatchee. Merge onto U.S. Highway 2 East and drive 1.9 miles, bearing right at the split to continue on U.S. Highway 2 East to Stevens Pass.

From Bellevue or the east side of Lake Washington, drive north on I-405 to exit 23 for State Route 522 East toward Woodinville. Drive 12.7 miles on State Route 522 East and take the exit for U.S. Highway 2 East toward Wenatchee. Merge onto U.S. Highway 2 East in Monroe and continue 50 miles to Stevens Pass.

Drive 4 miles past Stevens Pass, turning left into a highway divide toward Forest Road 6700/Smithbrook Road. After checking for oncoming westbound traffic, cross the highway onto Forest Road 6700/Smithbrook Road and drive 2.6 miles to the parking area on the left. No facilities are available at the trailhead.

GPS Coordinates: 47.802558, -121.076890 / N47° 48.137' W121° 04.633'

sandy views beyond Lake Valhalla to Lichtenberg Mountain

MOUNTAIN LOOP HIGHWAY

The official Mountain Loop Scenic Byway stretches

55 miles between the Snohomish towns of Granite Falls and Darrington. Hikes include old-growth forests and towering waterfalls, lakes enveloped in jagged mountain backdrops, and breathtaking 360-degree views. The highway cuts a narrow path between the peaks of the North Cascades as it winds east along the South Fork Stillaguamish River Valley and then north along the Sauk River Valley. The road passes distinctive mountains—Big Four, Sloan Peak, Vesper Peak, Mount Forgotten, Mount Pugh, and Whitehorse Mountain—each more than 6,000 feet in elevation. Southeast of the highway sits Glacier Peak, an active volcano named for the numerous glaciers covering its surface.

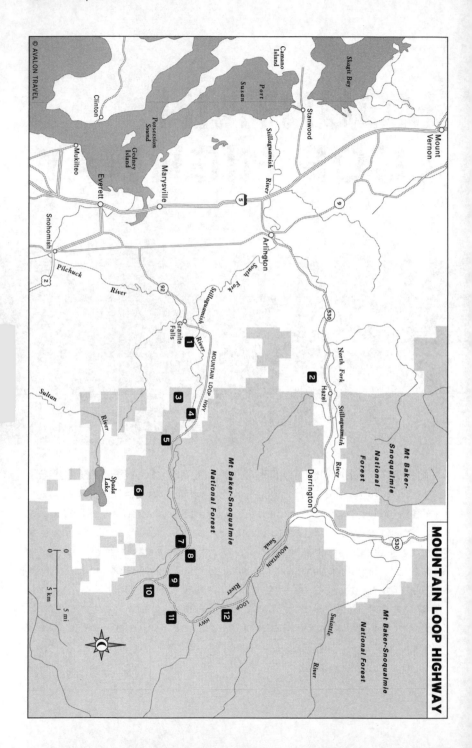

© AVALON TRAVEL

MOUNTAIN LOOP HIGHWAY

TRAIL NAME	LEVEL	DISTANCE	TIME	ELEVATION	PAGE
1 Lime Kiln Trail	Easy/moderate	5.1 mi	3 hr	400 ft	236
2 Boulder River	Easy/moderate	2.5-4.2 mi	1.5-2.5 hr	175-550 ft	240
3 Mount Pilchuck	Moderate	5.4 mi	3.5 hr	2,200 ft	243
4 Heather Lake	Easy/moderate	4.9 mi	3.5 hr	1,100 ft	247
5 Lake TwentyTwo	Moderate	6.2 mi	4 hr	1,500 ft	250
6 Cutthroat Lakes via Walt Bailey Trail	Moderate/strenuous	6.8 mi	6 hr	2,200 ft	254
7 Big Four Ice Caves	Easy	2.6 mi	1.5 hr	260 ft	258
8 Perry Creek Falls	Moderate	6.4 mi	4 hr	1,350 ft	262
9 Mount Dickerman	Strenuous	8.3 mi	7 hr	3,800 ft	266
10 Gothic Basin	Moderate/strenuous	9 mi	7 hr	3,000 ft	270
11 Goat Lake	Moderate	10.6 mi	5.5 hr	1,650 ft	274
12 Mount Pugh via Stujack Pass	Strenuous	9.2 mi	8 hr	3,800 ft	278

1 LIME KILN TRAIL
Robe Canyon Historic Park

Best: Historical

Distance: 5.1 miles round-trip

Duration: 3 hours

Elevation Change: 400 feet

Effort: Easy/moderate

Trail: Dirt paths, some rocky sections, wooden bridges

Users: Hikers, horses, mountain bikers, leashed dogs

Season: Year-round

Passes/Fees: None

Maps: Green Trails Map 109 for Granite Falls, USGS topographic map for Granite Falls

Contact: Snohomish County Parks and Recreation, www.snocoparks.org, 7am-dusk daily

---

This historic hike through a mossy forest leads to the site of a former railroad and a 100-year-old stone lime kiln.

Just east of Granite Falls, the Lime Kiln Trail makes for a quick getaway and a fascinating history lesson. Partial views of the South Fork Stillaguamish River, wooden bridges over rushing streams, and a pleasant, mossy forest complement the historic sites along the trail. Visit in the spring when the wildflowers are blooming, in summer to pick ripe blackberries, or in the fall when gold and auburn maple leaves warm the trail. This trail can get muddy, so bring shoes you don't mind getting dirty if you plan to hike in the rainy months.

Start the Hike
Start your hike from the **Robe Canyon Regional Park** sign located next to the parking lot. As you follow the wide, flat trail north, enjoy the mild path as it winds through mossy trees lit by a bright green understory of deer fern, lady fern, and sword fern. The trail undulates mildly for the first 0.6 mile, then steadily descends 340 feet to the former Everett to Monte Cristo railroad bed in Robe Canyon. Weathered, wooden signs are a frequent sight; they mark trail junctions

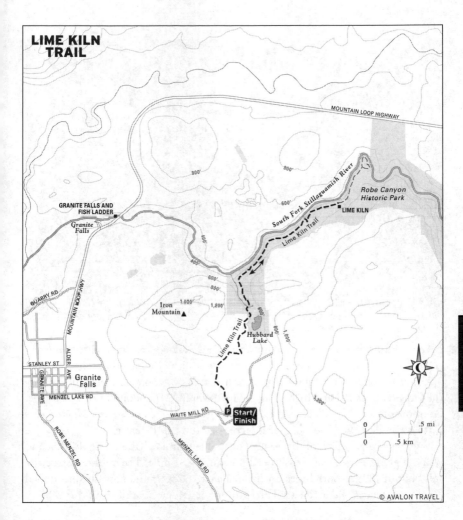

and historic places of interest along the way. Please follow the signs and stay on the trail, as it winds through private property along this stretch.

In 1.35 miles, turn left at a signed junction to continue north on the **Lime Kiln Trail.** Descend 0.2 mile to the former railroad bed, listening to the sounds of Hubbard Creek to the west and looking for bleeding heart and trillium in spring. A sign for the **Everett and Monte Cristo Railway Grade** marks the site of the former railway. It was completed in 1893 to transport gold and silver ore from the Monte Cristo mine to Everett. The decision to run the railroad through Robe Canyon was supported by financier John D. Rockefeller in order to make the railroad line cheaper—but it turned out to be a catastrophe. Almost as soon as the railroad was built, it was plagued by floods from the South Fork Stillaguamish River as well

The stalwart, mossy Lime Kiln stands beside the trail.

as rockslides along the steep canyon walls. Railroad workers were killed, railroad service was disrupted, and the tracks were periodically wiped out. After years of attempts to stabilize the railroad, it was ultimately abandoned in 1933, done in by the Great Depression and increasing competition from automobiles and roadways. For more on the railway's fascinating story, check out *The Everett and Monte Cristo Railway* by Phil Woodhouse, Daryl Jacobson, and Bill Petersen.

Enjoy peekaboo views of the South Fork Stillaguamish River along this flat and pleasant grade, arriving at the **Lime Kiln** in another 1 mile. The tall stone structure was built in 1899 to burn limestone from a nearby quarry and now sits surrounded by old saw blades and artifacts. Turn around here for a 5.1-mile round-trip hike.

Extend the Hike

Hike 0.75 mile northeast past the Lime Kiln to the short, 0.35-mile **River Shore Loop** and **Railroad Bridge Site** for a 6.8-mile round-trip hike (4 hours). While there isn't much remaining of the railroad bridge, it's neat to take a mental picture and then revisit the information kiosk at the trailhead (the side with the historical pictures) to see what the bridge over the South Fork Stillaguamish River looked like—right where you were just standing.

Make It a Day Trip

Stop to see the town's namesake waterfall: **Granite Falls.** From the intersection of Stanley Street and Alder Avenue, drive north on Alder Avenue for 1.3 miles.

Pull over into the dirt parking area on the left side of the road; look for a large wooden sign for the Granite Falls Fishway. Follow the steps down from the parking area and onto a gravel pathway, then turn right to descend the stairway to the fish ladder and waterfalls.

Looking for something more meditative? Visit the **Tsubaki Grand Shrine of America** (17720 Crooked Mile Rd., Granite Falls, 360/691-6389, www. tsubakishrine.org, 10am-4pm daily, free), a quiet Shinto shrine next to the Pilchuck River. Visitors can explore the peaceful grounds or sign up to take part in a Shinto ceremony (make an appointment ahead of time). From the intersection of Stanley Street and Alder Avenue, head west on Stanley Street. Pass through the town of Granite Falls and in 0.9 mile turn left onto Crooked Mile Road. The wooden gate entrance is 0.5 mile down the road on the left. Food and drink are not allowed, and pets are not permitted on the grounds.

Directions

From Seattle, take I-5 north to exit 194 for U.S. Highway 2 East toward Snohomish/Wenatchee. Drive 1.8 miles and then bear left, following the sign for State Route 204 East toward Lake Stevens. Merge onto State Route 204 East and drive 2.1 miles. Pass Vernon Road and turn left onto State Route 9 North. In 1.6 miles, turn right onto State Route 92 East toward Granite Falls. Drive 8.4 miles east to Granite Falls, staying straight through three traffic circles as the road transitions into 96th Street. Continue east through Granite Falls, arriving at an intersection with Stanley Street and Alder Avenue. Turn right onto Alder Avenue; at a stop sign in 0.2 mile, turn left onto Pioneer Street (Pioneer St. turns into Menzel Lake Rd.). In 0.9 mile, turn left onto Waite Mill Road signed for Lime Kiln Trailhead Parking. In 0.5 mile, bear left onto a gravel road signed for Lime Kiln Trail and follow the road to the parking area.

GPS Coordinates: 48.076813, -121.932039 / N48° 04.644' W121° 55.947'

2 BOULDER RIVER

Mount Baker-Snoqualmie National Forest, Boulder River Wilderness

Best: Waterfalls

Distance: 2.5-4.2 miles round-trip

Duration: 1.5-2.5 hours

Elevation Change: 175-550 feet

Effort: Easy/moderate

Trail: Dirt paths with rocky sections, log bridge crossings

Users: Hikers, leashed dogs

Season: March-November

Passes/Fees: None

Maps: Green Trails Map 111SX for Mountain Loop Highway, USGS topographic maps for Mount Higgins and Meadow Mountain

Contact: Mount Baker-Snoqualmie National Forest, Darrington Ranger District, www.fs.usda.gov

---

A family-friendly hike through an old-growth forest leads to a series of picturesque waterfalls along the Boulder River.

On upper Mountain Loop Highway, east of the town of Oso, the Boulder River Trail is a straightforward out-and-back hike to three waterfalls with peekaboo views of the rushing Boulder River. Hiking to the waterfalls makes for a family-friendly outing, or continue all the way to Boulder Ford Camp for waterside views.

Visit this trail in early spring, when water flows are strong from the snowmelt and wet weather. In winter, it may be possible to see the waterfalls frozen; call the ranger station beforehand as the road to the trailhead—and the trail itself—can become snowy, icy, and obstructed by blowdowns.

Start the Hike

From the parking lot, head south on the **Boulder River Trail** into the forest. The trail is wide and flat here, for good reason: This was the site of a former railroad used to harvest timber in the early 1900s. Enjoy the rushing sounds and peekaboo views of the Boulder River below and to the west as you hike among western redcedar, western hemlock, and Douglas fir. In 0.5 mile, listen as the rushing water

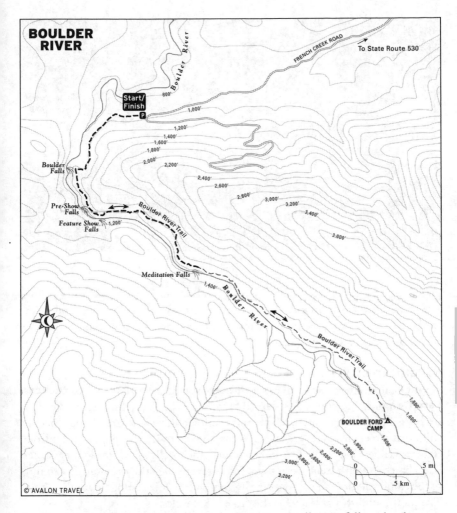

becomes more intense—the sound you hear is a small waterfall in the distance called Boulder Falls (unfortunately not visible from the trail).

In 1.2 miles, pause to admire a sinewy horsetail waterfall unofficially named **Pre-Show Falls,** your first waterfall along this route. Shortly after this stop is **Feature Show Falls,** arguably the showstopper of the hike with twin flows cascading 259 feet down a steep, rocky canyon into the Boulder River below. (For a shorter option, turn around here for a 2.5-mile round-trip hike with a 175-foot elevation change.)

Continue southeast on the trail, crossing a neat two-armed log bridge, and ascend a rubbly path through a gorgeous section of tall, imposing western redcedar scattered on either side of the trail. If it's sunny, the light will filter through the

approaching Feature Show Falls on the Boulder River Trail

green, mossy forest as you catch peeks of the Boulder River to the south below. Arriving at **Meditation Falls,** take a breather on one of the logs here and enjoy the last waterfall along the trail. Turn around here for a 4.2-mile round-trip hike with a 550-foot elevation change.

Extend the Hike

Continue hiking another 2 miles southeast beyond Meditation Falls to **Boulder Ford Camp,** a first-come, first-served campsite next to the Boulder River. The trail is generally rougher, narrower, and muddier along this stretch, but there is still plenty to enjoy. Deep-green deer ferns line the trail, with pops of color from trailing yellow violet and tufts of coltsfoot—their delicate white flowers cluster like a baseball atop a stout green stem. Cross several log bridges before descending to the camp and sit with your feet in the cool river before setting up for the night. The total round-trip mileage for this hike is 8.2 miles.

Directions

From Seattle, head north on I-5 to exit 208 for State Route 530 toward Arlington. At the end of the exit ramp, turn right onto State Route 530 and head east for 3.7 miles. Turn left onto State Route 9 North, then make a quick right to jump back onto State Route 530 East toward Darrington. Continue east on State Route 530 for 19.7 miles, passing the town of Oso. Turn right onto French Creek Road at milepost 41. Drive 3.7 miles to the trailhead. The road has several large potholes that are navigable at a slow speed. An ADA-accessible vault toilet is located 0.9 mile down French Creek Road, 2.8 miles from the trailhead.

GPS Coordinates: 48.250753, -121.814233 / N48° 15.050' W121° 49.009'

3 MOUNT PILCHUCK
Mount Baker-Snoqualmie National Forest, Mount Pilchuck State Park

Distance: 5.4 miles round-trip

Duration: 3.5 hours

Elevation Change: 2,200 feet

Effort: Moderate

Trail: Dirt paths, boulder fields

Users: Hikers, leashed dogs

Season: Late June-October

Passes/Fees: Northwest Forest Pass

Maps: Green Trails Map 109 for Granite Falls, Green Trails Map 111SX for Mountain Loop Highway, USGS topographic map for Verlot

Contact: Mount Baker-Snoqualmie National Forest, Darrington Ranger District, www.fs.usda.gov

Mount Pilchuck is a fun, yet challenging hike to a former fire lookout with magnificent views of several prominent peaks in the Cascades and Olympics.

Arrive early to get a jump start on the crowds—this is one of the most popular hikes in the Seattle area. While 5.4 miles doesn't seem very far, more than half the hike involves picking and scrambling your way up boulder fields—budget in some extra time to complete this hike. Snow can also linger on the mountain into summertime, making the boulders icy and slick. Use caution and check the trail conditions before you head out.

Start the Hike
From the parking lot, head south on **Mount Pilchuck Trail.** Bear right at a Y-junction (0.2 mile) to stay on the main path, hopscotching across Rotary Creek. The protective boughs of western hemlock, Pacific silver fir, and western redcedar reach over the trail above, while tiny, white-flowered foamflower and false lily-of-the-valley line the path. Listen for the sounds of Rotary Creek as you ascend several shallow, wooden staircases.

Arrive at a boulder field at 1.1 miles and turn left to follow the trail east. Take your time sighting the trail; orange markers are strategically placed to ease navigation, but watch for loose rocks below that can tweak an ankle. In 500 feet, bear a

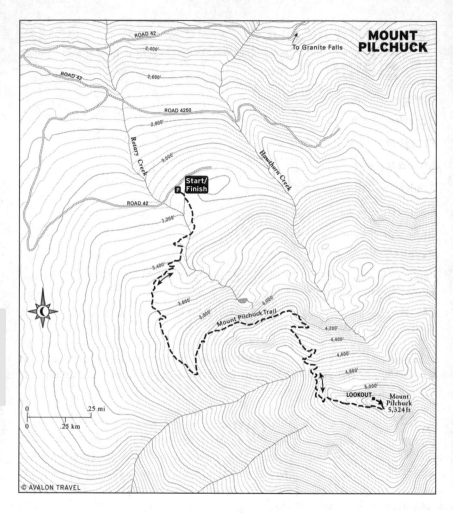

sharp right to climb an ambiguous rocky slope, picking up the trail as it continues east. Mount Baker, Whitehorse Mountain, and Three Fingers appear to the north. Soon you arrive at a large, north-facing meadow filled with boulders, mountain hemlock, and pink mountain-heather—a nice place for a snack or rest.

Hike southeast past the meadow, reaching the base of a short, steep pile of boulders at 2.7 miles that leads up to **Mount Pilchuck Lookout.** The last 70 feet to the lookout is a hand-over-hand scramble across steep boulders; take your time and climb carefully, continuing up the ladder to the lookout. Take in the magnificent 360-degree views of the Cascades, Olympics, and Puget Sound from the catwalk, spotting Mount Baker and Mount Shuksan to the north, Glacier Peak to

Mount Pilchuck Lookout sits high above the clouds.

the east, and Mount Rainier to the south. Inside the lookout, check out placards that identify more peaks in every direction and a photographic timeline of the lookout's construction and use. Rest and enjoy a snack or lunch before heading back to the trailhead.

Hike Nearby
Heather Lake is a 4.9-mile round-trip hike (3.5 hours) located off the same access road as Mount Pilchuck. The trailhead is well signed, and the hike is a nice alternative to Mount Pilchuck. *(See the Heather Lake hike in this chapter for more information.)*

Getaway for the Weekend
When not in use by a volunteer work party, the **Mount Pilchuck Lookout** is available for overnight stays on a first-come, first-served basis (free, open seasonally). Guests must bring their own sleeping bag, tent (in case the lookout is full), sleeping pad, food, and water; there is no running water and no toilet. A camp stove is permitted for outside use only. The lookout is notorious for having rodents; bring minimal food and keep any food you do bring in a tightly sealed container. You may also want to bring a hammock to sleep off the floor. The lookout relies on the honor system to stay clean, so please pack out all food and trash to keep it clean for the next visitor.

To confirm when a volunteer party is occupying the lookout, contact the **Everett Mountaineers** (www.everettmountaineers.org).

Directions

From Seattle, take I-5 north to exit 194 for U.S. Highway 2 East toward Snohomish/Wenatchee. Drive 1.8 miles and then bear left, following the sign for State Route 204 East toward Lake Stevens. Merge onto State Route 204 East and drive 2.1 miles, passing Vernon Road and turning left onto State Route 9 North. In 1.6 miles, turn right onto State Route 92 East toward Granite Falls. Drive 8.4 miles east to Granite Falls, staying straight through three traffic circles as the road transitions into 96th Street. Continue east through Granite Falls, arriving at an intersection with Stanley Street and Alder Avenue. Turn left onto Alder Avenue, following the road past a series of stop signs as it turns into the Mountain Loop Highway.

Mount Pilchuck Lookout

In 10.8 miles, pass the Verlot Public Service Center on the left. In another mile (just past the bridge over the South Fork Stillaguamish River), turn right at the sign for Mount Pilchuck Access Road onto Forest Road 42. In 0.1 mile, the pavement ends (the road can have significant potholes). Pass the Heather Lake Trailhead in another 1.2 mile. Continue 4.7 miles then bear left to stay on Forest Road 42. The trailhead and parking area appear in 2 miles. An ADA-accessible vault toilet is next to the trailhead.

GPS Coordinates: 48.070275, -121.814835 / N48° 04.208' W121° 48.888'

4 HEATHER LAKE

Mount Baker-Snoqualmie National Forest

Distance: 4.9 miles round-trip

Duration: 3.5 hours

Elevation Change: 1,100 feet

Effort: Easy/moderate

Trail: Dirt and gravel paths, rocky sections with exposed roots

Users: Hikers, leashed dogs

Season: May-October

Passes/Fees: Northwest Forest Pass

Maps: Green Trails Map 109 for Granite Falls, Green Trails Map 111SX for Mountain Loop Highway, USGS topographic map for Verlot

Contact: Mount Baker-Snoqualmie National Forest, Darrington Ranger District, www.fs.usda.gov

---

This short, yet rough trail leads to a picturesque lake basin that is partially encircled by the steep, rocky cliffs of Mount Pilchuck.

Heather Lake is a great option for when you have a few hikes under your belt and you're in the mood for a half-day hike to a lake. While short, the trail's roughshod tread of loose, uneven rocks, boulders, and thick, exposed roots carries on through substantial portions of the trail to the lake; wear sturdy shoes and bring hiking poles to help with balance. Even so, the trail is popular and parking can fill up quickly on sunny, summer weekends. Bring your bug spray and store any valuables out of sight in your locked vehicle.

Start the Hike

Start your hike on the **Heather Lake Trail** next to the parking area and ascend the dirt and gravel path lined with hemlock, cedar, and enormous nurse stumps. In 0.5 mile, descend 30 feet to a well-groomed gravel path under an airy tree canopy before reentering the forest on a rocky, pebbly trail. The uneven path seems keen to make you earn your views; take your time and stop for small breaks (especially with children). It's easy to lose your concentration and slip on the wet, slick rocks. One consolation to your rocky trek is the rushing and roaring sounds of Heather Creek to the west—although it's obscured by the forest, it's a welcome sound.

Break out of the forest at 2 miles and descend 35 feet to a Y-junction—the start

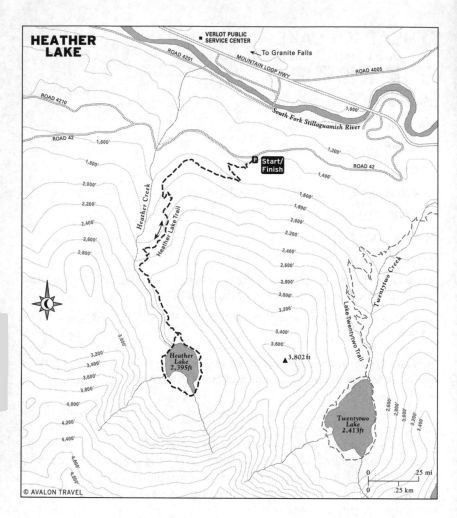

of a 0.9-mile loop around **Heather Lake.** It's your choice which way to go; I like heading left to start on the eastern side of the lake for the scenic views. Pass a couple of campsites and a spur trail to a pit toilet before emerging into the open-air lake basin. Walking on the wooden boardwalk that partially encircles the lake, enjoy the views of jagged, craggy peaks with rivulets of waterfalls flowing from the upper reaches. At the southern end of the lake, a field of boulders signals a resting place before finishing up your loop and heading back to the trailhead.

Make It a Day Trip
One mile west on the Mountain Loop Highway is the **Verlot Public Service Center** (33515 Mtn. Loop Hwy., Granite Falls, 360/691-7791, hours vary seasonally),

a great place to learn about local history and make a pre-hike rest stop. The service center was built in 1936-1938 by the Civilian Conservation Corps. It carries maps, books, and brochures and has separate rooms with historical exhibits. In the front office, friendly staff members are available to answer questions about trails, recreation, and weather. Clean restrooms are located next to the center, with occasional closures due to vandalism.

Directions

From Seattle, take I-5 north to exit 194 for U.S. Highway 2 East toward Snohomish/Wenatchee. Drive 1.8 miles and then bear left, following the sign for State Route 204 East toward Lake

jagged peaks at Heather Lake

Stevens. Merge onto State Route 204 East and drive 2.1 miles, passing Vernon Road and turning left onto State Route 9 North. In 1.6 miles, turn right onto State Route 92 East toward Granite Falls. Drive 8.4 miles east to Granite Falls, staying straight through three traffic circles as the road transitions into 96th Street. Continue east through Granite Falls, arriving at an intersection with Stanley Street and Alder Avenue. Turn left onto Alder Avenue and follow the road past a series of stop signs as it turns into the Mountain Loop Highway.

In 10.8 miles, pass the Verlot Public Service Center on your left. In another mile (just past the bridge over the South Fork Stillaguamish River), turn right onto Forest Road 42, signed for Mount Pilchuck Access Road. In 0.1 mile, the pavement ends. Follow the gravel, potholed road 1.2 miles to the signed trailhead on the left. An ADA-accessible vault toilet is next to the parking area.

GPS Coordinates: 48.082951, -121.773946 / N48° 04.966' W121° 46.436'

5 LAKE TWENTYTWO
Mount Baker-Snoqualmie National Forest

Best: Lakes

Distance: 6.2 miles round-trip

Duration: 4 hours

Elevation Change: 1,500 feet

Effort: Moderate

Trail: Dirt and gravel paths, shallow water crossings, wooden boardwalks

Users: Hikers, leashed dogs

Season: May-October

Passes/Fees: Northwest Forest Pass

Maps: Green Trails Map 109 for Granite Falls, Green Trails Map 110 for Silverton, Green Trails Map 111SX for Mountain Loop Highway, USGS topographic map for Verlot

Contact: Mount Baker-Snoqualmie National Forest, Darrington Ranger District, www.fs.usda.gov

---

Hike through a lush forest sprinkled with waterfalls to the dramatic setting of Lake Twentytwo.

The Lake Twentytwo Trail winds south along Twentytwo Creek to a lovely, clear lake set amid a glacially carved amphitheater. When the snow melts in the spring, hikers can follow the trail all the way around the lake for gorgeous views from different vantage points.

This trail is one of the most popular routes on the Mountain Loop Highway, and the parking lot fills quickly. Consider arriving by 7:30am on summer weekends or visiting during the week. Stow any valuables out of sight in your car and lock the vehicle.

Start the Hike
Start your hike at the **Lake Twentytwo Trail** sign next to the parking lot. Sign in at the trail register and begin hiking among old-growth stands of western hemlock and western redcedar that tower over lush pockets of deer fern and lady fern. The trail's tread alternates between dirt path, weathered wooden boardwalks, stretches of large, uneven rocks, wooden stairways, and shallow stream crossings

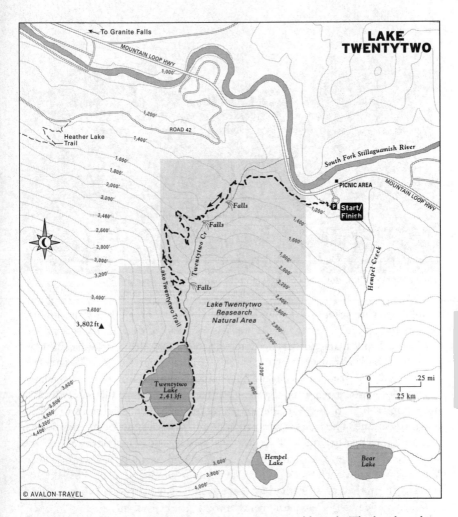

that can make for a wet, slippery, and sometimes muddy trek. The bright side to these trail conditions are the many water features along the way: pretty cascading waterfalls, the rushing, roaring sounds of Twentytwo Creek, and peekaboo views of the South Fork Stillaguamish River. In the spring, look for white, four-petaled flowers of western bunchberry popping up on tree trunks and along the ground throughout the trail.

In 0.6 mile, cross Twentytwo Creek on a sturdy **wooden bridge** and enjoy views of the modest waterfalls. Past the creek, ascend a set of shallow wooden staircases; more views of waterfalls appear from the trail. Soon you arrive at an open-air talus slope lined with pink-flowered salmonberry and crinkly, white-flowered

Wiry waterfalls flow down the craggy mountainside to Lake Twentytwo.

thimbleberry in spring. Pause to take in the views of Three Fingers and Liberty Mountain to the northeast—a scenic break as you pick your way up the rocky slope.

At the 2.5-mile mark, arrive at a T-intersection on a wooden boardwalk. Bear left to cross a wooden bridge and prepare for the dramatic sight of **Lake Twentytwo** surrounded by a steep, rocky cirque. Take a break along the east side of the lake.

In mid- to late spring, when the snow has receded, continue following the 1.2-mile loop around to the west side and enjoy the long, wiry waterfalls that flow down the cirque. The trail surface here alternates between wooden boardwalks, dirt and gravel paths, and rock fields; take care crossing the boardwalk on the southern side of the lake, as it can be damaged and partially sunken in places. When you're ready for a break, pick a rocky spot to sit on and relax. The lake and trail sit within the **Lake Twentytwo Research Natural Area,** a 790-acre swath of land set aside in 1947 to permanently protect the ecosystem.

Shorten the Hike
Skip the loop around the lake for a 5-mile round-trip hike (2.5 hours) to the lake and back. An even shorter option is the 1.2-mile round-trip hike to the **bridge** over Twentytwo Creek, with a nice view of shallow waterfalls from the bridge.

Directions
From Seattle, take I-5 north to exit 194 for U.S. Highway 2 East toward Snohomish/Wenatchee. Drive 1.8 miles and then bear left, following the sign for State Route 204 East toward Lake Stevens. Merge onto State Route 204 East and drive 2.1 miles, passing Vernon Road and turning left onto State Route 9 North. In 1.6

miles, turn right onto State Route 92 East toward Granite Falls. Drive 8.4 miles east to Granite Falls, staying straight through three traffic circles as the road transitions into 96th Street. Continue east through Granite Falls, arriving at an intersection with Stanley Street and Alder Avenue. Turn left onto Alder Avenue, following the road past a series of stop signs as it turns into the Mountain Loop Highway.

In 10.8 miles, pass the Verlot Public Service Center on the left. In 2 miles, turn right at the sign for Lake Twentytwo Trailhead and drive into the parking area. Two ADA-accessible vault toilets are located near the trailhead.

GPS Coordinates: 48.076917, -121.745926 / N48° 04.593' W121° 44.771'

6 CUTTHROAT LAKES VIA WALT BAILEY TRAIL

Mount Baker-Snoqualmie National Forest, Morning Star
Natural Resources Conservation Area (NRCA)

Best: Berry Picking

Distance: 6.8 miles round-trip

Duration: 6 hours

Elevation Change: 2,200 feet

Effort: Moderate/strenuous

Trail: Dirt and gravel paths, rocky and rooty stretches

Users: Hikers, leashed dogs

Season: July-October

Passes/Fees: Northwest Forest Pass

Maps: Green Trails Map 110 for Silverton, Green Trails Map 142 for Index, Green Trails Map 111SX for Mountain Loop Highway, USGS topographic maps for Mallardy Ridge and Wallace Lake

Contact: Mount Baker-Snoqualmie National Forest, Darrington Ranger District, www.fs.usda.gov

---

This challenging trek through meadows, creeks, tarns, and valleys rewards with the enchanting Cutthroat Lakes.

The Walt Bailey Trail to Cutthroat Lakes is located about 7 miles south of the Mountain Loop Highway on the northeastern side of Bald Mountain. This rough, challenging hike travels to the gorgeous Cutthroat Lakes basin. Numerous little lakes, carpets of blueberries, and backcountry campsites make this a fine day hike or weekend excursion. However, a patchwork of talus slopes, exposed roots, uneven rocks, and eroded ruts make the hiking slow going—budget extra time for this one. Ambiguous intersections and social trails are prevalent here; bring a map and compass to help get your bearings.

The trail is named in honor of Walt Bailey, an army veteran, volunteer firefighter, and member of the Civilian Conservation Corps, who championed the trail's construction. Bailey passed away in 2016 at the age of 96.

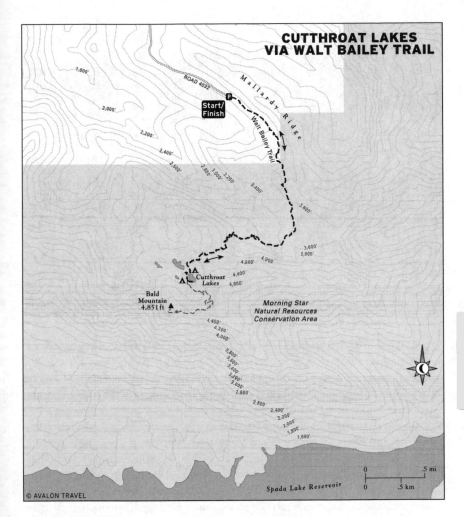

Start the Hike

From the parking lot, follow the **Walt Bailey Trail,** pausing at the Morning Star NRCA kiosk to check out the trail map. Head south on the dirt trail into the damp forest of western hemlock, Pacific silver fir, and maidenhair fern. In mid- to late August, plentiful blueberries and huckleberries linger over the trail—great for a quick energy boost. After ascending roughly 600 feet, the trail then descends into a scenic, open-air basin with meadows, creeks, and tarns at 1.5 miles. Follow the trail as it winds west, then stay straight through a talus slope to a dirt trail on the other side at 2 miles.

Hiking west on the trail, you'll gain a heart-pounding 230 feet over the next 0.3 mile. A brief, flat section offers a quick break and scenic forest views, followed

quiet lakeside views in the Cutthroat Lakes Basin

by the arrival of a second talus slope at 2.3 miles. Bear left, following **rock cairns** southwest up the slope to a rocky, defined trail just beyond. The next 0.6 mile is a steep 600-foot elevation gain through rocky passageways and wooden stairways. Take your time with your footing; it's easy to roll an ankle on the uneven rocks.

Cresting a ridge into the **Cutthroat Lakes basin** at 2.9 miles, follow the main trail around the north side of a large tarn. Head west for another 0.4 mile past lakes and tarns, and enjoy the view of Bald Mountain to the southwest, the carpets of blueberries flanking the trail, and the green, pastoral valley. Descend about 50 feet then bear left at a Y-junction heading south with a view of a lake straight ahead.

Arriving at an outlet of one of the larger **Cutthroat Lakes,** enjoy the view south along the lake's length and the reflections painting the perimeter. A maze of social trails can make it easy to get turned around. Stick to the wide, main trail and follow it south along the lake's western edge. At 3.4 miles, descend to a small peninsula jutting out into the lake, anchored by a lone mountain hemlock. This is a great spot for a snack or lunch before heading back to the trailhead.

Extend the Hike

The hike to **Bald Mountain** adds an extra 2.6 miles round-trip to the Cutthroat Lakes hike. From Cutthroat Lake, follow the main trail southeast; it will at first feel like you're hiking away from Bald Mountain. In about 0.6 mile, the trail winds west toward the mountain; bear right at a junction to hike downhill and stay on the trail. Continue hiking west under the peak and follow the trail as it switchbacks up the mountain. In 1.1 miles, cairns mark a turn-off to a boot path with plentiful boulders that are great for a rest. Soak in the views of Spada Lake Reservoir to the south and Culmback Dam to the southwest. The last part of the climb requires scrambling over steep boulders—best left to those with rock climbing experience.

Directions

From Seattle, take I-5 north to exit 194 for U.S. Highway 2 East toward Snohomish/Wenatchee. Drive 1.8 miles and then bear left, following the sign for State Route 204 East toward Lake Stevens. Merge onto State Route 204 East and drive 2.1 miles, passing Vernon Road and turning left onto State Route 9 North. In 1.6 miles, turn right onto State Route 92 East toward Granite Falls. Drive 8.4 miles east to Granite Falls, staying straight through three traffic circles as the road transitions into 96th Street. Continue east through Granite Falls, arriving at an intersection with Stanley Street and Alder Avenue. Turn left onto Alder Avenue, following the road past a series of stop signs as it turns into the Mountain Loop Highway.

In 10.8 miles, pass the Verlot Public Service Center on your left and, in another 7 miles, turn right onto Mallardy Road. Drive 1.3 miles, then turn right at a Y-junction, following the sign for Walt Bailey Trailhead onto Forest Road 4032. As of the writing of this book, in 2.7 miles there is a large tree angling across the road, which requires vehicles to drive in a rut on the side of the road to get around. Large trucks may find it difficult to pass under. The trailhead is another 2.9 miles beyond the tree and at the end of the road.

The small parking area only fits about four cars; park facing away from the trailhead for an easy exit. No facilities are available at the trailhead, so you may want to make a pit stop at the Verlot Public Service Center. Please practice Leave No Trace principles on the trail.

GPS Coordinates: 48.023901, -121.643752 / N48° 01.431' W121° 38.612'

7 BIG FOUR ICE CAVES

Mount Baker-Snoqualmie National Forest

Best: Easy Hikes

Distance: 2.6 miles round-trip

Duration: 1.5 hours

Elevation Change: 260 feet

Effort: Easy

Trail: Paved path, dirt and gravel, bridges and boardwalks

Users: Hikers, leashed dogs

Season: May-October

Passes/Fees: Northwest Forest Pass

Maps: Green Trails Map 110 for Silverton, Green Trails Map 111SX for Mountain Loop Highway, USGS topographic map for Silverton

Contact: Mount Baker-Snoqualmie National Forest, Darrington Ranger District, www.fs.usda.gov

---

A short but scenic hike to the ice caves at Big Four Mountain includes an option for picnicking nearby.

Nestled at the shady base of Big Four Mountain, the Big Four Ice Caves packs a scenic punch for such a short trail. Hikers of all abilities can enjoy up-close views of Big Four Mountain, colorful spring and summer wildflowers, flowing water-falls, and a fun crossing over the South Fork Stillaguamish River on a 224-foot aluminum bridge. The trail's short distance and easy tread make this a great option for families, as well as a quick add-on hike when tackling nearby trails along the Mountain Loop Highway.

Visit in summer when the snow caves have formed and the wildflowers are popping up, but try to time your trip during the week or get an early start on the weekend. The trail tends to get quite crowded on holidays and sunny weekends.

Though beautiful, the caves are part of an ever-changing environment that can be hazardous; please stay on the trail.

Start the Hike

Start your hike on the paved **Big Four Ice Caves Trail** located next to the information kiosk, taking a quick glance at the kiosk to learn about the trail system,

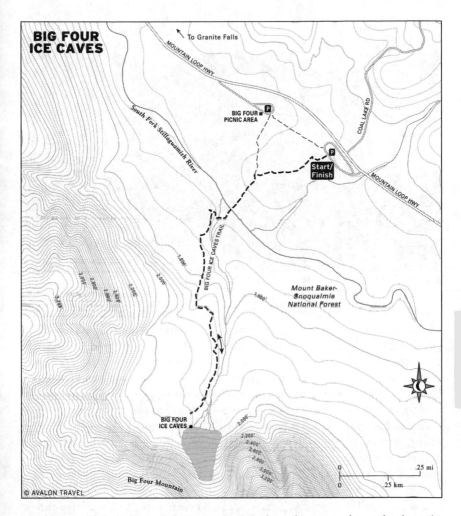

the history of the area, and the ice caves. Head southwest on the trail, where the partially shaded forest of western hemlock and Pacific silver fir leads through a wet marsh lined with yellow buttercup, delicate, fairylike foamflower, and stinky skunk cabbage in spring. In 0.3 mile, bear left at a signed T-junction toward the ice caves. (The trail to the right leads to a picnic area, a worthwhile detour for a snack or lunch on the return.)

In 0.1 mile, cross the 224-foot **aluminum bridge** over the South Fork Stillaguamish River. Look up to spot Big Four Mountain to the south and neighboring Hall Peak to the southwest. Past the bridge, enjoy sun-dappled forest views, cross wooden bridges, and listen to rushing creeks as you continue 0.9 mile on the dirt and gravel trail. Sturdy benches are available at regular intervals for a quick break.

trailside views of Big Four Mountain from the picnic area

Breaking out of the forest, the trail arrives at a **stone circle** 1.3 miles into the hike; this marks the end of the trail and your turnaround point. The grand, imposing sight of Big Four Mountain and Hall Peak are in front of you, waterfalls cascading down their steep faces to the **ice caves** below. The foundations for the caves begin in winter and spring when snow avalanches pile at the base of Big Four Mountain. Melting snow and warm air currents slowly penetrate the piled snow, causing openings—or caves—to form in mid- to late summer.

Please observe the ice caves from a safe distance, as they are unstable and typically melt and collapse in a seasonal cycle. (Since 1998, four people have been killed from falling snow and ice, the most recent in July 2015.) Signs highlight the potential for avalanches, falling rocks and chunks of ice, and holes and fissures in the snowfields, as well as collapsing caves. At the trail's end is a plaque honoring Grace Tam, an 11-year-old girl who was killed here in July 2010 by a large chunk of ice that fell from Big Four Mountain as she stood outside a cave.

Extend the Hike

Exploring the trail to the **Big Four Picnic Area** adds an extra 0.5 mile (about 30 minutes) to your hike. On your way back from the ice caves, stay straight at the T-junction and follow the sign toward the picnic area. Several picnic tables surround a large field, offering excellent views of Big Four Mountain. The stone chimney sitting next to the field was once part of the Big Four Inn, a popular resort that occupied this spot in 1921-1949. When ready, take the short scenic trail on the east side of the parking lot back to the main parking area.

Hike Nearby

Explore **Robe Canyon Historic Park** on a 2.3-mile round-trip trail, an easy 1.5-hour addition to the Big Four Ice Caves. The short, family-friendly trail descends 200 feet on a pleasant dirt path through the forest, emerging to up-close views of the South Fork Stillaguamish River and Robe Canyon. (Take care with young children, as there are some moderate drop-offs next to the trail.) At the end of the trail, walk along a short stretch of track from the ill-fated Everett and Monte Cristo Railway. Beyond this point the trail is blocked by a landslide—a reminder of the challenges the railway faced in its short lifetime.

To reach the trail from Granite Falls, start from the intersection of Alder Avenue and Mountain Loop Highway. Drive northeast on Mountain Loop Highway for 6.8 miles; look for a brick tombstone-like structure on the south side of the road signed Old Robe Trail. Pull over and park on the wide shoulder. The trail is open dawn-dusk; no pass or permit is required to park, and leashed dogs are allowed.

Directions

From Seattle, take I-5 north to exit 194 for U.S. Highway 2 East toward Snohomish/Wenatchee. Drive 1.8 miles and then bear left, following the sign for State Route 204 East toward Lake Stevens. Merge onto State Route 204 East and drive 2.1 miles, passing Vernon Road and turning left onto State Route 9 North. In 1.6 miles, turn right onto State Route 92 East toward Granite Falls. Drive 8.4 miles east to Granite Falls, staying straight through three traffic circles as the road transitions into 96th Street. Continue east through Granite Falls, arriving at an intersection with Stanley Street and Alder Avenue. Turn left onto Alder Avenue, following the road past a series of stop signs as it turns into the Mountain Loop Highway.

In 10.8 miles, pass the Verlot Public Service Center on the left. Drive another 14.4 miles, passing a sign for Big Four Picnic Area that leads to a parking area and alternate trailhead. In another 0.6 mile, turn right at the sign for the Ice Caves Trailhead. Enter the large parking area and main trailhead. Three ADA-accessible restrooms are next to the trailhead.

GPS Coordinates: 48.066005, -121.510506 / N48° 03.957' W121° 30.633'

8 PERRY CREEK FALLS

Mount Baker-Snoqualmie National Forest,
Perry Creek Research Natural Area

Distance: 6.4 miles round-trip

Duration: 4 hours

Elevation Change: 1,350 feet

Effort: Moderate

Trail: Dirt, gravel, and rocky paths

Users: Hikers, leashed dogs

Season: June-October

Passes/Fees: Northwest Forest Pass

Maps: Green Trails Map 111 for Sloan Peak, Green Trails Map 111SX for Mountain Loop Highway, USGS topographic map for Bedal

Contact: Mount Baker-Snoqualmie National Forest, Darrington Ranger District, www.fs.usda.gov

---

A moderately rocky hike through a lush, scenic valley includes an option to visit Mount Forgotten Meadows.

The scenic Perry Creek Trail traverses the grand valley between Stillaguamish Peak and Mount Dickerman. The Perry Creek rapids, an old-growth forest, wildflowers and berries, and the option to hike to Mount Forgotten Meadows make this a great, customizable trip. This trail generally sees less traffic than its neighbor, Mount Dickerman, so it's a good choice for a little more solitude. The trail falls within the Perry Creek Research Natural Area, so camping and campfires are discouraged (but not prohibited). Bring sturdy hiking shoes and hiking poles to help navigate the rocky, uneven talus slopes along the trail.

Start the Hike

Sign in at the trail register and start hiking northwest on the **Perry Creek Trail,** heading into a quiet, shady forest of towering Douglas fir, hemlock, and cedar. The grade is gentle here, a mostly flat walk past views of Big Four Mountain and Hall Peak to the southwest. In 1 mile, merge onto a wide gravel road heading northeast. The overgrown trail behind the road is the old Perry Creek Trail; it was rerouted in 2010 to share the parking lot with the Mount Dickerman Trail. Bear left at a sign for the Perry Creek Trail at 1.3 miles to emerge in a lush valley

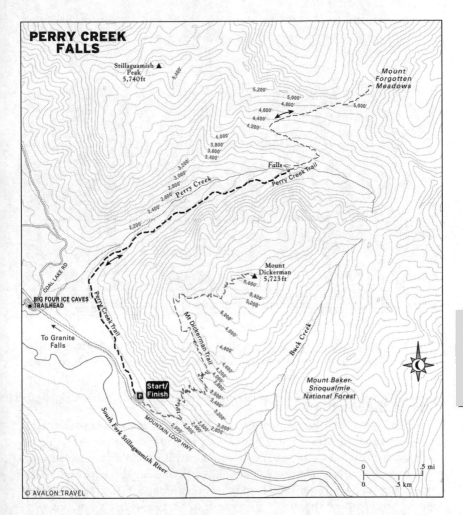

filled with bigleaf maple, vine maple, tufts of green ferns, and large rocks blanketed in a thick moss.

A rocky, uneven **talus slope** appears at 2.1 miles, the first of several talus slopes that may pose an avalanche risk when snow is present. Pick your way across the slope, bearing northeast to the trail on the other side. Look across the valley to spot a waterfall and keep a sharp eye out for pikas scurrying among the rocks. These small, rabbit-like mammals emit a high-pitched "eep! eep!" call that resembles a squeaky dog toy.

Arrive at a cool, shady alcove next to **Perry Creek Falls** at 3.2 miles. The falls are angled below the trail, giving you a top-down rather than a front-row view. There is plenty to enjoy here: Scattered rocks make a great perch for a picnic, the

Glacier Peak from Mount Forgotten Meadows

rushing rapids are right next to the trail, and there's ample shade from nearby trees. Enjoy a lunch or a snack before heading back to the trailhead. Or continue on to Mount Forgotten Meadows.

Extend the Hike

Continue hiking past Perry Creek Falls to **Mount Forgotten Meadows** for a 10.4-mile round-trip hike (about 7 hours) with a 3,350-foot elevation gain. From Perry Creek Falls, follow the trail northwest. Cross Perry Creek and pick up the trail beside the creek on the other side. (The creek crossing can have high water levels in the shoulder season; cross carefully or turn around if levels are too high.) Past the creek, ascend the rough, rocky trail to bear right at a Y-junction (4.5 miles) then right again (4.7 miles), taking your time to navigate the social trails near these junctions. Continue hiking northeast. Emerge onto a dirt path winding through an open meadow. At the top (5.2 miles), enjoy an iconic view of Glacier Peak reflected in a large tarn and views of Mount Baker, Mount Forgotten, and Mount Dickerman. Snow can linger on the trail up to Mount Forgotten Meadows into July; avoid travel when snow is present.

Directions

From Seattle, take I-5 north to exit 194 for U.S. Highway 2 East toward Snohomish/Wenatchee. Drive 1.8 miles and then bear left, following the sign for State Route 204 East toward Lake Stevens. Merge onto State Route 204 East and drive

2.1 miles, passing Vernon Road and turning left onto State Route 9 North. In 1.6 miles, turn right onto State Route 92 East toward Granite Falls. Drive 8.4 miles east to Granite Falls, staying straight through three traffic circles as the road transitions into 96th Street. Continue east through Granite Falls, arriving at an intersection with Stanley Street and Alder Avenue. Turn left onto Alder Avenue, following the road past a series of stop signs as it turns into the Mountain Loop Highway.

In 10.8 miles, pass the Verlot Public Service Center on your left and, in another 16.2 miles, turn left at the Forest Service sign for Dickerman/Perry Creek Trailhead into the parking lot. The trail starts from the west side of the parking lot; an ADA-accessible vault toilet is next to the trailhead. Be sure to take any valuable items with you; cars parked near trailheads that are easily accessed from the road occasionally experience break-ins and thefts.

GPS Coordinates: 48.053478, -121.490348 / N48° 03.296' W121° 29.484'

9 MOUNT DICKERMAN
Mount Baker-Snoqualmie National Forest

Best: Berry Picking, Mountain Views

Distance: 8.3 miles round-trip

Duration: 7 hours

Elevation Change: 3,800 feet

Effort: Strenuous

Trail: Rough, rocky dirt paths

Users: Hikers, leashed dogs

Season: July-October

Passes/Fees: Northwest Forest Pass

Maps: Green Trails Map 111 for Sloan Peak, Green Trails Map 111SX for Mountain Loop Highway, USGS topographic map for Bedal

Contact: Mount Baker-Snoqualmie National Forest, Darrington Ranger District, www.fs.usda.gov

---

This grinding hike up a series of switchbacks to majestic views of the North Cascades includes plentiful huckleberry shrubs.

Mount Dickerman is a classic on the Mountain Loop Highway. What makes this hike special are the sheer number of peaks visible from the trail—from Big Four Mountain to Mount Baker to Glacier Peak—and the rewarding grit it takes to reach the summit. This is a great option in summer, when the huckleberries ripen, or in fall for the changing colors of vine maple, bigleaf maple, and mountain ash. Pack extra water and food to keep yourself hydrated and energized. Bug spray isn't a bad idea either—especially at the summit on summer days.

Start the Hike
Start your hike from the **Dickerman Mountain Trail** sign on the east side of the parking lot and head east on the dirt path. Although the trail begins next to the highway, it soon fades into a quiet forest of Douglas fir, western hemlock, and sword fern. Sign the trail register before beginning an epic climb up numerous switchbacks, gaining a heart-pounding 2,000 feet in the first 2.1 miles. As you climb, spot Big Four Mountain (6,161 feet) and Hall Peak (5,452 feet) peeking through the trees to the southwest, marking your progress as you rise toward their heights.

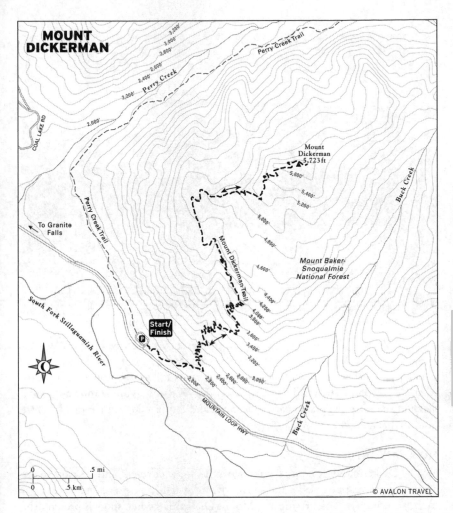

After the unrelenting ascent, the scenery starts to change at 2.1 miles. The switchbacks smooth out into longer stretches of trail lined with vine maple, Pacific silver fir, and mountain hemlock, and the tree canopy opens to direct sunlight. Meander through grassy meadows on the partially shaded, rocky trail, feasting on huckleberries in summer.

The trail emerges onto an open, exposed meadow at 3.5 miles. Peek behind you to the south for a tantalizing panorama of peaks as you climb: Del Campo Peak, the top of Mount Rainier, Mount Index and Mount Persis off in the distance, Sperry Peak, and Big Four Mountain. While scenic, the trail grinds 680 feet in the final 0.6 mile to the summit.

Arrive at the rocky north-facing summit at 4.1 miles and breathe in your

outstanding views of Glacier Peak and Mount Pugh from Mount Dickerman

accomplishment. A marvel of peaks line up before you: Three Fingers, White-horse Mountain, Mount Baker, Mount Shuksan, Mount Pugh, and Glacier Peak. Follow the trail another 350 feet to explore a second viewpoint; exercise care when taking photos to avoid the steep drop-offs. If the bugs aren't too bad, grab a patch of shade on the grass near the summit and rest or take a lunch break before heading back down.

Hike in Winter

Mount Dickerman is a popular hike when it's snow covered, and it's easy to see why: The snowcapped peaks and snow-covered meadows are a gorgeous contrast to the summer views. If attempting Mount Dickerman when snow is present, the trail will be more difficult to navigate, and a more difficult hike in general. Steer clear of snow cornices, which can form along the steep north face of the summit. Be prepared with layers, traction devices, and your 10 Essentials, and check the avalanche forecast before you go. Consider skipping this hike in winter if you are inexperienced in snow travel. It's also worth noting that the gate at Deer Creek (located 23.3 miles east of Granite Falls) closes annually in winter, limiting the accessibility of Mount Dickerman during winter months. Check the status of the gate at the **Darrington Ranger District** (360/436-1155, www.fs.usda.gov).

Directions

From Seattle, take I-5 north to exit 194 for U.S. Highway 2 East toward Snohomish/

Wenatchee. Drive 1.8 miles and then bear left, following the sign for State Route 204 East toward Lake Stevens. Merge onto State Route 204 East and drive 2.1 miles, passing Vernon Road and turning left onto State Route 9 North. In 1.6 miles, turn right onto State Route 92 East toward Granite Falls. Drive 8.4 miles east to Granite Falls, staying straight through three traffic circles as the road transitions into 96th Street. Continue east through Granite Falls, arriving at an intersection with Stanley Street and Alder Avenue. Turn left onto Alder Avenue, following the road past a series of stop signs as it turns into the Mountain Loop Highway.

In 10.8 miles, pass the Verlot Public Service Center on your left and, in another 16.2 miles, turn left at the Forest Service sign for Dickerman/Perry Creek Trailhead into the parking lot. The trail starts from the east side of the parking lot; an ADA-accessible vault toilet is next to the trailhead. Take any valuable items with you: Trailheads that are easily accessed from the road occasionally see car break-ins and thefts.

GPS Coordinates: 48.053478, -121.490348 / N48° 03.235' W121° 29.406'

10 GOTHIC BASIN
Mount Baker-Snoqualmie National Forest

Best: Strenuous

Distance: 9 miles round-trip

Duration: 7 hours

Elevation Change: 3,000 feet

Effort: Moderate/strenuous

Trail: Dirt paths, rough, rocky tread, scrambling

Users: Hikers, leashed dogs, mountain bikers

Season: Mid-July-October

Passes/Fees: Northwest Forest Pass

Maps: Green Trails Map 111 for Sloan Peak, Green Trails Map 143 for Monte Cristo, Green Trails Map 111SX for Mountain Loop Highway, USGS topographic maps for Bedal and Monte Cristo

Contact: Mount Baker-Snoqualmie National Forest, Darrington Ranger District, www.fs.usda.gov

---

Hike along the South Fork Sauk River, then climb to a rocky basin awash in meadows, lakes, and tarns.

Gothic Basin is a popular trail known for riverside views, deep-green valleys, jagged peaks, gushing waterfalls, and alpine lakes set amid tidal waves of orange-gray rock. The trail starts out deceptively easy, following the flat grade of a former mining route, before transitioning into a thigh-burning climb with uneven rocks and steep, slippery boulder slabs that require scrambling. In the shoulder season, high water levels and avalanche conditions can make this hike treacherous—prepare to turn around in adverse conditions. Hiking poles, sun protection, and waterproof boots will help with the uneven tread, sun exposure, and water crossings along the way.

Start the Hike
Head southeast from the parking area on the shoulder of Mountain Loop Highway. At a yellow Gate Ahead sign, turn right to skirt the gate and head south on Monte Cristo Road. The wide, gravel road was the former route of the Everett and Monte Cristo Railway, which transported silver and gold ore from the nearby mines to a smelter in Everett. Enjoy the sounds of the South Fork Sauk River to

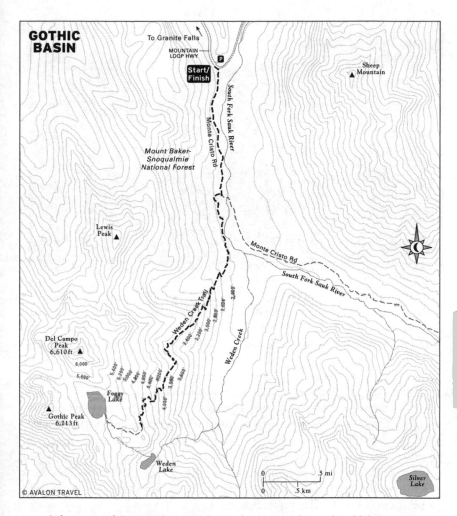

GOTHIC BASIN

To Granite Falls

MOUNTAIN LOOP HWY

Start/Finish

Sheep Mountain

South Fork Sauk River

Monte Cristo Rd

Mount Baker-Snoqualmie National Forest

Lewis Peak

Monte Cristo Rd

South Fork Sauk River

Weden Creek Trail

Weden Creek

Del Campo Peak 6,610 ft

6,000'
5,600'

5,400'
5,200'
5,000'
4,800'
4,600'
4,400'
4,200'
4,000'
3,800'
3,600'
3,400'
3,200'
3,000'
2,800'
2,600'
2,400'

Foggy Lake

Gothic Peak 6,213 ft

Weden Lake

0   .5 mi
0   .5 km

Silver Lake

© AVALON TRAVEL

your left, views of the North Cascades to the east, and ripe thimbleberries next to the trail in summer. An undulating reroute of the trail at 0.8 mile diverts around a slumping section of the road wiped out by a clay slide.

At 1.2 miles, pass a vault toilet and the **Weden Creek/Gothic Basin** kiosk. Veer west and follow the Weden Creek Trail sign. The Weden name can be traced to an early prospector of Monte Cristo, Otis N. Weeden (although some maps use the alternative Weden spelling). Over the next 0.5 mile, the narrow dirt trail weaves south through tall, open thickets of bracken fern and on wooden boardwalks across marshy wetlands. After one last glimpse of the South Fork Sauk River, begin climbing steeply, gaining a thigh-burning 1,300 feet in the next 1.3 miles. The trail ascends a long, grueling line southwest through the shady hillside.

heather meadows and rocky landscapes in Gothic Basin

Emerging from the forest at 3,700 feet, the trail briefly levels out onto an open hillside. Enjoy the views of Foggy Peak, Cadet Peak, and Silvertip Peak across the valley to the east, then arrive at the first in a series of waterfall and stream crossings at 3.1 miles. Pick your way carefully across the water's path; over the next 1.4 miles the trail becomes increasingly rugged, requiring you to use your hands to clamber over steep, slippery rocks, exposed roots, and damp boulder slabs.

Crest a ridge into **Gothic Basin** at 4.5 miles. This ocean of craggy peaks, bubbling streams, mirror-like tarns, and heather meadows hosts bright red patches of blueberry shrubs in the fall. Stay straight on the wide path to one of the larger tarns to enjoy a snack or break by the water's edge. Stretch out your visit by exploring the many rock formations, continuing on to Foggy Lake, or spending the night at one of several campsites. Whatever your plans, help protect the fragile meadows by practicing Leave No Trace principles.

Extend the Hike

A visit to **Foggy Lake** adds an extra 0.8-mile round-trip and 275 feet of elevation to your hike. Upon arrival at the large Gothic Basin tarn, bear right to skirt around its north side and follow the rock cairns for 0.4 mile on uneven, rocky terrain to the lake.

Hike Nearby

For an easier alternative to Gothic Basin, hike to historic **Monte Cristo Ghost Town** (9 miles round-trip, 5 hours, 800-foot elevation gain). Established in the late

1890s to support the mining activity in the area, the town was named after *The Count of Monte Cristo* by Alexandre Dumas—as you may have guessed.

Start from the same trailhead as Gothic Basin, taking Monte Cristo Road to the intersection with the Weden Creek Trail (1.2 miles). Ford the South Fork Sauk River and pick up the trail to Monte Cristo on the other side. (There is no bridge; cross the river at your own risk. Many people wait until summer, when the water level is lowest, to hunt for suitable crossings across the riverbed.) Once across the river, follow the road southeast for 3.25 miles to the Monte Cristo townsite.

Visit the **Monte Cristo Preservation Association** (www.mc-pa.org) online to print out an informative brochure with a map of the townsite to get a feel for the layout and town's history before you go.

Directions

From Seattle, take I-5 north to exit 194 for U.S. Highway 2 East toward Snohomish/Wenatchee. Drive 1.8 miles and then bear left, following the sign for State Route 204 East toward Lake Stevens. Merge onto State Route 204 East and drive 2.1 miles, passing Vernon Road and turning left onto State Route 9 North. In 1.6 miles, turn right onto State Route 92 East toward Granite Falls. Drive 8.4 miles east to Granite Falls, staying straight through three traffic circles as the road transitions into 96th Street. Continue east through Granite Falls, arriving at an intersection with Stanley Street and Alder Avenue. Turn left onto Alder Avenue and follow the road past a series of stop signs as it turns into the Mountain Loop Highway.

Drive 30.2 miles to the Barlow Pass Trailhead, passing the Verlot Public Service Center on your left at 10.8 miles. Turn left at the Barlow Pass Trailhead sign and enter the parking lot, or park on the wide shoulder to the south. There is a vault toilet in the parking lot. To reach the trailhead, walk 200 feet southeast on the shoulder of Mountain Loop Highway (toward the yellow Gate Ahead sign). Bear right at the sign and skirt the gate to pick up the trail.

GPS Coordinates:
Parking lot: 48.026539, -121.444299 / N48° 01.588' W121° 26.663'
Trailhead: 48.025933, -121.443602 / N48° 01.549' W121° 26.616'

11 GOAT LAKE

Mount Baker-Snoqualmie National Forest

Best: Hike to Lakes

Distance: 10.6 miles round-trip

Duration: 5.5 hours

Elevation Change: 1,650 feet

Effort: Moderate

Trail: Dirt and gravel paths

Users: Hikers, leashed dogs, mountain bikers, horses

Season: May-October

Passes/Fees: Northwest Forest Pass

Maps: Green Trails Map 111 for Sloan Peak, Green Trails Map 111SX for Mountain Loop Highway, USGS topographic maps for Bedal and Sloan Peak

Contact: Mount Baker-Snoqualmie National Forest, Darrington Ranger District, www.fs.usda.gov

---

This leg-stretcher travels to a large, picturesque lake encircled by peaks of the North Cascades.

Goat Lake is an excellent spring hike along the Mountain Loop Highway. Take your pick of one of two trails that meet below the lake; each has its own personality and distinctive scenery. While the long trail has a couple tricky areas to navigate, it offers a mostly gentle ascent—great for appreciating wildflowers, forest views, and the sounds of birds, waterfalls, and creeks along the way. The gorgeous lake with its refreshing clear water and stunning mountain scenery makes it worth the trek.

Arrive early on sunny spring and summer weekends to grab a good spot by the lake, and bring shoes you don't mind getting muddy.

Start the Hike

The hike to **Goat Lake** starts on a dirt and gravel trail next to the parking area. Sign the trail register and walk south to a signed junction in 0.25 mile. Bear left for the Upper Elliot Trail or right for the Lower Elliot Trail. The choice is yours: The trails merge 2 miles from the lake, and each has its own unique quirks. This hike takes one trail up and the second trail back to make a loop.

The **Upper Elliot Trail** is the longer of the two options, clocking in at 3.5

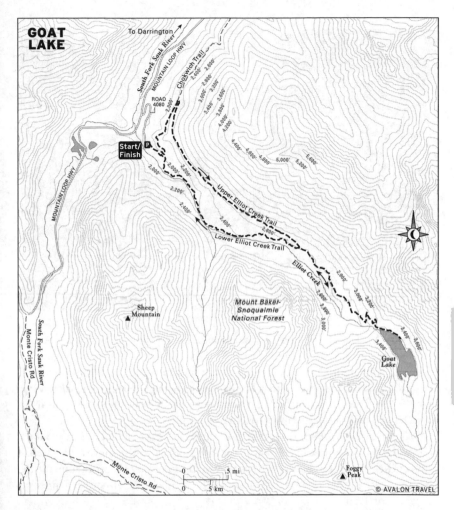

miles. The mostly dirt path is wide and well established, with partially obscured mountain views across the valley, pretty waterfalls along the last third of the trail, and beautiful stands of red alder. After 1 mile, bear right to stay on the trail as it makes a U-turn southeast, avoiding the Chokwich Trail.

The **Lower Elliot Trail** is a bit shorter at 2.4 miles. This trail follows an undulating dirt path that is somewhat brushy and narrow, but with beautiful up-close views of Elliot Creek. Take care crossing a rickety wooden bridge that leans precariously toward the creek.

The two trails merge into one at a signed junction for **Goat Lake,** 2.1 miles from the lake. As you hike through a grove of gorgeous, tall western redcedar, watch out for thorny devil's club lingering near the trail. After passing a sign for

stunning reflections of Cadet Peak and Foggy Peak at Goat Lake

the Henry M. Jackson Wilderness, you'll soon notice the trail becoming rough and steep, gaining 450 feet in the last 0.7 mile to the lake. Pick your way up the rocky, eroded path and keep your ears pricked for the sound of McIntosh Falls to the west; the falls are named after a family that once ran a lodge by the lake in the early 1900s. Bear a sharp left at an overturned tree stump and continue straight past a signed junction for **campsites** and a pit toilet.

Arriving at **Goat Lake,** marvel at the stunning peaks reflected in the lake's clear waters: Cadet Peak to the south and Foggy Peak to the southwest. Grab a spot on the sloping bank or down by the water and enjoy its cool temperature for a well-earned break before returning to the trailhead on either the Upper or Lower Elliot Trail.

From the late 1890s to the early 1900s, a small mining town existed at the lake, complete with a blacksmith shop, cabins, a mining office, and a hotel. Penn Mining, the major mining company here, opened several mining tunnels in Foggy Peak. Though they had some success unearthing common minerals, the town was eventually abandoned and destroyed; now hikers retrace the steps of the adventurous frontierspeople who came before them.

Shorten the Hike

Sticking to the **Lower Elliot Trail** both to and from Goat Lake shortens this hike to 9.5 miles round-trip (5 hours).

Directions

From Seattle, take I-5 north to exit 194 for U.S. Highway 2 East toward Snohomish/Wenatchee. Drive 1.8 miles and then bear left, following the sign for State Route 204 East toward Lake Stevens. Merge onto State Route 204 East and drive 2.1 miles, passing Vernon Road and turning left onto State Route 9 North. In 1.6 miles, turn right onto State Route 92 East toward Granite Falls. Drive 8.4 miles east to Granite Falls, staying straight through three traffic circles as the road transitions into 96th Street. Continue east through Granite Falls, arriving at an intersection with Stanley Street and Alder Avenue. Turn left onto Alder Avenue, following the road past a series of stop signs as it turns into the Mountain Loop Highway.

Drive 30.2 miles to Barlow Pass, where the pavement ends and the road transitions into a narrow, potholed dirt road. Continue northeast for 3.4 miles then turn right onto Forest Road 4080 signed for the Elliot Creek/Goat Lake Trailhead. Drive 0.7 mile to the parking area and trailhead at the end of the road where there is one vault toilet.

GPS Coordinates: 48.053841, -121.413061 / N48° 03.222' W121° 24.726'

12 MOUNT PUGH VIA STUJACK PASS

Mount Baker-Snoqualmie National Forest, Glacier Peak Wilderness

Best: Strenuous

Distance: 9.2 miles round-trip

Duration: 8 hours

Elevation Change: 3,800 feet

Effort: Strenuous

Trail: Dirt paths, uneven rocks, scrambling

Users: Hikers, dogs

Season: August-September

Passes/Fees: None

Maps: Green Trails Map 111 for Sloan Peak, Green Trails Map 111SX for Mountain Loop Highway, USGS topographic maps for White Chuck Mountain and Mount Pugh

Contact: Mount Baker-Snoqualmie National Forest, Darrington Ranger District, www.fs.usda.gov

---

This challenging hike offers fantastic views of the Cascades and the Sauk River Valley.

Mount Pugh is a mammoth day hike, notorious for its steep, rocky scramble in the last 0.5 mile to the summit. Strong hikers will have a great time trekking to Stujack Pass; those who are comfortable scrambling—and don't have a fear of heights—will enjoy the challenge of summiting Mount Pugh. While not a technical climb, the scramble to the summit includes a sharp ascent with steep drop-offs; the route can be tricky to sight and requires the use of your hands to grip bare rock. This is a long and difficult day hike with varying terrain and significant exposure. Be careful, use your best judgment, and bring hiking poles, plenty of snacks and water, sun protection, and layers.

Start the Hike

From the Mount Pugh kiosk, head southeast on **Mount Pugh Trail 644.** Wind through a cavernous forest of hemlock, Douglas fir, and alder on the narrow dirt path that crosses a few streams. The trail is shady and easy to follow, flanked by delicate ferns, spiny Oregon grape, and salal shrubs. The shade lasts for the

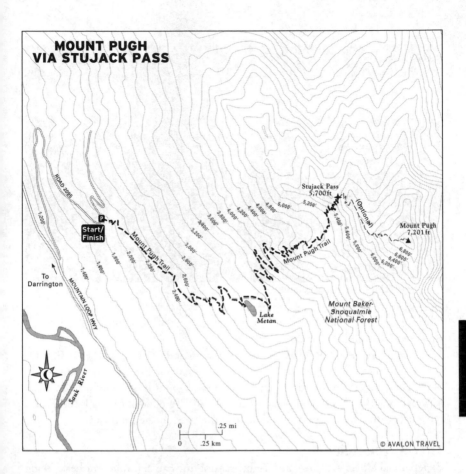

MOUNT PUGH
VIA STUJACK PASS

Stujack Pass
5,700 ft

Mount Pugh
7,201 ft

(Optional)

Start/
Finish

Mount Pugh Trail

Mount Pugh Trail

To
Darrington

MOUNTAIN LOOP HWY

ROAD 2095

Lake
Metan

Mount Baker-
Snoqualmie
National Forest

Sauk River

0   .25 mi
0   .25 km

© AVALON TRAVEL

first 3.9 miles before becoming fully exposed from the basin below Stujack Pass to the summit.

At 1.8 miles, arrive at **Lake Metan,** a good spot for a quick break. Look over the lake to spot Mount Pugh to the northeast—an almost inconceivable destination from this vantage point. After a quick rest and refuel, bear left on an unsigned path and follow the trail as it climbs steeply through the mossy forest to a sweeping, rocky basin interspersed with grassy meadows at 3.9 miles. Stujack Pass is to the northeast, located under the V-shaped outline of the rocky cliffs.

When ready, bear right to pick up the narrow dirt path (typically marked with a cairn) toward the basin. Continue north across an uneven boulder field, passing squeaking pikas and thickets of fireweed and thimbleberry. Switchback steeply toward Stujack Pass, gaining a sharp 800 feet in 0.7 mile; take small breaks to catch your breath and savor the panoramic views of the Sauk River Valley and

view of Glacier Peak at the summit

North Cascades to the west. Keep an eye out for eroded sections of the trail; cross these sections carefully on the angular slope.

At 4.6 miles, **Stujack Pass** (5,700 feet) is marked with a weathered sign for the Glacier Peak Wilderness. Enjoy fantastic views west to Mount Forgotten, Sloan Peak, and the Sauk River below, as well as Mount Baker and White Chuck Mountain to the north. Take shelter from the wind on one of the rocky cliffs and replenish with a snack or lunch before heading back to the trailhead.

Extend the Hike

Experienced hikers who are comfortable scrambling can continue southeast along the ridgeline up a steep rock face to **Mount Pugh,** an 11.2-mile round-trip hike (10 hours) with a 5,300-foot elevation gain. From Stujack Pass, switchback southeast through vibrantly colored meadows in fall and cross a narrow ridgeline that has a couple of scrambling sections. Pass a permanent snowfield to arrive at the base of a steep rock face at 5.1 miles. Look for a zigzagging path in the rock, scrambling carefully past an iron ring, and keep an eye out for cairns marking the route. Past the scramble section a hybrid trail appears, alternating between a dirt path and uneven, rocky tread to the summit of Mount Pugh at 5.6 miles. At the summit, marvel at the 360-degree views of Mount Baker, White Chuck Mountain, and Mount Shuksan to the north, Glacier Peak to the east, and Sloan Peak and Mount Rainier to the south. The rusted cables here were once used to hoist building materials for a former fire lookout, which stood here until 1965.

Directions

From Seattle, take I-5 north to exit 208 for State Route 530 toward Arlington. At the end of the exit ramp, turn right onto State Route 530, heading east for 3.7 miles. Take a left onto State Route 9 North, then a quick right to jump back on State Route 530 East. Drive 27.8 miles to Darrington and turn right at the Shell station onto the Mountain Loop Highway. Drive 12.5 miles (the pavement ends at 9.4 miles), then turn left at the sign for Mount Pugh Trailhead onto Forest Road 2095. Drive 1.6 miles to a sharp turn in the road and park in one of the pullouts. The trailhead is north of the turn, on the right side of the road. Parking is limited and there are no facilities.

descending the summit of Mount Pugh

GPS Coordinates: 48.145486, -121.415888 / N48° 08.751' W121° 24.943'

OLYMPIC PENINSULA

The Olympic Peninsula has a strikingly diverse natural profile—from sandy beaches to temperate rainforests to glacially carved peaks and valleys. Olympic National Park sits in the center of the peninsula and covers more than 1,400 square miles. The rugged, glacier-capped Olympic Mountains and Mount Olympus, the tallest peak on the peninsula, are located within the park. The Quinault, Queets, and Hoh rainforests call the southwestern part of the peninsula home, where up to 200 inches of rain falls annually. Sequim, in the northeastern corner, remains remarkably dry, receiving less than 18 inches of rainfall a year—quite a difference! Whether you love oceans and lakes or forests and mountain views, a wonderful range of hiking opportunities exist. Hikers can stroll along wide, rambling rivers, climb through misty old-growth forests, and walk across exposed ridgelines to views of Puget Sound, the Cascades, Mount Baker, and Mount Rainier.

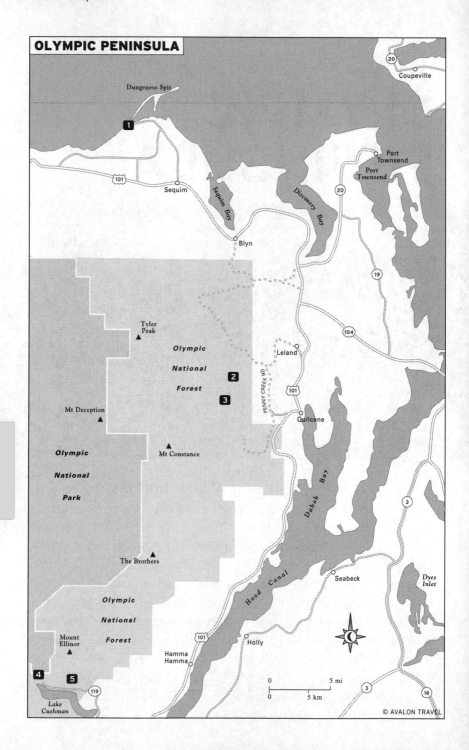

OLYMPIC PENINSULA

TRAIL NAME	LEVEL	DISTANCE	TIME	ELEVATION	PAGE
1 Dungeness Spit	Easy/moderate	10.4 mi	5 hr	150 ft	286
2 Mount Townsend	Moderate/strenuous	8.8 mi	6 hr	3,000 ft	290
3 Upper Big Quilcene-Marmot Pass	Moderate/strenuous	11 mi	7 hr	3,400 ft	295
4 Staircase Rapids Loop	Easy	2 mi	1 hr	200 ft	299
5 Mount Ellinor	Moderate/strenuous	6.6 mi	5 hr	3,250 ft	303

1 DUNGENESS SPIT

Dungeness National Wildlife Refuge, Sequim

Best: Beaches

Distance: 10.4 miles round-trip

Duration: 5 hours

Elevation Change: 150 feet

Effort: Easy/moderate

Trail: Paved walkway, sandy spit with pebbles, rocks, and driftwood

Users: Hikers

Season: Year-round

Passes/Fees: Entrance fee of $3 (cash or check)

Maps: USGS topographic map for Dungeness

Contact: U.S. Fish & Wildlife Service, Dungeness National Wildlife Refuge, www.fws.gov, 7am-sunset daily

---

A peaceful beach hike along Dungeness Spit in the Strait of Juan de Fuca offers wildlife-viewing and photo ops.

Dungeness Spit is a narrow finger of land jutting more than 5 miles into the Strait of Juan de Fuca on the northern coast of the Olympic Peninsula in Dungeness National Wildlife Refuge. This peaceful and engaging beach hike offers the opportunity to walk along one of the longest sand spits in the United States, view more than 200 different species of birds, take in waterfront and mountain views, and tour a lighthouse. Bring binoculars for up-close views of wildlife along the spit, and pack a sack lunch to enjoy on one of the lighthouse picnic tables.

Before you arrive, check the tide tables in order to time your hike with low tide; if the tide is too high, you can get pushed up to the rocky, driftwood-lined spine of the spit. (People have had accidents slipping on the driftwood trying to avoid the waves.) The spit is also very exposed, windy, and chilly; bring layers, rain protection, and sunscreen.

Due to the length of the hike and the more than two-hour drive from Seattle, consider making this a day trip. Enjoy the drive past quaint towns like Port Gamble, and stop in at the nearby city of Sequim after your hike.

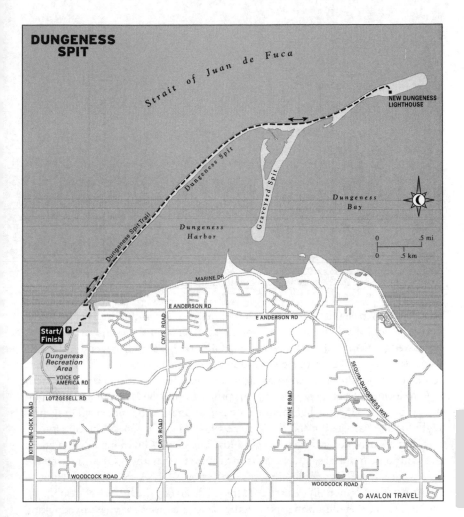

Start the Hike

Start your hike on the wide, paved trail next to the parking lot. The first 0.5 mile of the trail winds north through a dry conifer forest with madrone, red alder, western redcedar, and a green, brushy understory of sword fern and salal. Dungeness Harbor Overlook offers a peek of Dungeness Harbor and the spit in the distance with helpful interpretive signs about the wildlife and habitats in the refuge. The last 0.1 mile of this section descends a sharp 80 feet; enjoy the view of the spit curving out to the northeast, and try to spot the tiny lighthouse in the distance.

Upon reaching the sandy spit, begin your 4.6-mile trek northeast to the lighthouse. Breathe in the salty sea air, listen to the sound of the crashing waves, and gaze at the seemingly endless views of the Strait of Juan de Fuca. On a clear day,

Take a free tour of the New Dungeness Lighthouse on Dungeness Spit.

spot Vancouver Island to the northwest, Mount Baker and the Cascades to the northeast, and the Olympics to the south. The spit itself slopes upward from the water's edge: firm sand giving way to pebbles, rocks, and driftwood lining the spine of the spit. The north side of the spit (and the trail) is open to hikers year-round; the south side is closed to public access to protect the fragile coastal habitat.

A Welcome to Serenity signpost signals your arrival at the New Dungeness Lighthouse. Built in 1857, the lighthouse has been maintained by the New Dungeness Light Station Association (NDLSA) since 1994, when the Coast Guard removed their last resident keepers from the grounds. The Coast Guard intended to board the lighthouse buildings, but residents in Sequim formed the NDLSA to keep the lighthouse alive. Today, the lighthouse is staffed by NDLSA volunteers and is open for **tours** (9am-5pm daily year-round, free). Check out the historical exhibits on the first floor, then climb the spiral staircase to the tower for views overlooking the spit and Strait of Juan de Fuca. When you're ready to return, head back to the north side of the spit, following the wistfully painted signpost with big red letters: Reality 5 Miles.

Shorten the Hike
There's no need to walk all the way to the lighthouse to enjoy a breezy walk along Dungeness Spit. Wander the beach at your own pace, enjoying the salty sea air, views of the strait, crashing waves, and bustling wildlife.

Make It a Day Trip
In summer, fragrant, purple fields are in bloom at the multiple lavender farms

in Sequim. The annual **Sequim Lavender Festival®** (www.lavenderfestival. com, third weekend in July) features a street fair, live music, and farm tours. For a decadent treat, head to the friendly **Oak Table Cafe** (292 W. Bell St., Sequim, 360/683-2179, www.oaktablecafe.com, 7am-3pm daily) for their famous apple pancake, baked like a soufflé with sliced apples and gooey cinnamon.

Get Away for the Weekend
The **Dungeness Recreation Area** (554 Voice of America W., Sequim, 360/683-5847, www.clallam.net, $20-23) is located just south of the Dungeness Spit with 66 year-round campsites (including two ADA-accessible sites). For a vacation with a twist, volunteer at the **New Dungeness Lighthouse** (360/683-6638, www.newdungenesslighthouse.com, $35 membership fee, $50 deposit, $375 per adult per week, $195 youth age 6-17), located near the end of the Dungeness Spit. Volunteers commit to a weeklong stay, give lighthouse tours to the public, and perform light upkeep of the lighthouse and grounds.

Directions
From Seattle, take I-5 north to exit 177 for State Route 104 West, following the signs for Edmonds and the Kingston Ferry. Merge onto State Route 104 West; stay on the main road and follow signs for the Kingston Ferry. In 3.4 miles, exit the main road for the ferry terminal and holding area.

Take the **Edmonds-Kingston Ferry** (888/808-7977, www.wsdot.com, 30 minutes, fares vary). After exiting the ferry, drive 4 miles west on State Route 104. Turn right to stay on State Route 104 toward Port Angeles and Port Gamble. Drive 4.9 miles then turn right to cross the Hood Canal Bridge on State Route 104 toward Port Townsend. (There is no toll for the Hood Canal Bridge, but it closes periodically for maritime traffic; visit www.wsdot.com for information.)

Drive 15 miles and stay straight to merge onto U.S. Highway 101 North toward Port Angeles. Drive 24.4 miles on U.S. Highway 101 North, passing downtown Sequim. Turn right onto Kitchen-Dick Road. Follow the road for 3.3 miles as it turns into Lotzgesell Road. Just past the brown sign for Dungeness Wildlife Refuge/Dungeness County Park Entrance, turn left onto Voice of America Road. Follow the road through the Dungeness Recreation Area for 1 mile to the parking lot for the refuge. Restrooms are located next to the parking lot; a public restroom is also available at the lighthouse.
GPS Coordinates: 48.141285, -123.190514 / N48° 08.485' W123° 11.419'

2 MOUNT TOWNSEND

Olympic National Forest, Buckhorn Wilderness, Quilcene

Best: Wildflowers

Distance: 8.8 miles round-trip

Duration: 6 hours

Elevation Change: 3,000 feet

Effort: Moderate/strenuous

Trail: Dirt paths

Users: Hikers, leashed dogs, horses

Season: June-October

Passes/Fees: None

Maps: Green Trails Map 136 for Tyler Peak, Green Trails Map 168S for Olympic Mountains East, USGS topographic map for Mount Townsend

Contact: Olympic National Forest, Hood Canal Ranger District-Quilcene Office, www.fs.usda.gov

---

This heart-pumping hike to spectacular views of Puget Sound, the Olympics, and the Cascades offers plentiful pink rhododendrons in late spring.

Mount Townsend (16 miles west of Quilcene) is one of the finest hikes on the Olympic Peninsula. With 360-degree views of Puget Sound, the Cascades, and the Olympics from a long, undulating ridgeline, you'd be forgiven for singing and twirling à la Julie Andrews atop the ridgeline meadows.

Consider getting an early start on sunny spring and summer weekends; the trail is popular and there is limited parking at the upper trailhead. Pack a jacket, plenty of water, and sunscreen; two-thirds of the trail is exposed, and the 0.8-mile ridgeline at the top is windy and chilly. The travel time to the trailhead is a little more than two hours from Seattle: The Edmonds-Kingston Ferry is about 30 minutes with an additional 1.5-hour drive from Kingston to the trailhead.

Start the Hike

Start your hike from the upper trailhead, following the sign for **Mount Townsend Trail #839.** Your workout starts almost immediately on heart-pounding switchbacks that gain 1,250 feet in the first 1.5 miles of the well-groomed dirt trail. Take your time—enjoy the musical sound of Townsend Creek and the signature

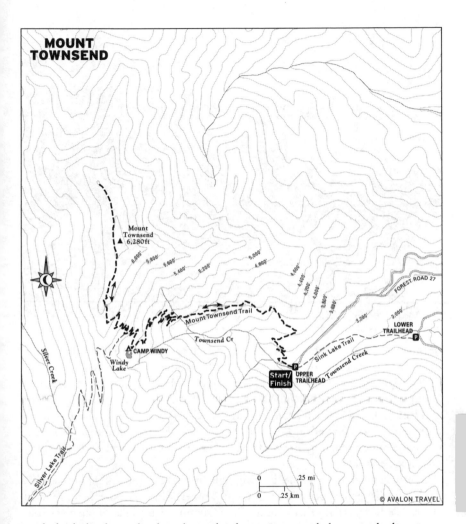

pink rhododendrons that line the trail in late spring, nestled among shady western hemlock, vine maple, and Douglas fir. As you hike west, shallow streams run through the trail feeding into Townsend Creek. Pretty purple lupine starts to appear in spring.

At 1.6 miles, the trail breaks out of the forest onto an east-facing slope. The scenic path is lined with purple-blue penstemon and bright, reddish-orange paintbrush. As you walk, pause to spot a pretty waterfall above to the west. On a clear day, the horizon line of the Cascade peaks will slowly reveal themselves as you climb, with stout, triangular Glacier Peak to the east as well as Mount Rainier and Mount Adams to the southeast. The waterways of Puget Sound become more visible, with views of the Kitsap Peninsula, Hood Canal Bridge, Magnolia bluff, and Seattle

fantastic views of the Olympics from the summit of Mount Townsend

to the east—wow! Passing through **Camp Windy,** follow the Trail sign as the path veers northwest to a signed junction with the **Silver Lakes Trail** (2.9 miles).

Bear right for **Mount Townsend,** passing through windswept shore pine trees with peekaboo views of Mount Baker to the north. After switchbacking a steep 600 feet in 0.7 mile, reach a long, rolling ridgeline at 3.6 miles. Take a moment to marvel at the views of the Olympics to the west. Bear right to follow the trail north, seemingly floating on a wide, green fairway above Puget Sound and the Olympic Peninsula.

Continue north for 0.8 mile, bearing right at a split in the trail after 0.6 mile. Arrive at a distinctive rocky outcropping (4.4 miles) with views north of the Strait of Juan de Fuca, the northern coast of the Olympic Peninsula, Dungeness Spit, the San Juan Islands, and peaks on Vancouver Island on a clear day—in addition to views of Puget Sound, the Cascades, and the Olympics! Slap on your sun hat and enjoy your lunch on the rocks, painted in neon orange and yellow splatters of lichen, before returning to the trailhead.

Extend the Hike

For a quiet start through a pleasant, shady forest, try the **Sink Lake Trail** from the lower trailhead; this adds an extra hour and 2 miles round-trip to your hike. This trailhead is also a great option if parking at the upper trailhead is full or covered in snow. To get to the lower trailhead, backtrack 2 miles from the upper trailhead to Forest Road 2760 (follow the driving directions directly to Forest Rd.

2760). Drive 0.7 mile west on Forest Road 2760; keep a sharp eye out for the easy-to-miss, signed trailhead on the right. Park on the cleared shoulder of the road. No pass is required at this trailhead, and dogs and horses are allowed on the trail.

Hike Nearby

Nearby **Silver Lakes** is a great option if you've already hiked Mount Townsend. Blending panoramic valley views and a scenic, mountain-filled lake setting, the Silver Lakes Trail is a 10.6-mile round-trip hike (8 hours) with 3,400 feet of elevation gain.

Starting from the upper trailhead for Mount Townsend, ascend 2.9 miles to the signed junction with the Silver

rhododendrons along the trail

Lakes Trail. Turn left, cresting a ridge and descending 600 feet in 1.6 miles toward Silver Creek—elevation you'll need to regain on the way back to the trailhead. At the bottom of the valley, stay straight on the trail, ascending 400 feet in the next 0.8 mile to Silver Lake. To turn your hike into an overnight camping trip, bed down at one of several first-come, first-served campsites at Silver Lake (campfires not permitted); these can be popular when the weather is nice.

Directions

From Seattle, take I-5 north to exit 177 for State Route 104 West, following the signs for Edmonds and the Kingston Ferry. Merge onto State Route 104 West, staying on the main road and following signs for State Route 104 West and the Kingston Ferry. In 3.4 miles, exit the main road for the ferry terminal and holding area.

Take the **Edmonds-Kingston Ferry** (888/808-7977, www.wsdot.com, 30 minutes, fares vary). After exiting the ferry, drive 4 miles on State Route 104 West, then turn right to stay on State Route 104 West toward Port Angeles and Port Gamble. Drive 4.9 miles then turn right to cross the Hood Canal Bridge on State Route 104 West toward Port Townsend. (There is no toll for the Hood Canal Bridge, but it can close periodically for maritime traffic; visit www.wsdot.com for more information.) In 11 miles, take the exit on the right for Center Street and Quilcene. At the stop sign, turn right onto Center Road toward Quilcene. Drive 8.1 miles then turn left onto U.S. Highway 101, heading south toward Shelton. In 1.4 miles, turn right at a Y-junction onto Penny Creek Road.

Reset your odometer to zero. At 1.4 miles, bear left onto Forest Road 27 and follow the sign for Mount Townsend Trail. At 3.4 miles, bear right to stay on Forest Road 27 and follow the Trails sign. At 4.5 miles, bear right and follow the sign for Mount Townsend Trail. At 6.8 miles, turn left to stay on Forest Road 27. At 7.1 miles, bear left to stay on the main road. At 10.7 miles, bear right to stay on Forest Road 27. At 12.1 miles, bear left to stay on the main road. At 13.7 miles, bear right and follow the sign for Mount Townsend Trail. (The road on the left is Forest Road 2760.) At 14.9 miles, turn left and follow the sign for Mount Townsend Trail. Drive carefully on the potholed road. At 15.7 miles, arrive at the trailhead at the end of the road. There is one ADA-accessible vault toilet.

GPS Coordinates: 47.856244, -123.035716 / N47° 51.365' W123° 02.172'

3 UPPER BIG QUILCENE-MARMOT PASS

Olympic National Forest, Buckhorn Wilderness, Quilcene

Best: Off the Beaten Path, Wildflowers

Distance: 11 miles round-trip

Duration: 7 hours

Elevation Change: 3,400 feet

Effort: Moderate/strenuous

Trail: Dirt paths

Users: Hikers, horses, leashed dogs

Season: June-October

Passes/Fees: Northwest Forest Pass

Maps: Green Trails Map 136 for Tyler Peak, Green Trails Map 168S for Olympic Mountains East, USGS topographic maps for Mount Townsend and Mount Deception

Contact: Olympic National Forest, Hood Canal Ranger District-Quilcene Office, www.fs.usda.gov

---

Hike to an amphitheater of mountain, river, valley, and wildflower views, with an option to summit Buckhorn Mountain.

Located in the northeast corner of the Olympic Peninsula, Marmot Pass is that rare hike with a little bit of everything: shady old-growth forest, riverside views, wildflower meadows, and an amphitheater of grand mountain and valley views.

Consider setting up a base camp at one of the campsites along the trail—an option for exploring trails in the Buckhorn Wilderness. Bring your sunscreen, bug hat, and bug spray; the trail is exposed with little shade the last third of the way to Marmot Pass, and the area boasts persistent, pesky bugs in spring and summer.

Start the Hike

The Big Quilcene Trail is divided between an Upper Trail and a Lower Trail. The main difference between the two is that the Upper Trail sits at a higher elevation than the Lower Trail and has a shorter hiking distance to Marmot Pass; it also isn't open to mountain bikes and motorbikes like the Lower Trail. Still, the Lower Trail is an option if the Upper Trail is snowed in or if the parking area is packed.

From the parking lot, follow the **Upper Big Quilcene Trail** west toward Shelter

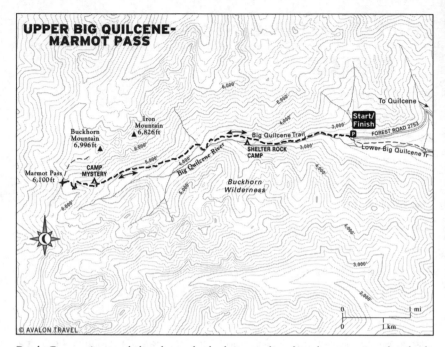

UPPER BIG QUILCENE-MARMOT PASS

Rock Camp. As you hike along the lush, moss-lined pathway, enjoy the shady forest of western hemlock, Douglas fir, and cedar. Enter the Buckhorn Wilderness to the sights and sounds of the Big Quilcene River to the south, passing by a pretty waterfall at 1.8 miles. Keep your eyes peeled for huckleberry shrubs lining the trail—an excellent snack when they ripen in summer. Past a wooden signed marked Stoves Only Beyond This Point, arrive at **Shelter Rock Camp** at 2.7 miles.

Bear right to continue west on the Upper Big Quilcene Trail toward **Camp Mystery.** The trail becomes more demanding, gaining 800 feet in the next mile, but oh, the views that await. Break out of the forest at 3.7 miles into the gorgeous, scenic Big Quilcene River Valley, surrounded by nearby peaks to the southwest and Buckhorn Mountain to the north. Pass through rocky talus slopes, enjoying the fields of wildflowers in spring and summer—yellow clumps of spreading stonecrop, purple aster, and deep-red paintbrush. Take a moment to turn around—on a clear day, you can see the triangular shape of Glacier Peak dominating the skyline to the east. At 4.7 miles, Camp Mystery offers a nice, shady option for a break.

Continue west toward **Marmot Pass.** After zigzagging up a series of switchbacks, the trail enters a grand, open meadow with views of the pass to the west and the imposing ridgeline of Buckhorn Mountain to the north. Shore pine trees and Pacific silver fir cluster the mountainside, while high-pitched marmot whistles can be heard near the pass—a warning call to their families that an intruder is near. A campsite sits just below the pass for those lucky enough to claim it.

mountain views and wildflowers along the Big Quilcene Trail

At 5.5 miles, arrive at **Marmot Pass** and take a moment to marvel at the views. The Olympics stretch out to the west: The trio of three peaks are Mount Mystery, Mount Fricaba, and Mount Deception (from left to right). Spot Gray Wolf to the northwest and enjoy the expansive view across the Dungeness River Valley. Marmot Pass is a three-way trail junction for the Tubal Cain Trail (north), the Dungeness Trail (south), and the Big Quilcene Trail (east). Grab a precious patch of shade if you can and enjoy the views before trekking back to the trailhead.

Extend the Hike

Are you ready for a grunt-worthy hike to panoramic views of the Olympics and Cascades? This trip to the west peak of **Buckhorn Mountain** adds an extra 2 miles round-trip and 1,000 feet of elevation gain to the Marmot Pass hike. From the trail junction at Marmot Pass, hike north on the **Tubal Cain Trail** for 300 feet, then turn right onto an obvious, but unsigned boot path. In the first 0.5 mile, ascend 700 steep feet up a pebbly, slippery slope, following the path northeast. The final ascent has a short section of hand-over-hand scrambling with steep drop-offs—proceed carefully. On a clear day from the summit, you can see Mount Baker, Glacier Peak, Mount Rainier, Mount Adams, Mount St. Helens, a panorama of peaks in the Olympics, Buckhorn Lake below you to the north, and the ridgeline of Mount Townsend to the northeast.

Get Away for the Weekend

Backpackers can snag free first-come, first-served campsites at **Shelter Rock** (2.7 miles), **Camp Mystery** (4.7 miles), or—if you're lucky—an unnamed campsite right before **Marmot Pass** (5.4 miles). Campfires are not allowed above 3,500 feet; please practice Leave No Trace principles during your stay.

Directions

From Seattle, take I-5 north to exit 177 for State Route 104 West, following signs for Edmonds and the Kingston Ferry. Merge onto State Route 104 West, staying on the main road and following signs for State Route 104 West and the Kingston Ferry. In 3.4 miles, exit the main road for the ferry terminal and holding area.

Take the **Edmonds-Kingston Ferry** (888/808-7977, www.wsdot.com, 30 minutes, fares vary). After exiting the ferry, drive 4 miles on State Route 104 West. Turn right to stay on State Route 104 West toward Port Angeles and Port Gamble. Drive 4.9 miles then turn right to cross the Hood Canal Bridge on State Route 104 West toward Port Townsend. (There is no toll for the Hood Canal Bridge, but it can close periodically for maritime traffic; visit www.wsdot.com for more information.) In 11 miles, take the exit for Center Street and Quilcene. At the stop sign, turn right onto Center Road toward Quilcene. Drive 8.1 miles then turn left onto U.S. Highway 101, heading south toward Shelton. In 1.4 miles, turn right at a Y-junction onto Penny Creek Road.

Reset your odometer to zero. At 1.4 miles, bear left onto Forest Road 27, following the sign for Big Quilcene Trail. At 3.4 miles, bear right to stay on Forest Road 27 following the Trails sign. At 4.5 miles, bear right following the sign for Big Quilcene Trail. At 6.8 miles, turn left to stay on Forest Road 27. At 7.1 miles, bear left to stay on the main road. At 10.7 miles, bear left onto Forest Road 2750 (watch out for large potholes). At 15.3 miles, arrive at the parking area and trailhead. A vault toilet is located at the trailhead.

GPS Coordinates: 47.827904, -123.041102 / N47° 49.671' W123° 02.466'

4 STAIRCASE RAPIDS LOOP
Olympic National Park, Staircase Area

Best: Easy Hikes

Distance: 2 miles round-trip

Duration: 1 hour

Elevation Change: 200 feet

Effort: Easy

Trail: Dirt paths

Users: Hikers

Season: Year-round

Passes/Fees: National Park Pass

Maps: Green Trails Map 167 for Mount Steel, USGS topographic map for Mount Skokomish

Contact: Olympic National Park, Staircase Area, www.nps.gov

This family-friendly hike through old-growth forest in the North Fork Skokomish River Valley crosses a cable bridge spanning the rapids.

Sitting just beyond the northwestern tip of Lake Cushman, the Staircase Rapids Loop is a quiet, shady walk along the wide, rushing North Fork Skokomish River. The first 0.25 mile of the trail is ADA-accessible (with assistance) to the Big Cedar and a river viewpoint just beyond; the first 0.1 mile of the nearby Shady Lane Trail is also accessible. (The trail is unpaved, and you may encounter some rocks and roots that require some extra oomph.) Visit in spring or fall to enjoy the changing seasons and avoid the summer crowds. In the winter, the gate at the park boundary (1 mile from the trailhead) may close in poor snow conditions; call the park if you plan to visit then.

Start the Hike
From the ranger station, head northwest to cross a pedestrian bridge over the North Fork Skokomish River, pausing to take in the picturesque views of the valley. Continue northwest on the **Staircase Rapids Loop Trail,** stepping into an old-growth forest of tall, thick western redcedar and Douglas fir. In spring, yellow-green vanilla-leaf, with its squiggle-edged leaves, carpets the shady understory. Take time to explore the signed spur trail to Big Cedar, a fallen western

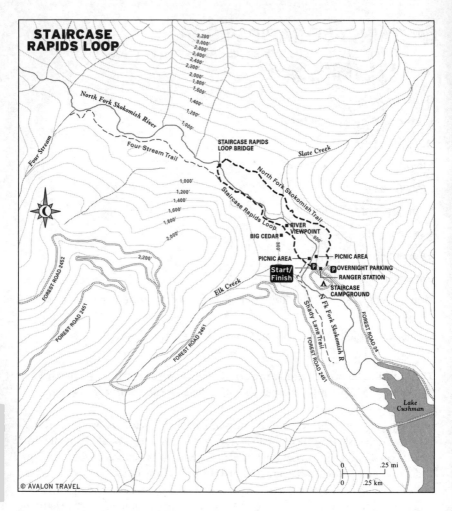

STAIRCASE
RAPIDS LOOP

redcedar, and other spur trails with views of the river. In 0.8 mile, bear right at a
signed junction for the **Staircase Rapids Loop Bridge,** a charming cable bridge.

Cross the Staircase Rapids Loop Bridge and follow the trail 175 feet to an intersection with the **North Fork Skokomish River Trail.** Turn right and follow a
sign marked Ranger Station to take the trail southeast for 1 mile. While the North
Fork Skokomish River isn't as visible from this side of the trail, there is a gorgeous
viewpoint of Slate Creek in 0.4 mile, with water rushing and bubbling over rocks
framed by the leafy forest. After the **river viewpoint,** bear left to cross a narrow
one-armed bridge and pick up the dirt trail on the other side of the creek. Climb a
set of shallow wooden steps before descending to the North Fork Skokomish River

The Staircase Rapids Loop Bridge is a cable bridge built in 2013.

Trailhead. Follow the gravel road back to the day-use parking area and pedestrian bridge to complete your loop.

Extend the Hike
Take a side trip on one of two out-and-back trails through beautiful, mossy, old-growth forest with views of the North Fork Skokomish River. The first option, **Four Stream Trail** (2.2 miles round-trip), adds an extra hour to the loop and offers nice views of the valley. At the signed intersection of the Rapids Loop Bridge and Four Stream Trail, bear left to follow Four Stream Trail northwest for 1.1 miles to Four Stream, the turnaround point.

The **Shady Lane Trail** (1.6 miles round-trip) adds 45 minutes to the loop. Pick up this trail just after crossing the pedestrian bridge from the day-use parking area; turn left (south) and follow the sign for Shady Lane. The trail leads 0.7 mile to a Y-junction; bear right for another 0.1 mile to Forest Road 2451, the turnaround point.

Make It a Day Trip
Enjoy a picnic at one of the picnic tables near the trailhead or at one of the established picnic sites right off Lake Cushman on Forest Road 24. Pick up doughnuts, cookies, or sandwiches at **IGA Hood Canal Grocery** (24151 U.S. 101 N, Hoodsport, 360/877-9444, www.iga.com, 7am-10pm daily, call to confirm hours). **Hoodsport Coffee** (24240 U.S. 101 N., Hoodsport, 360/877-6732, www.hoodsportcoffee. com, hours vary), located just south of the intersection of State Route 119 and U.S. Highway 101, is a friendly cafe with a selection of tea and espresso beverages,

build-your-own sandwiches, and locally made Olympic Mountain ice cream (www. olympicmountainicecream.com).

Directions

From Seattle, take I-5 south to exit 104 for U.S. Highway 101 North toward Aberdeen and Port Angeles. Merge onto U.S. Highway 101 North, and in 5.4 miles bear right to stay on U.S. Highway 101 North toward Shelton and Port Angeles. Drive 28.6 miles to Hoodsport, following the signs for the Cushman-Staircase Recreation Area. Turn left onto State Route 119 North and drive 9.2 miles to a T-intersection with a stop sign. Turn left to stay on State Route 119 North/Forest Road 24 and continue toward the Staircase Area. (The pavement ends in 1.6 miles and converts to a gravel road.) In 5.3 miles, stay straight, passing a causeway on your left leading to the Dry Creek and Copper Creek Trailheads. In 0.2 mile, pass a gate and Olympic National Park boundary, arriving at the parking area after another mile. An ADA-accessible vault toilet is located next to the pedestrian bridge.
GPS Coordinates: 47.515888, -123.330470 / N47° 30.939' W123° 19.800'

5 MOUNT ELLINOR

Olympic National Forest, Mount Skokomish Wilderness

Distance: 6.6 miles round-trip

Duration: 5 hours

Elevation Change: 3,250 feet

Effort: Moderate/strenuous

Trail: Dirt paths, rough, steep rock tread

Users: Hikers, leashed dogs

Season: July-October

Passes/Fees: Northwest Forest Pass (upper trailhead)

Maps: Green Trails Map 167 for Mount Steel and Green Trails Map 168 for The Brothers, Green Trails Map 168S for Olympic Mountains East, USGS topographic maps for Mount Washington and Mount Skokomish

Contact: Olympic National Forest, Hood Canal Ranger District, www.fs.usda.gov

---

A sharp ascent leads to 360-degree views of the Cascades, Olympics, and Puget Sound.

If you were to draw a straight line west from Seattle across the Kitsap Peninsula to the Olympic National Forest, and bend it a little south toward Hoodsport, you would hit the spiky ridgeline where Mount Ellinor resides. This popular trail is known for its rough, steep ascent, mountain goat sightings, and resounding views of Mount Rainier, the Olympics, Puget Sound, and Lake Cushman. Bring hiking poles and expect plenty of company from day hikers, trail runners, tourists, and even mountain goats. (While spotting a mountain goat can be a memorable experience, follow the safety guidelines posted on trail kiosks.) Mount Ellinor is a little more than a two-hour drive from the Seattle area, but well worth the time and trip.

There are two options for reaching Mount Ellinor: a 3.4-mile hike from the upper trailhead or a 6.6-mile hike from the lower trailhead. The trail from the upper trailhead gets down to business straightaway, climbing steeply from the parking area. The trail from the lower trailhead is a longer, gentler warm-up through a pleasant, shady forest. The trails merge 1.4 miles below the summit for a mutually steep ascent. A Northwest Forest Pass is required for the upper trailhead, which has a vault toilet; no pass is required for the lower trailhead (which doesn't). If starting from the lower trailhead, please observe Leave No Trace principles and pack out any used toilet paper.

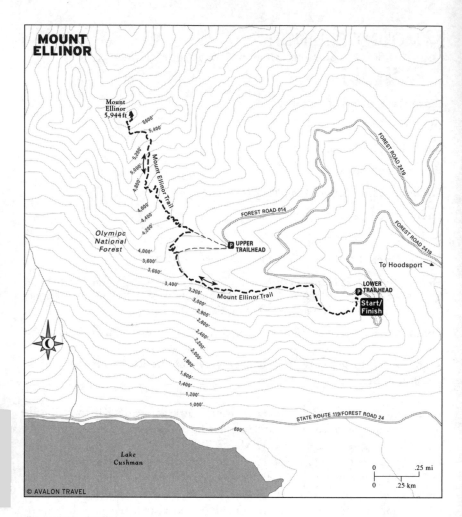

Start the Hike

Start your hike from the **lower trailhead,** picking up **Mount Ellinor Trail 812** on the south side of the road. Hike through an airy forest of tall western hemlock and Douglas fir on a clear and well-maintained dirt pathway where occasional wooden benches line the trail. Pass a signed junction for a trail to Big Creek Camp (0.2 mile), following the path as it veers west through leafy passageways and mossy hillsides.

Upon arriving at the first of two signed junctions (1.6 miles), stay straight. Past this point, the grade loses its gentle character, earnestly ascending to a second junction (1.9 miles) with the upper trailhead. Bear left to head northwest on a staircase of roots along the mountain's spine. The tread soon evens out to a dirt

looking southeast toward Hood Canal

pathway, with the still-shady forest a welcome relief as you ascend a steep series of switchbacks.

At 2.3 miles, you'll pass a trail for the winter route; stay straight for the summer trail. Breaking out of the forest, look to your right for a small landing with a plaque on a tree. The plaque honors members of the Mount Rose Trail Crew, a volunteer group that has maintained the Mount Ellinor Trail for more than 30 years. Pause for a moment to give a silent tip of your hat before continuing northwest, climbing a rough, steep, and bouldery section that transitions to a scree field with wooden steps at 2.8 miles. Take small breaks to catch your breath, admiring the sweeping views of Lake Cushman emerging to the south.

Upon reaching a ridgeline, turn right to gain a calf-burning 400 feet in the last 0.3 mile to the summit at 3.3 miles. This last section is a moderately steep rock face; use your hands for balance and leverage. On a clear day, take in the beautiful mountain and water views: Mount Baker to the northeast, Hood Canal to the east, Mount Rainier and Mount St. Helens to the southeast, and Lake Cushman to the south. The summit area is small, so let others have a turn after you've taken your pictures. Enjoy your snack or lunch break before heading back to the trailhead.

Shorten the Hike

Starting from the **upper trailhead** makes for a steep 3.4-mile round-trip hike (3 hours) that gains 2,400 feet in 1.7 miles. A Northwest Forest Pass is required, and parking is limited for the upper trailhead. Plan to arrive early to get a jump start on the crowds.

Make It a Day Trip

Take a drive up the coast to visit friend-ly **Hama Hama Oysters** (35846 N. U.S. 101, Lilliwaup, 360/877-5811, www.hamahamaoysters.com, hours vary), a family-owned shellfish farm about a 15-minute drive north of Hoodsport. Savor a sample platter of fresh-shucked oysters at the Hama Hama Oyster Saloon, taking in the sea-side views of the Hood Canal from the low-key outdoor seating area. If you'd rather pick up something to cook later, visit the farm store located next door to the saloon and choose from a variety of fresh seafood as well as snacks and ice cream.

Mount Ellinor Trail

Directions

From Seattle, take I-5 south to exit 104 for U.S. Highway 101 North toward Ab-erdeen and Port Angeles. Merge onto U.S. Highway 101 North. In 5.4 miles, bear right to stay on U.S. Highway 101 North toward Shelton and Port Angeles. Drive 28.6 miles to Hoodsport, following the signs for the Cushman-Staircase Recreation Area. Turn left onto State Route 119 North and drive 9.2 miles, arriving at a T-intersection with a stop sign. Turn right onto Forest Road 24, following the sign for the Mount Ellinor Trail. In 1.5 miles, turn left onto Forest Road 2419. Drive 4.6 miles to the lower trailhead. For the upper trailhead, drive 1.6 miles past the lower trailhead, then turn left onto Forest Road 014. Drive 1 mile to the upper trailhead at the end of the road. A vault toilet is available at the upper trailhead; there are no facilities at the lower trailhead.

GPS Coordinates:

Upper trailhead: 47.510456, -123.247998 / N47° 30.614' W123° 14.885'
Lower trailhead: 47.506777, -123.231905 / N47° 30.409' W123° 13.910'

MOUNT RAINIER

Majestic. Ethereal. Silent. Mount Rainier, the tallest
and most iconic mountain in Washington State, leaves many people speechless
upon first sight. Designated a national park in 1899 and christened a federally
protected wilderness area in 1988, Mount Rainier National Park is so awe-
inspiring it makes hikers of all ages and abilities feel like kids on a playground.
Stroll through open fields of lupine, beargrass, and paintbrush; take in the clear,
larger-than-life views of glaciers spilling out from the top of Mount Rainier; spot
marmots, deer, elk, and bears; or rest by a picturesque lake surrounded by fall
foliage. There are more than 250 miles of trail in Mount Rainier National Park,
as well as opportunities for camping, geocaching, mountaineering, snowshoe-
ing, cross-country skiing, and sledding.

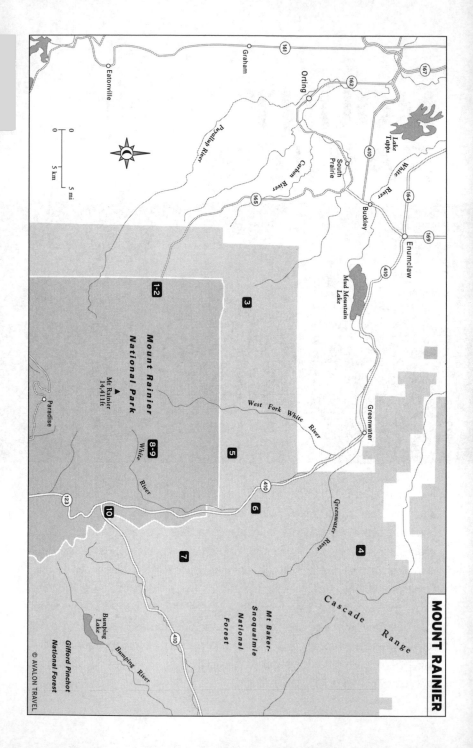

TRAIL NAME	LEVEL	DISTANCE	TIME	ELEVATION	PAGE
1 Tolmie Peak Lookout	Moderate	6 mi	3.5 hr	1,500 ft	310
2 Spray Park	Moderate	8.4 mi	5.5 hr	2,250 ft	314
3 Summit Lake	Moderate	4.8-6.2 mi	3-4 hr	1,100-1,500 ft	319
4 Kelly Butte Lookout	Easy/moderate	3.5 mi	2.5 hr	1,050 ft	323
5 Grand Park via Lake Eleanor	Moderate	8.8 mi	5 hr	1,400 ft	327
6 Snoquera Falls Loop	Easy/moderate	3.9 mi	2 hr	900 ft	331
7 Norse Peak	Moderate/strenuous	10 mi	6 hr	2,900 ft	334
8 Second Burroughs	Moderate	6 mi	4 hr	1,200 ft	338
9 Dege Peak	Easy/moderate	4.1 mi	2.5 hr	900 ft	343
10 Tipsoo Lake-Naches Peak Loop	Easy/moderate	3.6-4.1 mi	2.5 hr	700 ft	347

1 TOLMIE PEAK LOOKOUT

Mount Rainier National Park, Mowich Lake

Best: Mountain Views

Distance: 6 miles round-trip

Duration: 3.5 hours

Elevation Change: 1,500 feet

Effort: Moderate

Trail: Dirt paths

Users: Hikers

Season: July–mid-October

Passes/Fees: National Park Pass

Maps: Green Trails Map 269 for Mount Rainier West, Green Trails Map 269S for Mount Rainier Wonderland, USGS topographic maps for Mowich Lake and Golden Lakes

Contact: Mount Rainier National Park, Carbon River Ranger Station, www. nps.gov

---

Hike to a dramatic lake setting and a former fire lookout with outstanding views of Mount Rainier.

Snug in the northwest corner of Mount Rainier National Park, Tolmie Peak Lookout hits several hiking sweet spots—an enjoyable forest walk, a pretty alpine lake with shallow lagoons, and a lookout with dominating views of Mount Rainier. And all this while boasting a doable mileage and challenging yet not-too-difficult elevation gain.

The combination of scenery and easy hiking makes this hike a favorite for Seattleites and tourists in the summer. Plan to visit during the week or get an early start on the crowds—a long line of cars has been known to stretch down Mowich Lake Road on sunny, summer weekends, as well as on Memorial Day and Labor Day weekends. Bring your bug spray too; bugs can be especially pesky at Eunice Lake in the summer.

It may take more than 2 hours to reach the Tolmie Peak Trailhead due to long, gravelly Mowich Lake Road. The road closes in winter months due to snowfall and typically reopens in late June or early July depending on road and weather conditions; check with the Carbon River Ranger Station for opening dates. If you

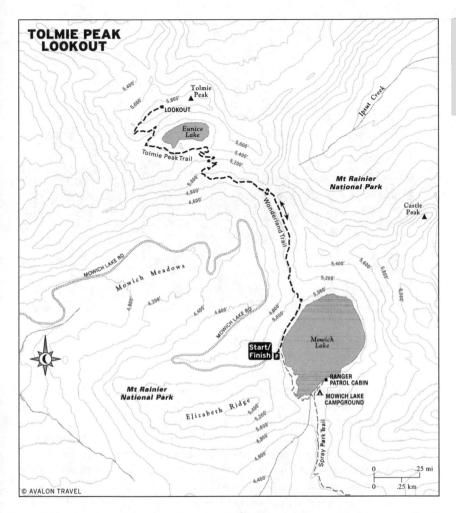

TOLMIE PEAK LOOKOUT

Tolmie Peak

LOOKOUT

Eunice Lake

Tolmie Peak Trail

Ipsut Creek

Mt Rainier National Park

Castle Peak

Wonderland Trail

Mowich Lake Rd

Mowich Meadows

Mowich Lake Rd

Start/Finish P

Mowich Lake

RANGER PATROL CABIN

MOWICH LAKE CAMPGROUND

Mt Rainier National Park

Elizabeth Ridge

Spray Park Trail

0   .25 mi
0   .25 km

© AVALON TRAVEL

need a national park pass, a self-service kiosk is located about 12 miles on Mowich Lake Road; pay the fee in exact cash or with a check.

Start the Hike

Start your hike from the signed Tolmie Peak Trailhead, descending to Mowich Lake. Bear left to head north on the **Wonderland Trail** toward Ipsut Pass and hike along the western edge of the lake. The dirt trail is nice and wide here, with some stretches of rocks and roots. Enjoy the shady forest of tall mountain hemlock, Pacific silver fir, and white rhododendron, taking a moment to turn around and spot Mount Rainier peeking through the trees to the southeast.

In 1.1 miles, arrive at a split in the trail and bear left for the **Tolmie Peak Trail**

Mount Rainier rises over Eunice Lake from Tolmie Peak Lookout.

toward Eunice Lake. Descending more than 200 feet through the forest, you'll pass impressive rock walls, pockets of thimbleberry, and colorful patches of paintbrush. Keep your eyes peeled for round-eared pikas darting among the rocks and black-tailed deer quietly foraging in the forest beyond the trail. The trail bottoms out at 1.5 miles then gains a heart-pounding 450 feet in elevation as you ascend northwest on a series of switchbacks to the lake basin.

Break out of the forest at **Eunice Lake** (2.1 miles) and enjoy the dramatic setting: the lake's blue-green waters ringed by tall pillars of columnar basalt and spire-like subalpine fir. Look northwest to spot Tolmie Peak Lookout impossibly perched above the lake. Several dirt paths lead from the main trail to the lake; shallow, lagoon-like spots are perfect for a cool splash on hot summer days. The fragile vegetation here sees lots of annual visitors; please protect it by staying on the main paths.

To press on, follow the trail around the western edge of Eunice Lake, climbing more than 500 feet in 0.9 mile to **Tolmie Peak Lookout** at 3 miles. Take in the impressive 360-degree views on a clear day: Mount Rainier presides over Eunice Lake to the southeast, Mount St. Helens is visible to the south, Mount Baker is to the northwest, the top of Glacier Peak lies north, and Mount Stuart is northeast. If you look carefully in the direction of Mount Rainier, you can also spot a sliver of Mowich Lake below as well as Mowich Lake Road snaking up the mountainside—a neat way to gauge how far you've come. The lookout is open for visitors and staffed by park service employees most summer days; it is closed to overnight stays.

Shorten the Hike
The hike to Eunice Lake is a perfectly acceptable destination in its own right: a 4.2-mile round-trip trek (2.5 hours).

Extend the Hike
If you've got more gas left in the tank, explore the trails around pretty **Mowich Lake.** The Wonderland Trail winds close to the lake's southern side (near the campground) and is perfect for cooling off on a hot day. From the trailhead, take Wonderland Trail south along Mowich Lake to the ranger patrol cabin for a 1.2-mile round-trip addition (45 minutes) to the Tolmie Peak hike.

You can also start your Tolmie Peak hike from the **Mowich Campground area** for more lakeside hiking. This route adds 1 mile round-trip (about 30 minutes) to the hike. From the parking area, pick up the Wonderland Trail from Mowich Campground and follow the trail north for 0.5 mile along Mowich Lake until it meets with the shorter route to Tolmie Peak.

Directions
From Seattle, take I-90 east to exit 10A for I-405 South toward Renton. Continue on I-405 South to exit 4 for State Route 169 South toward Enumclaw. At the end of the exit ramp, continue straight through the intersection with 3rd Street. Turn left at the next intersection for State Route 169 South toward Maple Valley/Enumclaw. Drive 25 miles on State Route 169 to Enumclaw, then turn left onto State Route 164 East/Griffin Avenue. In 0.5 mile, turn right onto State Route 410 West/Roosevelt Avenue.

Drive 4 miles to Buckley then turn left for State Route 165 toward Wilkeson. Follow the road as it curves sharply to the right and stay straight at a stop sign. In 1.5 miles, turn left at a T-intersection to stay on State Route 165 South toward Wilkeson and Carbonado. Drive 8 miles and cross the Fairfax Bridge. At 0.5 mile past the bridge, bear right and follow the Mount Rainier National Park sign for Mowich Lake. Drive 16.3 miles on the rough, potholed road to the Tolmie Peak Trailhead on your left. Park on the wide shoulder along the left side of the road (the side closest to Mowich Lake). No facilities are available, but there are two vault toilets at Mowich Campground at the end of the road in 0.3 mile.

GPS Coordinates: 46.937280, -121.867537 / N46° 56.236' W121° 52.051'

2 SPRAY PARK
Mount Rainier National Park, Mowich Lake

Best: Wildflowers

Distance: 8.4 miles round-trip

Duration: 5.5 hours

Elevation Change: 2,250 feet

Effort: Moderate

Trail: Dirt paths, log footbridges

Users: Hikers

Season: July–mid-October

Passes/Fees: National Park Pass

Maps: Green Trails Map 269 for Mount Rainier West, Green Trails Map 269S for Mount Rainier Wonderland, USGS topographic map for Mowich Lake

Contact: Mount Rainier National Park, Carbon River Ranger Station, www. nps.gov

---

An undulating trail to wildflower-filled meadows offers views of Mount Rainier with the option to explore Spray Falls.

Spray Park ticks off items that are high on a hiker's wish list: a stunning lake near the trailhead, a towering waterfall, meadows of wildflowers in the summer, satisfying views of Mount Rainier, and camping. The rolling trail can be somewhat deceiving as it descends more than 400 feet in elevation in the first 2 miles (elevation you'll regain back to the trailhead) before climbing sharply to Spray Park. At Spray Park, the trail continues to climb more than 750 feet through wildflower-filled meadows to a high point in the trail—the turnaround point. Bring plenty of water, sun protection, and bug spray; the top third of this trail is fully exposed with little shade, and the bugs can be voracious.

Spray Park is located in the northwest corner of Mount Rainier National Park, and it can be more than a 2-hour drive from the Seattle area. You may make it to Mowich Lake Road in 1.5 hours, but it can be slow going on the 16-mile potholed gravel road to the trailhead. Mowich Lake Road closes annually due to snowfall (mid-Oct.-late June or early July). If hiking on the edge of the season, call the Carbon River Ranger Station to check the status of the road before you make the drive.

This corner of Mount Rainier National Park sees substantial crowds in summer,

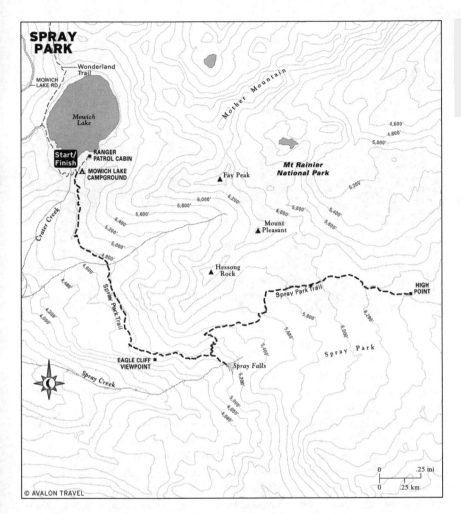

especially during August and on Memorial Day and Labor Day weekends. Plan to get an early morning start (even on weekdays) in order to grab a parking space and start your hike before the crowds descend.

Start the Hike

Start your hike from the Mowich Campground. Follow signs for Spray Park and the **Wonderland Trail** on the southern end of campground, just past the vault toilets. The Wonderland Trail is a strenuous 93-mile loop that circles Mount Rainier; it typically takes hikers 10-14 days to complete the whole loop. If you start early, you may hear tired hikers still snoozing in their tents; many campsites at Mowich are reserved for Wonderland Trail hikers, and it is also a popular resupply stop.

fields of wildflowers and views of Mount Rainier from the Spray Park Trail

The Wonderland Trail descends a dirt path for 0.25 mile into a shady forest of hemlock, cedar, and Douglas fir. Bear left at a well-signed junction onto the **Spray Park Trail** and enjoy crossing creeks on log footbridges and winding through an airy, sun-dappled forest on this rolling trail. After climbing a series of wooden steps, look right for a sign for the **Eagle Cliff Viewpoint** at 1.5 miles; the 0.1-mile round-trip spur trail leads to a view of Mount Rainier. Back on the trail, pass a sign for Eagle's Roost Camp, staying straight on the Spray Park Trail.

Arrive at a Y-junction with the **Spray Falls Viewpoint** at 2 miles and bear right to take the short 0.3-mile round-trip trail to the falls. The best view is across a rushing creek, which can be slippery and tricky to cross in high water; please proceed with caution. If you're traveling with young children or looking for a short hike, this is a good destination for the day. The trail to Spray Park climbs steeply beyond the Y-junction.

Back on the Spray Park Trail, bear left at the Y-junction toward **Spray Park.** Ascend a thigh-burning series of switchbacks, gaining more than 500 feet in 0.6 mile. Cross a log footbridge and enter meadows with a view of Mount Rainier rising above the trail at 2.6 miles. As you climb east another 1.2 miles, enjoy the view of nearby peaks with a colorful foreground of magenta paintbrush, purple lupine, and yellow cinquefoil bursting in summer.

Continue through a talus field at 3.8 miles, with expansive views to the north. Prominent yet tiny-sized peaks include Mount Baker to the northwest, triangle-shaped Glacier Peak to the north, and Mount Stuart to the northeast. In another 0.2

Spray Falls

mile, you'll reach a high point on the trail at 6,400 feet. Beyond this point, the trail descends sharply into Cataract Valley. Turnaround here and return 4 miles back to the trailhead.

Shorten the Hike
The trail to Spray Falls and back is a quick 4.3-mile round-trip hike (2.5 hours).

Extend the Hike
Pretty lakeside trails surround **Mowich Lake,** offering shallow access points and shady, rocky promontories perfect for picnics and cooling off after a hot day. Pick up lakeside trails from the northern side of Mowich Lake Campground, next to a sign marked Wonderland Trail and Lakeshore Walk. Bear right toward the ranger patrol cabin on the southeastern side of the lake, then swing left to explore the southwest side for a 1.6-mile round-trip hike (1 hour).

Get Away for the Weekend
Mowich Lake Campground is located at the start of the trail and offers an overnight option for this hike. Campsites are first-come, first served, and there is no fee to camp. The campground is open early July-early October. Self-issue permits are available at the trailhead. Call the ranger station to see how full the campgrounds are before you arrive; August is the busiest month and campsites fill quickly.

The seven **Eagle's Roost** campsites are located off a signed spur on the Spray Park Trail. Campers at Eagle's Roost will need a backcountry camping permit (free). Permits can be picked up in person 24 hours in advance at the **Carbon River Ranger Station** (35415 Fairfax Forest Reserve Rd. E., Carbonado, 360/829-9639, hours vary, free). While camping is free, a Mount Rainier National Park entrance fee applies.

Directions
From Seattle, take I-90 east to exit 10A for I-405 South toward Renton. Continue on I-405 South to exit 4 for State Route 169 South toward Enumclaw. At the end of the exit ramp, stay straight through the intersection with 3rd Street, then turn left at the next intersection for State Route 169 South toward Maple Valley/

Enumclaw. Drive 25 miles on State Route 169 to Enumclaw, then turn left onto State Route 164 East/Griffin Avenue. In 0.5 mile, turn right onto State Route 410 West/Roosevelt Avenue.

Drive 4 miles to Buckley then turn left for State Route 165 toward Wilkeson. Follow the road as it curves sharply to the right, staying straight at a stop sign. In 1.5 miles, turn left at a T-intersection to stay on State Route 165 South toward Wilkeson and Carbonado. Drive 8 miles, crossing the Fairfax Bridge. At 0.5 mile past the bridge, bear right and follow the Mount Rainier National Park sign for Mowich Lake. Drive 16.6 miles (the pavement ends in 1.6 miles) on a rough and potholed gravel road. The road ends at the parking area for Mowich Campground. Two vault toilets are located next to the campground.

If you can't find a parking spot in the lot, then park along the north shoulder on Mowich Lake Road (the side closest to the lake).

GPS Coordinates: 46.933164, -121.864578 / N46° 55.958' W121° 51.804'

3 SUMMIT LAKE

Mount Baker-Snoqualmie National Forest, Clearwater Wilderness

Distance: 4.8-6.2 miles round-trip

Duration: 3-4 hours

Elevation Change: 1,100-1,500 feet

Effort: Moderate

Trail: Dirt paths, some rocky sections

Users: Hikers, horses, leashed dogs

Season: Late June-September

Passes/Fees: Northwest Forest Pass

Maps: Green Trails Map 237 for Enumclaw, USGS topographic map for Bearhead Mountain

Contact: Mount Baker-Snoqualmie National Forest, Snoqualmie Ranger District-Enumclaw Office, www.fs.usda.gov

---

This deep, forested hike passes wildflowers and meadows on the way to a peaceful lake with mountain views.

Summit Lake is a stunning alpine lake atop a forested mesa 13 miles north of Mount Rainier. The hike's not-too-difficult grade and distance, along with berry-picking and lakeside exploring, make it a great option for beginning hikers and families. For more exploring after Summit Lake, press on to Summit Lake Peak for fantastic views of Mount Rainier on a clear day.

Altogether, this is a very popular hike; consider arriving early on weekends or on a weekday, or visit in the shoulder season for a quieter experience. Bugs can be voracious in the summer, so pack bug spray or wait until later in the season to tackle the trail. The road to the trailhead is notoriously rough—a high-clearance vehicle is strongly recommended.

Start the Hike

Start your hike on **Summit Lake Trail 1177,** heading east on the rocky dirt path into the forest. As you hike beneath towering stands of Pacific silver fir and noble fir, the trail evens out to a smoother dirt path and crosses into the Clearwater Wilderness at 0.7 mile. In summer, keep an eye out for plump blueberries and huckleberries along the trail.

Bear left at a signed junction (0.9 mile) next to Twin Lake to continue east on

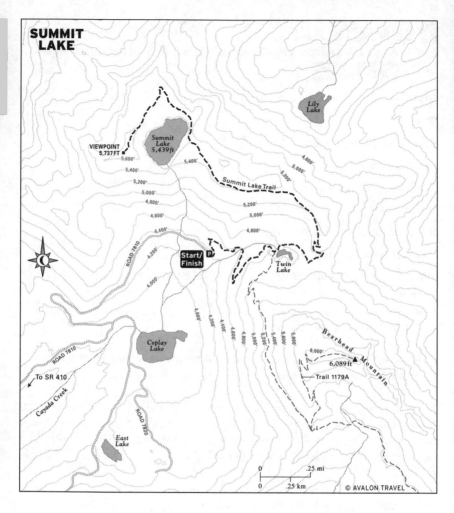

the **Summit Lake Trail.** (A right turn takes you toward Bearhead Mountain, a worthy alternative or a satisfying addition to your hike.) Past Twin Lake, the trail gains a steady 650 feet as it switchbacks north, passing thick columns of mountain hemlock, a beargrass-filled meadow, and a sneak peek of Mount Rainier to the south at 2.1 miles.

Arrive at the **Summit Lake** basin at 2.4 miles; the basin is bordered by a meadow to the west and the rounded top of Summit Peak to the north. Stop here for a 4.8-mile round-trip hike, or continue to the viewpoint atop Summit Lake Peak for a 6.2-mile round-trip trek.

Bearing right at Summit Lake, follow the dirt trail past some campsites and

Summit Lake sparkles beneath Bearhead Mountain and Mount Rainier.

around the lake's east side. In 0.3 mile, bear left to follow the trail southwest, gaining a few hundred feet in the next 0.4 mile to Summit Lake Peak at 3.1 miles.

Summit Lake Peak is exposed and windy, but offers plenty of rocky perches to rest and refuel. Enjoy the views of Bearhead Mountain to the southeast and Mount Rainier, Little Tahoma, and Carbon Glacier to the south. As you descend, the light catches on sparkling royal-blue Summit Lake and its shallow, fade-to-aqua shoreline. On a clear day, look north and you can just make out the outlines of Mount Baker to the northwest, Glacier Peak to the north, and Mount Stuart to the northeast.

Hike Nearby

Hike to **Bearhead Mountain** (6 miles round-trip, 4 hours, 1,800 feet elevation gain) for fantastic views of the Olympics, Summit Lake, Mount Baker, Glacier Peak, Mount Stuart, and Mount Rainier. From the parking lot, follow the Summit Lake Trail for 0.9 mile to the signed junction at Twin Lake. Turn right toward Bearhead Mountain and head south. In 1.3 miles, turn left to hike north on Trail 1179A. Follow the sign for Bearhead Mountain and arrive at the summit in 0.8 mile.

Get Away for the Weekend

Camping at one of the many sites bordering Summit Lake leaves time to explore nearby Bearhead Mountain. Campsites are first-come, first-served; no fees or permits are required. Campfires are prohibited. For more information, contact the **Mount Baker-Snoqualmie National Forest** (Snoqualmie Ranger District-Enumclaw Office, 450 Roosevelt Ave. E., Enumclaw, 360/825-6585, www.fs.usda.gov).

Directions

From Seattle, take I-90 east to exit 10A for I-405 South toward Renton. Continue on I-405 south to exit 4 for State Route 169 South toward Enumclaw. At the end of the exit ramp, stay straight through the intersection with 3rd Street, then turn left at the next intersection for State Route 169 South toward Maple Valley/ Enumclaw. Drive 25 miles on State Route 169 to Enumclaw, then turn left onto State Route 164 East/Griffin Avenue. In 0.5 mile, turn right onto State Route 410 West/Roosevelt Avenue.

Drive 4 miles to Buckley, then turn left for State Route 165 toward Wilkeson. Follow the road as it curves sharply to the right, staying straight at a stop sign. In 1.5 miles, turn left at a T-intersection to stay on State Route 165 South toward Wilkeson and Carbonado. Drive 8 miles, crossing the Fairfax Bridge. At 0.5 mile past the bridge, bear left at a Y-junction onto Carbon River Road, following the sign for Carbon River. Drive 7.5 miles then turn left onto unsigned Forest Road 7810 to cross a bridge over the Carbon River. Drive 6.5 miles on Forest Road 7810 to the end of the road and parking area (you will pass a target shooting area on your left in 0.2 mile). The bone-rattling drive on Forest Road 7810 is filled with troughs and bowling ball-sized rocks: A high-clearance vehicle is strongly recommended. No facilities are available at the trailhead, but there is a pit toilet at the lake. **GPS Coordinates:** 47.031503, -121.827122 / N47° 01.875' W121° 49.602'

4 KELLY BUTTE LOOKOUT
Mount Baker-Snoqualmie National Forest, Greenwater

Distance: 3.5 miles round-trip

Duration: 2.5 hours

Elevation Change: 1,050 feet

Effort: Easy/moderate

Trail: Dirt paths

Users: Hikers, leashed dogs

Season: July-October

Passes/Fees: Northwest Forest Pass

Maps: Green Trails Map 239 for Lester, USGS topographic map for Lester

Contact: Mount Baker-Snoqualmie National Forest, Snoqualmie Ranger District-Enumclaw Office, www.fs.usda.gov

---

Kelly Butte Lookout is an excellent option for a short trail that boasts fantastic views of Mount Rainier and the opportunity to peek inside a former fire lookout.

While this hike is on the shorter side, it is exposed in the last mile to the summit and can feel brutal on sunny days; bring plenty of water and sun protection. The last 6 miles to the trailhead have some narrow, one-lane sections, potholes, and small troughs that are close calls for low-clearance vehicles. Consider taking a high-clearance vehicle or, if you have a low-clearance vehicle, go slow and take your time.

Start the Hike
From the parking area, head west past a modest, unsigned kiosk to hike the **Kelly Butte Trail.** Enjoy the wide, gravel path (a former logging road) under a partial canopy of tall Douglas fir. Emerge at a small clearing in 0.7 mile with a view of Mount Rainier to the south. Bear right and follow the Trail sign, ascending more than 500 feet up a tight series of switchbacks on a narrow, rocky path—the steepest part of the hike. The gorgeous, unobstructed views of Mount Rainier continue as you climb, with colorful paintbrush, penstemon, lupine, and thimbleberries framing the trail in the summer. The trail soon gentles out and meanders northwest through a grassy meadow at 1.25 miles. Enjoy the low huckleberry shrubs lining the trail—a great snack in summer. This section of the trail can be a bit overgrown with brushy plants, a gentle reminder that we're visitors in nature's home.

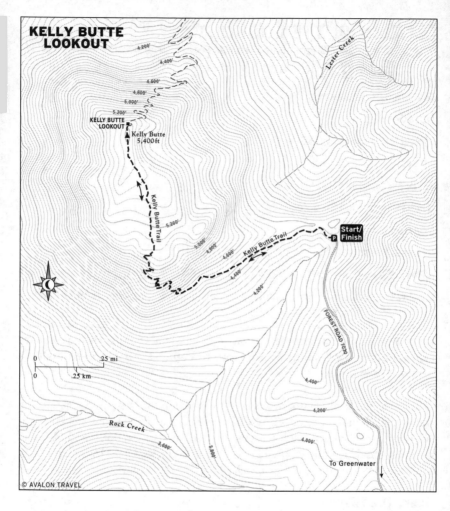

As you ascend a ridge, marvel at the view to the west of the Olympics. Just north is your destination: **Kelly Butte Lookout** at 1.75 miles. At 5,400 feet, Kelly Butte Lookout was a functioning fire lookout until the 1980s. After being vandalized, the lookout was restored in September 2011 with the help of volunteers from the U.S. Forest Service and Washington Trails Association. Today, it's staffed by U.S. Forest Service volunteers in summer; visitors are welcome to take a look inside.

Inside the lookout, enjoy the 360-degree mountain and valley views and use the panoramic map to help identify peaks: spot the top of Glacier Peak to the north, Mount Stuart to the northeast, Mount Rainier to the south, and even Suntop Mountain. If you have binoculars, you can even spot teeny-tiny Suntop Lookout

peaking out from Kelly Butte Lookout to views of Mount Rainier

and the road leading up to it. Explore the lookout and the ridge to the north before heading back to the trailhead.

Get Away for the Weekend

Volunteers with the U.S. Forest Service can spend the night at Kelly Butte Lookout. Duties include greeting fellow hikers and light upkeep of the lookout during your stay. Prospective volunteers must attend an orientation meeting where they can sign up for volunteer slots by lottery. (Attending the orientation does not guarantee a slot; the Forest Service has seen increasing interest in overnight stays in recent years.) To attend an orientation, call the **Enumclaw Ranger District** (450 Roosevelt Ave. E., Enumclaw, 360/825-6585, www.fs.usda.gov, hours vary seasonally) in late April or early May to be added to their volunteer email list. Applicants then receive an email notification when the orientation meeting is scheduled, typically in June.

Directions

From Seattle, take I-90 east to exit 10A for I-405 South toward Renton. Continue on I-405 South to exit 4 for State Route 169 South toward Enumclaw. At the end of the exit ramp, stay straight through the intersection with 3rd Street, then turn left at the next intersection for State Route 169 South toward Maple Valley/Enumclaw. Drive 25 miles on State Route 169 to Enumclaw, then turn left onto Griffin Avenue/State Route 164 East. In 0.5 mile, turn left onto State Route 410 East/Roosevelt Avenue.

Drive 18 miles on State Route 410 East to Greenwater. In another 2 miles, turn left onto Forest Road 70, which is located between mileposts 44 and 45. Drive 8.1 miles on paved Forest Road 70, then turn left onto Forest Road 7030, which is marked with a small brown sign and arrow. The paved road turns to gravel past this point. Drive 3.8 miles on Forest Road 7030, crossing a bridge and passing several campsites. At a T-junction, turn left to stay on Forest Road 7030. In 0.5 mile, stay straight on Forest Road 7030 and follow the sign for Kelly Butte. In 0.6 mile, bear right at a Y-junction and follow the sign for Forest Road 7030. Drive 1.2 miles farther on Forest Road 7030; turn left at the third road on the left to a small parking area and the trailhead. No facilities are available; come prepared to pack out any waste.

GPS Coordinates: 47.163320, -121.474362 / N47° 09.796' W121° 28.452'

5 GRAND PARK VIA LAKE ELEANOR

Mount Baker-Snoqualmie National
Forest, Mount Rainier National Park

Best: Wildflowers

Distance: 8.8 miles round-trip

Duration: 5 hours

Elevation Change: 1,400 feet

Effort: Moderate

Trail: Dirt paths

Users: Hikers

Season: June-October

Passes/Fees: None

Maps: Green Trails Map 270 for Mount Rainier East, USGS topographic map for Sunrise

Contact: Mount Rainier National Park, www.nps.gov

Hike through a shaded forest into Grand Park, an expansive meadow with sweeping views of Mount Rainier.

Grand Park offers something very few hikes can claim—a vista of Mount Rainier from a grand meadow. This route to Grand Park is the shorter of two approaches, heading south to Lake Eleanor instead of north from the Sunrise area. Parking is limited on this approach, so it's a good idea to get an early start if you're heading out on a sunny summer weekend. Pack your sun hat, bug spray, and sunscreen—the mosquitoes can be voracious in the summer and the meadows are fully exposed to the sun. Wear shoes or boots you don't mind getting mucked up—a few stretches of trail tend to be muddy and waterlogged.

Start the Hike

Start your hike on the unsigned dirt path near the **Eleanor Creek** sign and head southwest into the forest. Enjoy hiking under the shady canopy of mountain hemlock with pretty white rhododendron lining the trail. The trail officially enters Mount Rainier National Park in 475 feet, continuing past an extended muddy section of the trail. This area is a bit tricky; in some places it's possible to sink up to your ankles in mud. Take your time navigating this section.

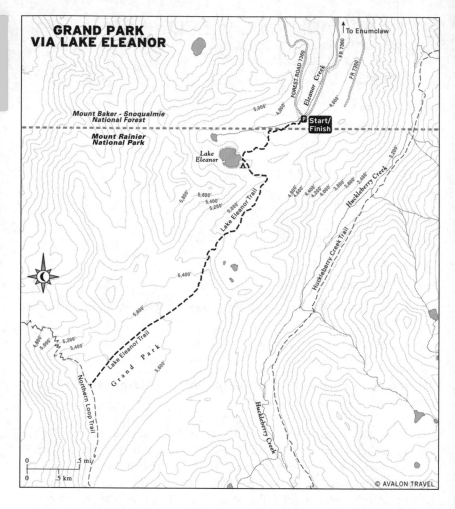

Arrive at **Lake Eleanor** in 1 mile and admire the pretty, tree-ringed lake. When you're ready to press on, take the unsigned dirt path opposite the lake to head southeast through a roomy forest of Douglas fir and western hemlock. Soon you'll swing back southwest, descending more than 150 feet to a small, open meadow at 1.6 miles; this area is sometimes referred to as Baby Grand Park. After a teasing view of the top of Mount Rainier, reenter the forest on the quiet dirt path and climb 675 feet over the next 1.5 miles to Grand Park. (This is the most elevation you'll gain in one spot on this hike.)

Cresting a hill into **Grand Park** at 3.1 miles, the trail evens out to a flat, gentle grade in the large, open meadow. Keep hiking southwest for another 0.9 mile

A hiker heads south through Grand Park.

for the best views of Mount Rainier—they get better and better as you go. Take in the dominating view of the mountain and the fields of aster, paintbrush, and lupine that bloom in summer. See if you can spot teeny-tiny Fremont Lookout atop Mount Fremont to the south, as well as Skyscraper Mountain, Little Tahoma, and Steamboat Prow to the southwest. Turn around here, or continue another 0.4 mile to a signed junction with the Northern Loop Trail (4.4 miles) for a bit of shade before heading back.

Hike Nearby

Suntop Lookout boasts panoramic views of Mount Rainier and the Cascades during the day and stargazing at night. The 1.4-mile round-trip hike gains a steep 500 feet in 0.7 mile, so be prepared for a workout.

The access gate to the lookout is typically open during the day (closes at 8pm); when open, you can drive directly to the lookout on a rough, bumpy road. If the gate is closed, park outside the gate (do not block it) and look for the **Trail 1183 Suntop Lookout** trail sign posted south of the gate.

Volunteers staff the lookout seasonally (June-Oct.), and nearby picnic tables offer lunch with a view. Dogs are allowed on the trail. A Northwest Forest Pass is required. There is a vault toilet at the lookout.

To get there, follow the directions for Grand Park. At the intersection of Forest Road 73 and State Route 410, drive south on Forest Road 73 for 1.3 miles and turn left at the Y-junction onto Forest Road 7315. Continue 4.8 miles to a Y-junction and bear right through the access gate to the lookout.

Directions

From Seattle, take I-90 east to exit 10A for I-405 South toward Renton. Continue on I-405 South to exit 4 for State Route 169 South toward Enumclaw. At the end of the exit ramp, stay straight through the intersection with 3rd Street, then turn left at the next intersection for State Route 169 South toward Maple Valley/Enumclaw. Drive 25 miles on State Route 169 to Enumclaw, then turn left onto Griffin Avenue/State Route 164 East. In 0.5 mile, turn left onto State Route 410 East/Roosevelt Avenue.

Drive 24 miles on State Route 410 East. Pass milepost 49 at the Mount Rainier Viewpoint and in 0.3 mile turn right onto unmarked Forest Road 73. Drive 1.3 miles on Forest Road 73, passing a vault toilet in 0.4 mile. At an unsigned Y-junction, bear right. In 0.5 mile, bear left to stay on Forest Road 73. Drive 7.1 miles on the rough, rocky road and stay straight at a junction onto unsigned Forest Road 7360. Drive 1.1 miles, passing the sign for Eleanor Creek, and park in the small area on the right. Hike down the road about 80 feet to pick up the obvious, but unsigned, dirt trail near the sign for Eleanor Creek.

GPS Coordinates: 46.996298, -121.641723 / N46° 59.780' W121° 38.500'

6 SNOQUERA FALLS LOOP

Mount Baker-Snoqualmie National Forest, Greenwater

Distance: 3.9 miles round-trip

Duration: 2 hours

Elevation Change: 900 feet

Effort: Easy/moderate

Trail: Dirt and rock paths

Users: Hikers, mountain bikers, leashed dogs

Season: April-November

Passes/Fees: Northwest Forest Pass

Maps: Green Trails Map 238 for Greenwater, USGS topographic map for Sun Top

Contact: Mount Baker-Snoqualmie National Forest, Enumclaw Ranger Station, www.fs.usda.gov.

Snoquera Falls is an adventurous loop hike past a dramatic, 449-foot waterfall.

The trailhead is located next to Camp Sheppard, a former Civilian Conservation Corp camp that now operates as a Boy Scout camp. When the trail reaches Snoquera Falls, it crosses the falls through a rocky section that can get flooded and slippery; those with younger children might want to skip this crossing and instead turn back at the falls. Whichever option you decide, it's a good idea to bring a map, as the signs and junctions can be confusing. Visit in spring when the falls are rushing from the snowmelt and lingering rainy season; the falls tend to dry out significantly in the summer.

Start the Hike

From the parking lot, follow the sign for **Snoquera Falls 1167,** hiking east. Enjoy the sight of massive Douglas fir, western redcedar, and western hemlock dotting the trail, bearing left to skirt behind a small wooden amphitheater. Continue straight past an intersection with the Moss Lake Trail and follow the sign for Snoquera Falls. In 475 feet, arrive at a signed junction with Snoquera Falls Trail and White River Trail. Bear right to take the upper trail for Snoquera Falls Trail 1167; the lower trail is White River Trail 1199.

The next 1.4 miles to Snoquera Falls is a peaceful hike through a sun-dappled forest carpeted with treelike yellow-green moss, sprigs of pointy Oregon grape,

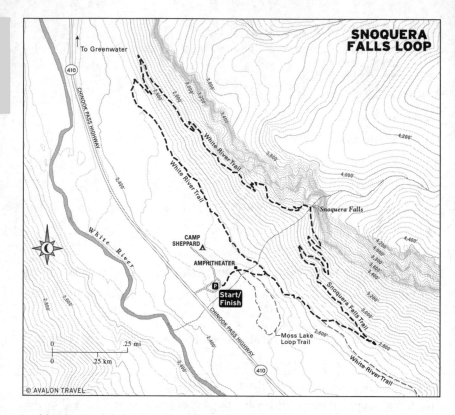

and leathery salal shrubs. Climb steadily, first to the southeast and then to the northwest on long switchbacks with peekaboo views west across the White River Valley. You'll emerge onto an exposed, rocky talus field with the plunging 287-foot upper part of the falls above. Enjoy the view, then either turn back and descend the trail the way you came, or continue another 2.1 miles to finish the loop. The loop involves crossing through the base of the falls, which may be slippery and impassable depending on weather conditions.

Continue on the loop and cross the wet, rocky base of **Snoquera Falls** to find the dirt path on the other side. Make a hard left to switchback down the path, pausing to enjoy the better vantage point of the waterfall and its cascading 162-foot fan-shaped lower part. Descending northwest, you'll notice that the trail on this side of the falls is narrower, rockier, and more exposed, passing through talus fields before reentering the cool, mossy, canopied forest. Enjoy the open views of the mountains across the valley.

In 1.4 miles, turn left at a signed junction onto **White River Trail 1199** and follow the trail southeast. Cross an open field to pick up the trail on the other side (it's marked with a Trail sign). Complete your loop in 0.7 mile, arriving back at the junction with the Snoquera Falls Trail and White River Trail. Bear right toward Camp Sheppard to return to the trailhead in 0.2 mile.

Shorten the Hike

For a shorter outing (or when water flow obstructs the path through the falls), turn back when reaching the waterfall for a 3.2-mile, 1.5-hour hike.

Extend the Hike

The 0.6-mile **Moss Lake Loop** makes a nice addition to the Snoquera Falls Trail. The quiet, peaceful walk is scattered with a few wooden benches. From the amphitheater, follow the sign east for Moss Lake Loop Trail. The side trip adds 20 minutes to your hike.

Snoquera Falls

Make It a Day Trip

Wapiti Woolies (58414 SR 410 E., Greenwater, 800/766-5617, www.wapitiwoolies.com, open daily) is a fun and friendly shop selling everything from tea and espresso to sunglasses, T-shirts, and their signature hats, or "woolies." Stop in for huckleberry ice cream, a caffeine fix, or to pick up some huckleberry honey.

To get there from the intersection of Camp Sheppard and State Route 410 East, head west on State Route 410 East for 9.6 miles to Greenwater. Wapiti Woolies is on the left, just before Naches Tavern.

Directions

From Seattle, take I-90 east to exit 10A for I-405 South toward Renton. Continue on I-405 South to exit 4 for State Route 169 South toward Enumclaw. At the end of the exit ramp, stay straight through the intersection with 3rd Street, then turn left at the next intersection for State Route 169 South toward Maple Valley/Enumclaw. Drive 25 miles on State Route 169 to Enumclaw, then turn left onto Griffin Avenue/State Route 164 East. In 0.5 mile, turn left onto State Route 410 East/Roosevelt Avenue. Drive 27.7 miles east then turn left onto Forest Road 7155 at the sign for Camp Sheppard Trailhead. Turn right into the parking lot. Two vault toilets are located next to the parking lot.

GPS Coordinates: 47.035845, -121.560175 / N47° 02.149' W121° 33.603'

7 NORSE PEAK
Mount Baker-Snoqualmie National Forest, Enumclaw

Best: Day Trips

Distance: 10 miles round-trip

Duration: 6 hours

Elevation Change: 2,900 feet

Effort: Moderate/strenuous

Trail: Narrow dirt paths

Users: Hikers, horses, leashed dogs

Season: July-October

Passes/Fees: Northwest Forest Pass

Maps: Green Trails Map 271 for Bumping Lake, Green Trails Map 269S for Mount Rainier Wonderland, USGS topographic map for Norse Peak

Contact: Mount Baker-Snoqualmie National Forest, Snoqualmie Ranger District-Enumclaw Office, www.fs.usda.gov

---

This dry yet forested hike climbs a ridgeline with 360-degree views of the Cascades, Olympics, and Silver Creek Valley.

Norse Peak sits on a ridgeline straddling the Silver Creek Valley to the west and the brawny, steep-bowled basins of the Norse Peak Wilderness to the east. The summit boasts bold views of Mount Rainier, Mount Adams, the North Cascades, and the Stuart Range.

While the trail winds along forest for the first half, it is dry, exposed, and windy on the second half; bring plenty of water, sun protection, and wind protection. You may see local outfitters bringing folks up here on horseback. Please yield to any horses you encounter on the trail by stepping to the downhill side to let them pass.

Start the Hike
From the intersection of Gold Hill Road and Crystal Mountain Boulevard, head south on the wide, gravel road. In 0.25 mile, turn left at the sign for **Norse Peak Trail 1191** and follow the dusty, dirt path into the forest. Pass a junction with the Half Camp Trail at 0.4 mile, then ascend 1,800 feet over the next 2.4 miles, climbing long switchbacks that wind lazily northeast up the mountain. The cool shade of hemlock, Douglas fir, and vine maple lines the trail, with triangle-shaped

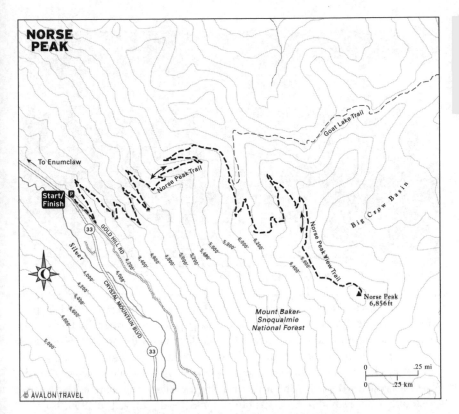

bracken fern poking out from the dry hillside. A number of weathered trails intersect with the Norse Peak Trail throughout the hike; some sport signs marked Closed For Restoration, while other rogue paths cut the switchbacks. Stay on the main trail to prevent further erosion of the mountainside.

Reaching a signed junction with Goat Lake at 2.8 miles, bear right to stay on **Norse Peak Trail 1191.** The trail's grade eases as you traverse meadows with stands of subalpine fir; their sharp, pointed profiles help the trees shed snow in winter. Emerge onto an exposed, windy ridgeline at 4.4 miles with a direct view of Norse Peak to the southeast. Take in the grand view of Big Crow Basin to the east, with the Pacific Crest Trail winding through the basin below.

Bear right onto the unsigned **Norse Peak View Trail 1191.1** and head southeast, following an established path along the ridgeline. Take care through this section as there are steep drop-offs next to the trail. The grand mountain and valley views get prettier and prettier over the next 0.6 mile, with purple lupine painting the mountain in the summer. As you round a bend, spot Basin Lake below to the east. Bear right at an unsigned junction and head west on a short spur trail through the trees.

Mount Rainier from a wind shelter at Norse Peak

Arrive at **Norse Peak** at 4.9 miles. The peak is topped with a shallow, U-shaped wind shelter and a dead-on view of Mount Rainier to the southwest. Farther south, you can spot Mount Adams as well as Crystal Mountain Resort and its gondola carrying passengers to the summit of Crystal Mountain. Swinging around to the northeast, a lineup of peaks stretches across the horizon—Mount Stuart, the North Cascades, and a teeny-tiny Mount Baker. Rusted cables are a reminder that an old fire lookout once stood here; it was built in 1931 and removed in 1956. Enjoy a snack or lunch and leave time to savor the views from the ridgeline on your way back to the trailhead.

Make It a Day Trip

Visit nearby **Crystal Mountain Resort** (33914 Crystal Mountain Blvd., Enumclaw, 360/663-2265, www.crystalmountainresort.com, hours and rates vary seasonally) and take a gondola ride up Crystal Mountain. From the summit, take a seat in a sling-back chair facing Mount Rainier, or enjoy lunch at one of the picnic benches near the gondola or at the Summit House restaurant. You can also hike to the top of Crystal Mountain and take the gondola back down or vice-versa.

To get to Crystal Mountain Resort, drive 2 miles south on Crystal Mountain Boulevard to the Crystal Mountain Resort at the end of the road. Parking is free; leashed dogs are allowed on the gondola and the hiking trails. The gondola is wheelchair-accessible.

Directions

From Seattle, take I-90 east to exit 10A for I-405 South toward Renton. Take

I-405 South to exit 4 for State Route 169 South toward Enumclaw. At the end of the exit ramp, stay straight through the intersection with 3rd Street, then turn left at the next intersection for State Route 169 South toward Maple Valley/Enumclaw. Drive 25 miles on State Route 169 to Enumclaw, then turn left onto State Route 164 East/Griffin Avenue. In 0.5 mile, turn left onto State Route 410 East/Roosevelt Avenue.

Drive 32.5 miles on State Route 410 East, then turn left onto Crystal Mountain Boulevard and continue toward Crystal Mountain Resort. Drive 4.2 miles to an unsigned gravel road (Gold Hill Rd.) on the left. Park on the wide shoulder on the right side of the road, marked by the Crystal Mountain Ski Area sign. Carefully cross the road (there is no pedestrian crosswalk) and hike 0.25 mile south on Gold Hill Road to the trailhead.

GPS Coordinates: 46.964171, -121.482775 / N46° 57.858' W121° 28.960'

8 SECOND BURROUGHS

Mount Rainier National Park, Sunrise Area

Best: Off the Beaten Path, Mountain Views

Distance: 6 miles round-trip

Duration: 4 hours

Elevation Change: 1,200 feet

Effort: Moderate

Trail: Dirt paths

Users: Hikers

Season: Late June-October

Passes/Fees: National Park Pass

Maps: Green Trails Map 270 for Mount Rainier East, Green Trails Map 269S for Mount Rainier Wonderland, USGS topographic map for Sunrise

Contact: Mount Rainier National Park, www.nps.gov

Second Burroughs is a fantastic hike for vision-dominating views of Mount Rainier.

Named after naturalist John Burroughs, Second Burroughs is one of three distinct peaks on Burroughs Mountain; First, Second, and Third Burroughs each rises progressively higher than the last. Aside from visiting Second Burroughs, there are great opportunities to customize your hike: Shorten the trip to a family-friendly jaunt to First Burroughs, lengthen it to explore Third Burroughs, or make it a loop by taking the Sunrise Rim Trail on your return. You can also make a day trip out of your hike by exploring nearby trails, visiting the Sunrise Visitor Center, or taking a break at Sunrise Lodge.

Snow can linger into the summer on Burroughs Mountain. It can be chilly and windy on Second Burroughs, and there are no water sources along the way. Pack layers, check trail conditions before you head out, and take advantage of the water bottle refill station at the Sunrise Lodge. A sun hat and sunscreen will come in handy too—these trails are generally exposed with little tree cover.

The Sunrise area is the highest point you can drive to on Mount Rainier. The roads are paved all the way to the Sunrise parking lot, roughly a 2-hour, 20-minute traffic-free drive from downtown Seattle. On clear, sunny days, holiday weekends, and fee-free days, wait times at the entrance can be an hour or more: Plan to arrive

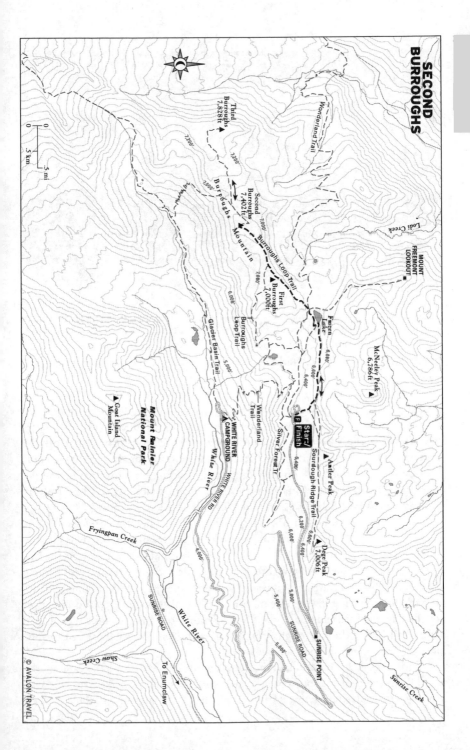

SECOND BURROUGHS

Third Burroughs 7,828ft

Second Burroughs 7,402ft

First Burroughs 7,000ft

Burroughs Loop Trail

Burroughs Mountain

Burroughs Loop Trail

Wonderland Trail

Lodi Creek

MOUNT FREEMONT LOOKOUT

McNeeley Peak 6,786ft

Frozen Lake

Glacier Basin Trail

Wonderland Trail

WHITE RIVER CAMPGROUND

Goat Island Mountain

Mount Rainier National Park

White River

WHITE RIVER RD

Silver Forest Tr.

Star/ Finish

Souralough Ridge Trail

Antler Peak

Dege Peak 7,006ft

Fryingpan Creek

White River

SUNRISE ROAD

SUNRISE POINT

SUNRISE ROAD

To Enumclaw

Shaw Creek

Sunrise Creek

© AVALON TRAVEL

0   5 km
0   .5 mi

view of Mount Rainier and Second Burroughs from First Burroughs

before 10am or after 2:30pm to avoid peak travel times. Due to lingering snow and a short summer season, Sunrise harbors a dry, subalpine environment with fragile meadows. Help the National Park Service restore the meadows by staying on the hiking trails.

Start the Hike

From the Sunrise parking lot, head north on the wide trail (next to the restrooms) toward **Sourdough Ridge.** In 0.1 mile, bear right at an information kiosk; in another 0.1 mile, bear left at a signed junction toward Burroughs Mountain Trail. In 0.2 mile, join the Sourdough Ridge Trail, heading west toward Burroughs Mountain. Enjoy the gorgeous view of Mount Rainier looming southwest of the trail, as well as Huckleberry Basin and McNeeley Peak to the north.

About 1.6 miles into your hike, arrive at a five-way junction and the Mount Fremont Lookout Trail. Stay straight toward **First Burroughs** for 0.8 mile, gaining 400 feet as you hike southwest along the ridge toward Mount Rainier. At the flat top of First Burroughs, enjoy the break in the grade and the direct view of Mount Rainier and Second Burroughs ahead. Keep your eyes peeled for mountain goats that might be grazing in the large meadow. If First Burroughs is your destination for the day, turn around here for a 4.8-mile round-trip hike, or take the Sunrise Rim Trail (called the Burroughs Loop Trail on Green Trails Maps) east toward Shadow Lake to make a picturesque loop.

Continuing on to **Second Burroughs,** stay straight and climb 0.6 mile southwest. Reaching the flat-topped peak, take a seat on a turtleback-like structure with a built-in bench facing Mount Rainier. If it's chilly, slip on your windbreaker then enjoy the view of Steamboat Prow chugging up the mountain, dividing Emmons Glacier on the left with Winthrop Glacier on the right. Chipmunks and birds haunt this area, poking and skittering among the rocks (please don't feed them). Take some pictures, enjoy your lunch break, and when you're ready, head back to the trailhead.

Extend the Hike
The hike to **Third Burroughs** (9.2 miles round-trip, 6 hours) includes a 2,500-foot elevation gain. From Second Burroughs, follow the Burroughs Mountain Trail west, descending 300 feet in 0.4 mile—elevation you'll need to regain on the way back. Upon reaching a signed junction for the Burroughs Mountain Trail, turn right onto an unsigned and unmaintained path heading west and climb more than 800 feet in the next 1.25 miles to Third Burroughs. Take care, as the summit has steep drop-offs and the route can be dangerous in fog and snow conditions. (Snow can linger on Third Burroughs well into the summer, so check the trail conditions before you go.)

Make It a Loop
Create a loop hike on your way back from Second Burroughs by taking the **Sunrise Rim Trail** to visit Shadow Lake. This loop adds an extra 30 minutes and 0.4 mile to your Second Burroughs hike, for a total distance of 6.4 miles round-trip. After you've reached Second Burroughs, head back down to First Burroughs. Turn right at the signed junction for the Sunrise Rim Trail and head southeast toward Shadow Lake. Continue following signs for the Sunrise Rim Trail and you'll reach Shadow Lake in 1.4 miles. After exploring the lake, continue northeast for another 1.4 miles and follow the signs for Sunrise back to the parking lot.

Hike Nearby
Visit **Mount Fremont Lookout,** a former fire lookout built in the mid-1930s. The 5.8-mile round-trip hike (3.5 hours) starts from the Sunrise parking area and gains 1,200 feet of elevation. Head west on the Sourdough Ridge Trail toward Frozen Lake. In 1.6 miles, turn right at a five-way junction for the signed Mount Fremont Lookout Trail. Follow the trail northwest along the ridge for 1.3 miles to the lookout with panoramic views of Mount Rainier, Burroughs Mountain, and Grand Park. The lookout is not open for overnight stays, but you're welcome to peek inside when the park service is staffing the lookout.

Make It a Day Trip
The **Sunrise Visitor Center** (360/663-2425, 10am-6pm daily early July-early Sept.) and **Sunrise Lodge** (day-use only, early July-late Sept., hours vary seasonally) are both adjacent to the Sunrise parking lot. The visitors center offers exhibits, trail

maps, and guided interpretive programs. At Sunrise Lodge, you can rest at one of the cafeteria tables and enjoy some hot food or a snack, pick up some bug spray or a water bottle, or refill your water bottle at the refill station. If a picnic lunch is more your style, follow the signs from the Sunrise parking lot to the picnic area for a scenic spot at one of the picnic tables behind the visitors center.

Directions

From Seattle, take I-90 east to exit 10A for I-405 South toward Renton. Continue on I-405 South to exit 4 for State Route 169 South toward Enumclaw. At the end of the exit ramp, stay straight through the intersection with 3rd Street, then turn left at the next intersection for State Route 169 South toward Maple Valley/Enumclaw. Drive 25 miles on State Route 169 to Enumclaw, then turn left onto State Route 164 East/Griffin Avenue. In 0.5 mile, turn left again onto State Route 410 East/Roosevelt Avenue.

Drive 37 miles east and turn right at the Mather Memorial Parkway sign onto Sunrise Park Road. In 1.2 miles, pass through the pay station and White River Wilderness Information Center. Drive another 14 miles to the end of the road and the Sunrise parking lot. Restrooms are located next to the parking lot.

Note that **Sunrise Road closes** in the off-season.

GPS Coordinates: 46.914520, -121.639485 / N46° 54.884' W121° 38.543'

9 DEGE PEAK
Mount Rainier National Park, Sunrise Area

Best: Mountain Views

Distance: 4.1 miles round-trip

Duration: 2.5 hours

Elevation Change: 900 feet

Effort: Easy/moderate

Trail: Dirt paths

Users: Hikers

Season: Late June-October

Passes/Fees: National Park Pass

Maps: Green Trails Map 270 for Mount Rainier East, Green Trails Map 269S for Mount Rainier Wonderland, USGS topographic maps for Sunrise and White River

Contact: Mount Rainier National Park, White River Ranger Station, www.nps.gov

---

This short hike leads to 360-degree views of the Cascades with stunning views of Mount Rainier from the peak.

Dege Peak is a short hike with big, bold views of Mount Rainier. Save this hike for a summer day with clear weather; the main draw on this trail is the view of Mount Rainier and you won't want to miss this due to clouds. Or, if you're comfortable hiking with a headlamp, Dege Peak also makes a wonderful sunrise hike with the added bonus of watching tiny, pinprick lights from climbers' headlamps form an ant trail up Mount Rainier during their early morning ascent.

The Sunrise Visitor Center and parking area is roughly a 2-hour, 20-minute drive from the Seattle area. Consider squeezing in some extra time while you're here, or make a day trip out of your visit. This is also a popular tourist destination; wait times at the entrance can be an hour or more in peak season. To bypass the summer crowds, avoid peak travel times (10am-2:30pm) on clear, sunny days in August, or on holiday weekends and fee-free days. Early fall, when the meadows surrounding Sunrise give off a golden hue, is a great time to visit. Bring a hat and sunscreen as trails in the Sunrise area are exposed with little shade.

Start the Hike
From the Sunrise parking lot, head north on the wide trail toward **Sourdough**

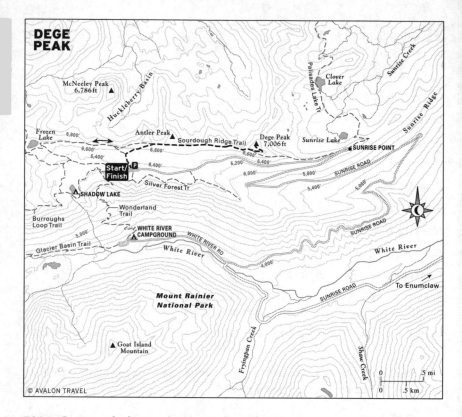

Ridge. In 0.1 mile, bear right at an information kiosk; in another 0.1 mile, bear right again at a signed junction for Dege Peak and the Sourdough Ridge Trail. Hiking east, you'll reach the Sourdough Ridge Trail in 0.3 mile. Bear right to continue east for 1.2 miles along the gently undulating trail that links Antler Peak with Dege Peak. Enjoy the views of Huckleberry Basin and McNeeley Peak to the north, and take a quick peek behind you for a preview of Mount Rainier views for your way back.

About 1.8 miles into the hike, turn left at a signed junction for Dege Peak. The trail gains 230 feet in 0.25 mile to the summit at 7,006 feet. Dege Peak is named for James H. Dege, a clothier who moved to Tacoma from Atlanta, Georgia, in 1889 (he owned a large clothing store called Dege and Milner on Pacific Avenue). Enjoy the 360-degree views from the summit, but take care, as there are steep drop-offs surrounding three-quarters of the peak. On a clear day, you can see Mount Adams rising clearly in the southeast and Mount Rainier dominating the view southwest. If you squint, you can also spot tiny Mount Baker to the northwest, Glacier Peak to the north, and even Mount Stuart and the Stuart Range to

views of Mount Rainier on the way back from Dege Peak

the northeast. Look southwest to spy Sunrise Road snaking its way to the visitors center and parking lot. Heading back, enjoy the fantastic view of Mount Rainier as you hike west back to the parking lot and Sunrise Visitor Center.

Hike Nearby

The **Silver Forest Trail** is a wonderful option for families or those with limited mobility. This easy 2-mile round-trip hike packs exceptional views of Mount Rainer and the Glacier Basin, with only 250 feet of elevation gain.

Pick up the inconspicuous trail on the south side of the parking lot across from Sunrise Lodge. Hike south on the dirt trail toward Shadow Lake and Sunrise Camp. In 450 feet, bear left to head east on the Silver Forest Trail. Continue past the first overlook for a great view of Emmons Glacier from the second overlook; keep going for more beautiful vistas toward the end of the maintained trail.

Get Away for the Weekend

White River Campground (late June-Sept., $20) is just 11 miles from the Sunrise Visitor Center and offers an opportunity to spend the night nearby. The 112 first-come, first-served campsites come with drinking water, fire grates, and flush toilets. Call ahead to confirm that the campground and park roads are open before you go.

Looking to camp in the backcountry? There are several backcountry campsites off the Sunrise area trails. A free permit is required for campsites and is only issued in person from the **White River Wilderness Information Center** (White River Entrance, 360/569-6670, www.nps.gov, 7:30am-5pm daily late May-early Oct.).

Directions

From Seattle, take I-90 east to exit 10A for I-405 South toward Renton. Continue on I-405 South to exit 4 for State Route 169 South toward Enumclaw. At the end of the exit ramp, stay straight through the intersection with 3rd Street, then turn left at the next intersection for State Route 169 South toward Maple Valley/Enumclaw. Drive 25 miles on State Route 169 to Enumclaw, then turn left onto State Route 164 East/Griffin Avenue. In 0.5 mile, turn left onto State Route 410 East/Roosevelt Avenue.

Drive 37 miles east and turn right at the Mather Memorial Parkway sign onto Sunrise Park Road. In 1.2 miles, pass through the pay station and White River Wilderness Information Center. Drive another 14 miles to the end of the road and the Sunrise parking lot. Men's and women's ADA-accessible restrooms are next to the parking lot.

Note that **Sunrise Road closes** in winter.

GPS Coordinates: 46.914520, -121.639485 / N46° 54.884' W121° 38.543'

10 TIPSOO LAKE-NACHES PEAK LOOP

Mount Rainier National Park, William O. Douglas Wilderness

Best: Wildflowers

Distance: 3.6-4.1 miles round-trip

Duration: 2.5 hours

Elevation Change: 700 feet

Effort: Easy/moderate

Trail: Dirt paths

Users: Hikers, leashed dogs (PCT section only)

Season: Early July-early October

Passes/Fees: None

Maps: Green Trails Map 270 for Mount Rainier East, Green Trails Map 271 for Bumping Lake, USGS topographic maps for Chinook Pass and Cougar Lake

Contact: Mount Rainier National Park, White River Ranger Station, www.nps.gov

---

The Tipsoo Lake-Naches Peak Loop boasts showy wildflower displays, picturesque tarns, and outstanding views of Mount Rainier, all wrapped up in a family-friendly hike.

Plan to arrive early on summer weekends, as the popular trail sees large tourist crowds. Dogs are only allowed on the northeastern section of the loop (the Pacific Crest Trail side). You can pick up the Pacific Crest Trail from a separate parking area past the main Tipsoo Lake parking lots. While you can hike the loop in either direction, most people travel clockwise for a gentler elevation gain and a nice vista of Mount Rainier.

Start the Hike

From the Tipsoo Lake parking lot, head northeast on the **Naches Peak Loop Trail** toward Chinook Pass. Explore the 0.5-mile trail around Tipsoo Lake and enjoy the modest reflection of Mount Rainier in the water and the fields of lupine that decorate the meadows in summer. (Bugs run rampant here; pack bug spray and wear long sleeves and pants.) Returning to the trail, pass beneath Yakima Peak and hike northeast toward the pass.

The trail emerges at State Route 410 in 0.3 mile. Cross a pedestrian bridge over the highway and onto the **Pacific Crest Trail.** Enjoy views of a picturesque

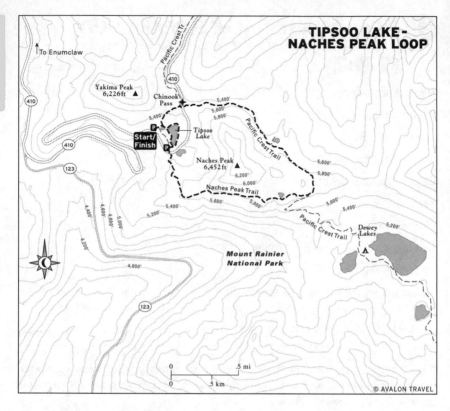

TIPSOO LAKE-NACHES PEAK LOOP

© AVALON TRAVEL

tarn and seasonal waterfalls as you hike southeast beneath Naches Peak. Time your hike for when the wildflowers are blooming to experience a dazzling carpet of lupine blanketing the hillsides. (Wildflower blooms vary annually; check trip reports online at www.wta.org in summer.)

About 1.9 miles into your hike, you'll arrive at a signed junction for **Dewey Lakes.** Stay straight on the loop trail toward Tipsoo Lake. Dewey Lakes sparkle below as you head west for another 0.1 mile to a grand, tree-lined meadow bursting with lupine and magenta paintbrush in the summer. Mount Rainier dominates the view on the horizon, anchored by a pretty tarn at the base of the meadow.

Past the tarn, enjoy further views of Mount Rainier as you wind north, descending 550 feet in 1.4 miles to the trail intersection with State Route 410. There is no pedestrian walkway here; take care crossing the highway. To finish the loop, pick up the trail at the edge of the sidewalk next to the small parking lot. A couple of trails head back to the larger parking lot—it's your choice. If you're looking for a place to have a snack or lunch, there are several picnic tables next to the parking lot.

Mount Rainier on the Tipsoo Lake-Naches Peak Loop

Extend the Hike
The hike to **Dewey Lakes,** located southeast of the Tipsoo Lake-Naches Peak Loop on the Pacific Crest Trail, adds an extra 2.3 miles round-trip and 650 feet of elevation gain. From the intersection of the Tipsoo Lake-Naches Peak Loop and the Pacific Crest Trail (PCT), head southeast on the PCT for about 1.1 miles, descending 650 feet to the lakes. Explore the lakes and pick a shady campsite for a nice snack or lunch break.

For a 5.5-mile dog-friendly hike (about 3 hours), hike the **PCT to Dewey Lakes** and back. To get to the trailhead, drive 0.5 mile on State Route 410 East past the main Tipsoo Lake parking area. Cross under the pedestrian bridge and park in the pullout on the side of the road. From here, follow the signs to pick up the PCT.

Get Away for the Weekend
Spend the night at one of several established backcountry campsites near Dewey Lakes. Campsites are available first-come, first-served; there is no fee to camp. A free wilderness-use permit is required and is available at the PCT and Tipsoo Lake-Naches Peak Loop junction. Campfires are prohibited within 0.25 mile of Dewey Lakes, and camping is prohibited within 100 feet of the shoreline. For more information, contact the **Okanogan-Wenatchee National Forest, Naches Ranger District** (10237 Hwy. 12, Naches, 509/653-1401, www.fs.usda.gov).

Directions
From Seattle, take I-90 east to exit 10A for I-405 South toward Renton. Continue on I-405 South to exit 4 for State Route 169 South toward Enumclaw. At the

end of the exit ramp, stay straight through the intersection with 3rd Street, then turn left at the next intersection for State Route 169 South toward Maple Valley/Enumclaw. Drive 25 miles on State Route 169 to Enumclaw, then turn left onto State Route 164 East/Griffin Avenue. In 0.5 mile, turn left again onto State Route 410 East/Roosevelt Avenue.

Drive 37 miles east, staying straight past the Mather Memorial Parkway sign at the junction with Sunrise Park Road. Continue straight for 6.4 miles on State Route 410 east toward Yakima, bearing left to follow the sign for Tipsoo Lake/Chinook Pass. There is a large parking area on the left with two ADA-accessible vault toilets, as well as a smaller parking area 0.2 mile down the road near Tipsoo Lake.

Note that **Chinook Pass closes** in winter.

GPS Coordinates: 46.867149, -121.518257 / N46° 52.177' W121° 31.196'

RESOURCES

City and County Parks

**Cedar River Watershed
Education Center**
19901 Cedar Falls Rd. SE
North Bend, WA 98045
206/733-9421
www.seattle.gov

City of Sammamish
801 228th Ave. SE
Sammamish, WA 98075
425/295-0500
www.sammamish.us

King County Parks
18201 SE Cougar Mountain Dr.
Bellevue, WA 98027
206/296-4232
www.kingcounty.gov

Seattle Parks and Recreation
100 Dexter Ave. N.
Seattle, WA 98109
206/684-4075
www.seattle.gov

**Snohomish County Parks
and Recreation**
6705 Puget Park Dr.
Snohomish, WA 98296
425/388-6600
www.snocoparks.org

**Snohomish County Public
Utility District**
P.O. Box 1107
Everett, WA 98206-1107
425/783-1712
www.snopud.com

**University of Washington
Botanic Gardens**
P. O. Box 354115
Seattle, WA 98195-4115
206/543-8616
www.uwbotanicgardens.org

Washington State Parks

Mailing address:
P.O. Box 42650
Olympia, WA 98504-2650
360/902-8844
www.parks.wa.gov

Cama Beach State Park
1880 SW Camano Dr.
Camano Island, WA 98282
360/387-1550
www.parks.state.wa.us

Deception Pass State Park
41020 SR 20
Oak Harbor, WA 98277
360/675-3767
www.parks.state.wa.us

Joseph Whidbey State Park
Crosby Road
Oak Harbor, WA 98277
360/678-4519
www.parks.state.wa.us

Olallie State Park
51350 SE Homestead Valley Rd.
North Bend, WA 98045
425/455-7010
www.parks.state.wa.us

South Whidbey State Park
4128 S. Smugglers Cove Rd.
Freeland, WA 98249

360/331-4559
www.parks.state.wa.us

Squak Mountain State Park
21430 SE May Valley Rd.
Issaquah, WA 98029
360/902-8844
www.parks.state.wa.us

Wallace Falls State Park
14503 Wallace Lake Rd.
Gold Bar, WA 98251
360/793-0420
www.parks.state.wa.us

Washington State Agencies
Washington State Department of Natural Resources
1111 Washington St. SE
Olympia, WA 98504
360/902-1000
www.dnr.wa.gov

Northwest Region
919 N. Township St.
Sedro Woolley, WA 98284-9384
360/856-3500
www.dnr.wa.gov

South Puget Sound Region
950 Farman Ave. N.
Enumclaw, WA 98022-9282
360/825-1631
www.dnr.wa.gov

Washington State Department of Fish and Wildlife
Physical address:
Natural Resources Building
1111 Washington St. SE
Olympia, WA 98501

Mailing address:
600 Capitol Way N.
Olympia, WA 98501-1091
360/902-2200
www.wdfw.gov

Washington State Department of Transportation
310 Maple Park Ave. SE
P.O. Box 47300
Olympia, WA 98504-7300
Ferries: 888/808-7977
www.wsdot.wa.gov

National Forests
Mount Baker-Snoqualmie National Forest
Darrington Ranger District
1405 Emens Ave. N.
Darrington, WA 98241
360/436-1155
www.fs.usda.gov

Skykomish Ranger District
74920 NE Stevens Pass Hwy.
P.O. Box 305
Skykomish, WA 98288
360/677-2414
www.fs.usda.gov

Snoqualmie Ranger District-Enumclaw
450 Roosevelt Ave. E.
Enumclaw, WA 98022
360/825-6585
www.fs.usda.gov

Snoqualmie Ranger District-North Bend
902 SE North Bend Way, Bldg. 1
North Bend, WA 98045

425/888-1421
www.fs.usda.gov

Verlot Public Service Center
33515 Mountain Loop Hwy.
Granite Falls, WA 98252
360/691-7791
www.fs.usda.gov

**Okanogan-Wenatchee
National Forest
Cle Elum Ranger District**
803 W. 2nd St.
Cle Elum, WA 98922
509/852-1100
www.fs.usda.gov

Wenatchee River Ranger District
600 Sherbourne St.
Leavenworth, WA 98826
509/548-2550
www.fs.usda.gov

**Olympic National Forest
Hood Canal Ranger
District-Quilcene Office**
295142 Hwy. 101 S.
Quilcene, WA 98376
360/765-2200
www.fs.usda.gov

National Wildlife Refuges and Reserves
**Billy Frank Jr. Nisqually
National Wildlife Refuge**
100 Brown Farm Rd.
Olympia, WA 98516
360/753-9467
www.fws.gov

Dungeness National Wildlife Refuge
Physical address:
554 Voice of America Rd.
Sequim, WA 98382

Mailing address:
715 Holgerson Rd.
Sequim, WA 98362
360/457-8451
www.fws.gov

**Padilla Bay National Estuarine
Research Reserve**
10441 Bayview-Edison Rd.
Mount Vernon, WA 98273
360/428-1558
www.padillabay.gov

**Trust Board of Ebey's Landing
National Historic Reserve**
Physical address:
The Cottage at Sunnyside
162 Cemetery Rd.
Coupeville, WA 98239

Mailing address:
P.O. Box 774
Coupeville, WA 98239
360/678-6084
www.nps.gov/ebla

National Parks
Mount Rainier National Park
55210 238th Ave. E.
Ashford, WA 98304
360/569-6575
www.nps.gov

Carbon River Ranger Station
35415 Fairfax Forest Reserve Rd. E.

Carbonado, WA 98323
360/829-9639
www.nps.gov

White River Ranger Station
Wilderness Information Center
70002 Washington 410
Enumclaw, WA 98022
360/569-6670
www.nps.gov

Olympic National Park
600 E. Park Ave.
Port Angeles, WA 98362-6798
360/565-3130
www.nps.gov

Map Resources
Green Trails Maps
P.O. Box 77734
Seattle, WA 98177
206/546-6277
www.greentrailsmaps.com

REI Seattle
222 Yale Ave. N.
Seattle, WA 98109
206/223-1944
www.rei.com

U.S. Geological Survey
Western Regional Office
Federal Office Building
909 1st Ave., 8th Floor
Seattle, WA 98104
206/220-4600
888/275-8747
www.usgs.gov

CalTopo
www.caltopo.com

Passes and Permits
Discover Pass
866/320-9933
discoverpass@dfw.wa.gov
www.discoverpass.wa.gov

Northwest Forest Pass
800/270-7504
www.fs.usda.gov
www.discovernw.org

National Park Pass
www.nps.gov

America the Beautiful Pass
www.nps.gov
www.usgs.gov

Rescue Organizations
King County Explorer Search and Rescue
P.O. Box 1266
North Bend, WA 98045
www.kcesar.org

Seattle Mountain Rescue
P.O. Box 67
Seattle, WA 98111
425/243-2144
www.seattlemountainrescue.org

Washington State Animal Response Team
P.O. Box 21
Enumclaw, WA 98022
425/681-5498 (emergencies)
www.washingtonsart.org

HIKING RESOURCES
Outdoor Organizations
Mountains to Sound Greenway
Mountains to Sound Greenway Trust
2701 1st Ave., Ste. 240
Seattle, WA 98121
206/382-5565
www.mtsgreenway.org

North Cascades Institute
North Cascades Institute (Main Office)
810 State Route 20
Sedro Woolley, WA 98284
360/854-2599
www.ncascades.org

Pacific Crest Trail Association
North Cascades Region
902 SE North Bend Way
North Bend, WA 98045
425/888-8798
www.pcta.org

Pacific Northwest Trail Association
North Cascades Gateway Center
1851 Charles Jones Memorial Circle,
Unit #4
Sedro-Woolley, WA 98284
360/854-9415
www.pnt.org

Sierra Club
Washington State Chapter
180 Nickerson St., Ste. 202
Seattle, WA 98109
206/378-0114
www.sierraclub.org

The Mountaineers
Seattle Program Center
7700 Sand Point Way NE
Seattle, WA 98115
206/521-6000
www.mountaineers.org

Washington Trails Association
705 2nd Ave., Ste. 300
Seattle, WA 98104
206/625-1367
www.wta.org

Hiking and Volunteer Groups
Search for hiking, volunteering, climbing, camping, and adventure groups based on your interests.

Backcountry Horsemen of Washington
www.bchw.org

Hike It Baby
www.hikeitbaby.com

Issaquah Alps Trails Club
www.issaquahalps.org

Latino Outdoors
www.latinoutdoors.org

Meetup
www.meetup.com

Northwest Hikers
www.nwhikers.net

Outdoor Afro
www.outdoorafro.com

OutVentures
www.outventures.org

SummitPost
www.summitpost.org

The Mountaineers
www.mountaineers.org

Washington Trails Association
www.wta.org

Gear Resources
Backpacking Light
www.backpackinglight.com

CampSaver
www.campsaver.com

Moosejaw
www.moosejaw.com

Northwest Hikers
www.nwhikers.net

OutdoorGearLab
www.outdoorgearlab.com

REI
www.rei.com

Second Ascent
www.secondascent.com

Section Hiker
www.sectionhiker.com

Sierra Trading Post
www.sierratradingpost.com

Summit Post
www.summitpost.org

The Mountaineers
www.mountaineers.org

Washington Trails Association
www.wta.org

Plant and Mycological Resources
King County Native Plant Guide
www.kingcounty.gov

Oregon State University Common Trees of the Pacific Northwest
www.oregonstate.edu/trees

Puget Sound Mycological Society
www.psms.org

Washington Native Plant Society
www.wnps.org

WTU Image Collection Plants of Washington
www.burkemuseum.org

Weather Resources
AccuWeather
www.accuweather.com

Air Sports Net
www.usairnet.com

American Avalanche Association
www.avalanche.org

Cliff Mass Weather Blog
www.cliffmass.blogspot.com

Mountain Forecast
www.mountain-forecast.com

National Oceanic and Atmospheric Administration
www.noaa.gov

Northwest Avalanche Center
www.nwac.us

Tides and Currents
www.tidesandcurrents.noaa.gov

Road and Traffic Conditions
U.S. Forest Service
www.fs.usda.gov

Washington State Department of Transportation
www.wsdot.wa.gov

Public Transit
Backpacking by Bus
www.backpackingbybus.com

Seattle Metro Bus Hiking
https://sites.google.com/site/seattlemetrobushiking

Seattle Transit Hikers
www.meetup.com

TOTAGO
(Turn Off The App Go Outside)
www.totago.com

SUGGESTED READING

Adlen, Peter, and Dennis Paulson. *National Audubon Society Field Guide to the Pacific Northwest.* New York, NY: Alfred A. Knopf, 1998.

Alaback, Paul, Joe Antos, Trevor Goward, Ken Lertzman, Andy MacKinnon, Jim Pojar, Rosamund Pojar, Andrew Reed, Nancy Turner, and Dale Vitt. *Plants of the Pacific Northwest Coast: Washington, Oregon, British Columbia & Alaska.* Compiled and edited by Jim Pojar and Andy MacKinnon. Auburn, WA: Lone Pine Publishing, 1994.

Link, Russell. *Living with Wildlife in the Pacific Northwest.* Seattle, WA: University of Washington Press in association with the Washington Department of Fish and Wildlife, 2004.

Mathews, Daniel. *Cascade-Olympic Natural History: A Trailside Reference.* Portland, OR: Raven Editions, 1988.

The Mountaineers. *Mountaineering: The Freedom of the Hills.* United Kingdom: Quiller, 2010.

Turner, Mark, and Phyllis Gustafson. *Wildflowers of the Pacific Northwest.* Portland, OR: Timber Press, Inc., 2006.

Zobrist, Kevin. *Native Trees of Western Washington.* Pullman, WA: WSU Press, 2014.

Index

Acknowledgements

Thank you to Avalon Travel, my family and friends, and the outdoor community in Washington for making this book possible. My editor, Sabrina Young, helped me navigate this process and made this book better with her editing expertise.

The Washington Trails Association has been an invaluable resource to me and to thousands of other hikers across the state. Thank you for the opportunity to learn and grow through your organization.

Thank you, Anna Roth, for taking the time to answer my questions and sharing your encyclopedic hiking knowledge of Washington State. Thank you to Stewart Wechsler and Laura Blumhagen for helping me with plant identification and terminology. Thank you to Ken Giesbers for answering my questions regarding navigation technologies. Thank you to Larry Colagiovanni from Seattle Mountain Rescue and Michaela Eaves from the Washington State Animal Response Team for sharing your insights. Thank you, Margaret Schwertner, for sharing your pictures and tips on hiking with Badger. Thank you, Ken Stanback, for sharing your photography expertise for this book, and for your friendship.

Thank you to Katie Woolsey, Matt Mechler, Tom Anderson, Marc Chirico, the Issaquah Alps Trails Club, Kristen Griffin, Holly Richards, Rick Oakley, the Breazeale Interpretive Center, and the rangers at Cama Beach State Park for the trail information, stories, and history.

Thank you, Craig Romano, for your time. Thank you, Sheila and George Saul, for introducing me to hikes on Whidbey Island and teaching me the waterways of the Salish Sea. Thank you, Kate Spiller, for sharing your thoughtful contribution on hiking with kids.

Thank you to my hiking buddy, Grace Abbott, for your unbridled enthusiasm and support throughout this project. Thank you to Bobbi Wilhelm, for opening your home to me, your friendship, and your generosity. Thank you to my parents, Mary Grace Kristian and Irv Siebrecht, and my brother, Steve Siebrecht, for your support and encouragement. Thank you, Bill Payne, for your gifts beyond price. Thank you to my husband, Onur Ozbek, for sharing the highs and lows of this journey with me, for being a critical sounding board, and for believing in me when I doubted myself. Thank you for your love, support, good humor, and patience. You are my heart and the light of my life. This is for you.

MOON OUTDOORS

Your Adventure Starts Here

MOON 75 GREAT HIKES SEATTLE
Avalon Travel
An imprint of Perseus Books
A Hachette Book Group company
1700 Fourth Street
Berkeley, CA 94710, USA
www.moon.com

Editor and Series Manager: Sabrina Young
Copy Editor: Ann Seifert
Production and Graphics Coordinator:
    Lucie Ericksen
Cover Design: Faceout Studios, Charles Brock
Moon Logo: Tim McGrath
Map Editor: Mike Morgenfeld
Cartographers: Moon Street Cartography,
    Durango, CO., Brian Shotwell
Proofreader: Alissa Cyphers

ISBN-13: 978-1-63121-498-1
ISSN: 1559-1778

Printing History
1st Edition – May 2017
5 4 3 2 1

Front cover photo: Tipsoo Lake - Naches Peak
    Loop © Melissa Ozbek
Back cover photo: © Melissa Ozbek
All interior photos: © Melissa Ozbek

Printed in Canada by Friesens

Keeping Current

We are committed to making this book the most accurate and enjoyable camping
guide to the state. You can rest assured that every campground in this book has been
carefully reviewed in an effort to keep this book as up-to-date as possible. However,
by the time you read this book, some of the fees listed herein may have changed and
campgrounds may have closed unexpectedly.

If you have a favorite gem you'd like to see included in the next edition, or see
anything that needs updating, clarification, or correction, please drop us a line. Send
your comments via email to feedback@moon.com, or use the address above.